Reconstructing the Canadian Family: Feminist Perspectives

Edited by

Nancy Mandell
Department of Sociology
York University
North York, Ontario

and

Ann Duffy
Department of Sociology
Brock University
St. Catharines, Ontario

Butterworths

Toronto and Vancouver

Reconstructing the Canadian Family: Feminist Perspectives
©1988 Butterworths Canada Ltd.

Printed and bound in Canada.

The Butterworth Group of Companies
Canada:
Butterworths Canada Ltd.,
2265 Midland Avenue,
TORONTO, Ontario M1P 4S1
        and
409 Granville St., Suite 1455,
VANCOUVER, B.C. V6C 1T2
Australia:
Butterworths Pty. Ltd., SYDNEY, MELBOURNE, BRISBANE, ADELAIDE, PERTH, CANBERRA and HOBART
Ireland:
Butterworth (Ireland) Ltd., DUBLIN
Malaysia:
Malayan Law Journal Sdn. Bhd., KUALA LUMPUR
New Zealand:
Butterworths of New Zealand Ltd., WELLINGTON and AUCKLAND
Singapore:
Butterworth & Co. (Asia) Pte. Ltd., SINGAPORE
United Kingdom:
Butterworth & Co. (Publishers) Ltd., LONDON and EDINBURGH
United States:
Butterworth Legal Publishers, ST. PAUL, Minnesota, SEATTLE, Washington, BOSTON, Massachusetts, AUSTIN, Texas and D & S Publishers, CLEARWATER, Florida

Canadian Cataloguing in Publication Data
Main entry under title:

Reconstructing the Canadian family : feminist perspectives

Bibliography: p.
Includes index.
ISBN 0-409-80528-9

1. Women—Canada—Family relationships.
2. Family—Canada. I. Mandell, Nancy.
II. Duffy, Ann Doris.   7/562
HQ559.R42 1988   306.8′5′0971   C88-093917-6

Sponsoring Editor: Janet Turner
Cover Design: Patrick Ng
Production: John Stein

To Our Mothers:

Margaret Louise Pennal

and

Elizabeth Matilda Kaiser

Introduction

Why a 'feminist' book on the family?

The Canadian family has not lacked analytical attention. Over the years numerous books and articles have addressed family topics. The reader, then, might reasonably wonder why it is useful to bring out yet another tome on this much-studied topic and why a specifically 'feminist' perspective is a necessary addition to the literature.

Feminists, as the reader will learn from the selections in this text, are a varied lot. They not only may not agree with one another on every subject, they may disagree vehemently over important issues. Some feminists are men (though not every feminist would agree that men can be feminists). Since two of the contributors here are men it is clear that we believe that men can make important contributions to feminist thought. While these disagreements help make feminist scholarship a lively and dynamic field, they make defining 'feminism' a difficult task (Jaggar and Struhl 1978).

In a very basic sense, feminists are concerned with studying the world through women's eyes (Smith 1977). This means, for example, paying attention to the experiences of wives, mothers and daughters; secretaries, nurses and waitresses; nuns and mother superiors; women revolutionaries, writers, artists and philosophers, rather than only their male counterparts. Throughout history, the accomplishments, concerns and ideas of women have been mostly eclipsed by philosophies, sciences and arts which were premised on a male perspective (Spender 1982). Feminists want to correct this unbalanced and inaccurate approach to human experience.

When feminists examine women's 'hidden history', they discover considerable evidence of the oppression, subordination and exploitation of women (Rowbotham 1973; Lerner 1986). Even though many men faced difficult and oppressive conditions in their lives, it has been women who generally have had the fewest rights, opportunities and freedoms.

In many societies, a 'respectable' woman was always subject to male control. Father, husband and, in old age, the eldest son, dictated her existence. Frequently, women could not own property, were expected to turn their earnings over to their father or husband and had no rights over their own children. A woman's life, unlike that of her brother, was "normally" restricted to a domestic role. The world of adventure, exploration and power was distinctly male.

Today, this patriarchal social structure—rights and opportunities for men; restrictions and subordination for women—has not entirely vanished. Certainly, many of the most glaring inequalities have been erased. Women have been legally deemed "persons" in Canada and have been eligible to vote for more than 60 years. It is no longer legal to rape your wife (as of 1985). Women are no longer barred from institutions of higher learning (the University of Toronto, for example, allowed the first women undergraduates some 100 years ago). Women no longer make half the income of men (it's up to 64%) (Statistics Canada 1985). However, patriarchal structures and attitudes are far from being completely dismantled.

Women's concerns and experiences still often are ignored or trivialized. The 1982 incident in the House of Commons in which members of the House greeted a report on wife abuse with laughter testifies to the persistent devaluation of women's issues. As does the failure of the government to provide adequate child care for the growing numbers of employed mothers. Women are still far from being equally represented in spheres of power and influence. In the 1984 general election, women constituted only 15% of the candidates and 10% of the M.P.s (Brodie 1985, 4). Women remain scarce in the highest echelons of every profession, corporation and branch of the public service. Women continue to be ghettoized in low-paying, low-status "women's jobs" (Armstrong 1984). Violence against women remains a pressing public concern. It is estimated that one million women are abused by their husbands or live-in partners each year (MacLeod 1987) and at least one in 17 women are raped at some point in their lives (Brickman and Briere 1984).

All too frequently, women learn about patriarchal realities, not in sociology courses, but through their lived experiences. At 16, a young woman finds that her sports get less money, time and support from her high school than do sports for boys (Hall and Richardson 1982). At 18, a young woman discovers her professor, boss or co-worker is more preoccupied with her sexuality than with her work skills or academic potential. At 25, she finds herself stuck in a dead-end "female" job while her male college friends have gone on to more income and more promotions. At 30, unlike her male colleagues, she has to make difficult choices between parenthood and career. At 35, despite a loving, supportive husband, she is juggling a "double day" of housework, childcare and paid employment. If her marriage ends in divorce, she may find herself joining the growing ranks of single mothers struggling to get by on too little income and inadequate government assistance (Weitzman 1985). Even in old age, she may find the societal dice loaded against her. She probably will be considered less attractive and desirable than men her age. (Pierre Trudeau married Margaret Sinclair when he was 60 years old. Imagine a 60-year-old woman Prime Minister taking a 25-year-old husband.) More importantly, the aging woman is likely to discover that she has substantially less income and fewer economic prospects than her male counterpart (Gee and Kimball 1987). The permutations and possibilities are endless. The bottom line is that our social system provides fewer opportunities, less support and more obstacles to her, simply because she was born a woman.

Feminists want women and men to be aware of these basic inequalities and injustices. They want to tear down the centuries-old myths and ideologies which keep women "in their place". They challenge the old notions that women are ruled by their biology (from sexpot to dishpot); that women are naturally inferior in intellect, judgement or skills and that women's sole or essential destiny is as wife and mother. Women and men have many of the same hopes, dreams and aspirations; they both deserve the chance at human fulfillment.

In short, there are two basic ingredients in the feminist perspective. Feminists are individuals who recognize the importance of (1) understanding women's life experiences, and (2) working towards fuller lives for women (and men). Strategies for accomplishing these tasks vary considerably amongst feminists. For example, some work from a more structural viewpoint and emphasize the economic basis of gender inequality, while others focus on the ideological pressures (biological determinism, sexism, traditional gender socialization) which justify women's subordination. Some feminist work examines the personal (micro) level of women's experience (patterns of non-verbal communication, women's attitudes and values), while other work looks at the societal (macro) dimensions of gender inequality (rates of poverty, patterns of wife abuse).

No one viewpoint will characterize this book. Rather, the intent here is to satisfy the two basic tenets of feminism. First, the goal is to provide women and men with up-to-date, reliable information on women's issues and women's concerns in the Canadian family. This knowledge—of the rights of children, reproductive technology, men's lives, women and the economy—helps to provide the basis for reasoned discussion, choice and action. By focusing on specifically women's issues and women's perspective on the family, information is provided which is often absent from other sources. Secondly, by implicitly and explicitly challenging the gender inequalities in the family and in society at large, the aim is to contribute to the greater freedom of men and women, both inside and outside the family.

An Overview

This book is organized into three major sections. In the first part, the three principal participants in the modern nuclear family are introduced—wife/mother, husband/father and children. Roberta Hamilton traces the roles of women as wives, mothers and kin-keepers as they were transformed through industrialization and the development of capitalism. From her discussion it is clear that there have been significant changes in women's day-to-day family activities. "Rough and ready equality" (where women were productive partners in family enterprises) gave way to isolation and dependency for women. Although the nature of patriarchal relations changed as the economic order changed, the liberation of women—"the longest revolution"—has yet to be achieved.

Robert Stebbins examines the roles of husbands and fathers from a male perspective. As he points out, men have generally wanted to be members of families and have benefited from their participation in families. Family life for men, however, contains strains and contradictions. It is, for example, often difficult for men to reconcile the conflicting demands of their work life, family responsibilities and leisure interests. The resolution of these personal conflicts will probably result in changes in the basic models of masculinity in our society.

Lastly, Nancy Mandell discusses children and their pivotal connection to women's familial and social roles. Childhood is as much a social construction as a biological reality. Ideas and attitudes towards children vary considerably depending on historical period, class, gender and cultural context. At times in our past, children were treated as independent beings capable of working alongside adults. Now, our society seems ambivalent about children (and their mothers). Fuller lives for children and women depends upon new ways of integrating both children and their mothers into family life and public life.

The second major section examines the dynamic quality of the family—from both a macro and micro perspective. Monica Boyd discusses the dramatic demographic changes which have transformed the Canadian family. Contemporary family living takes many and varied shapes. More and more Canadians live alone, in common-law marriages, in reconstituted families, in dual-earner families and in lone-parent families.

Family life, in these new forms, manages to survive, despite the social and economic upheavals of the past three decades. As Boyd points out, women living in these new family forms play a considerably different role from that of the traditional homemaker at home with the children. Understanding women's role in the family means taking into consideration the proliferating variations on family life.

Ann Duffy takes a more micro perspective on changes in the family. She focuses on the power politics of marriage and the ways in which inequality is lived out in the day-to-day routine of family life. Although the modern feminist movement has made us more aware of power relations between men and women, inequality between husbands and wives remains a problem and still exacts a heavy toll in terms of unhappiness, dissatisfaction and violence. We are developing, however, a better grasp of the subtleties and complexities of family power and a clearer understanding of the connections between familial inequality and the socioeconomic structure. This improved understanding will, one hopes, contribute to the creation of families that are truly more egalitarian and companionate.

In the final section, the authors explore the powerful social forces which set the stage for family life. Pat and Hugh Armstrong detail the impact of large-scale economic alterations on the lives of family members. Starting with the early European settlers, they trace changes in the political economy of Canada and in women's familial role. The connections between the economy and the family are complex and contradictory. For example, increasingly women are under pressure to combine their domestic work with wage work. While the resultant "double day" oppresses women, movement into the paid labour force has helped to expand women's choices and alter ideas about women's role. Women's lives in the family and in the economy are continuing to change. Understanding the complex interconnections between the two will help us to "shape a future" in which men and women share equally in work in and out of the labour force.

Susan McDaniel focuses on the new reproductive technologies and their impact on women's family roles. These scientific developments—surrogate mothers, test-tube babies, glass wombs—are changing our notions about motherhood. Although these advances promise to benefit infertile women and men, they allow for increasing intervention in women's reproductive role. These and other scientific advances raise troubling questions about who should "be allowed" to become pregnant and what constitutes appropriate mothering. To avoid becoming passive recipients of this new scientific expertise, women must take a leading role in deciding how much and what kind of intrusion into mothering is socially desirable.

Finally, Norene Pupo considers the impact of the state on women's experience of family life. She explains that throughout Canadian history the actions of legislators have dramatically affected women. For example, legislation on childcare and family law establishes the concrete realities of many women's family lives. The implications of state actions for women have been both positive and negative. Under pressure from women's organizations, the Canadian state has produced policies which provide women with some protection and justice. Pupo argues, however, that, in the long run, the actions of the state have served to maintain patriarchal relations in society. Women must continue to pressure the state to provide more equitable policies.

Four central themes are woven throughout these contributions. First, those who promulgate feminist perpectives on the family are keenly aware of the varied nature of family life. Individuals live out their family lives in many different ways; the family cannot be approached or understood as a monolith (Eichler 1983). By implication, no one form of the family should be considered "right" or "natural". Boyd's attention to new family forms along with Hamilton's, Mandell's and the Armstrongs' emphasis on historical and class variations in family living reflect this fundamental assumption.

Second, the family has been and still is in a continuous process of change. In order to understand and examine the family it must be located within and relative to its historical context. For example, Pupo's work on the state and McDaniel's on reproductive technology are located in a distinct historical reality. To appreciate the degree and nature of change the family undergoes, this historical perspective is a necessity.

Third, many of the articles work from a "materialist" perspective. Instead of looking simply at the ideas about family life, they examine the day-to-day and generation-to-generation realities of men and women's work, producing and reproducing their lives. Rather than focusing on ideas about wives and mothers, Hamilton considers the real labours of women inside and outside the home. Similarly, Mandell is interested in the relations of children to productive labour and the implications of these real activities for children's lives.

Finally, the family is approached here as a social and political issue. Informing all of these articles is the view that for numerous people, particularly many women, family life does not provide sufficient intimacy, nurture and support. Women continue to experience domination, subordination and, too frequently, abuse in their family lives. Reforming the family is not an abstract exercise. Each author assumes not only that a more egalitarian family life is desirable, but that each of us has a responsibility to work towards achieving the end of patriarchy and the beginning of equality.

The task of editing the articles was shared equally by both Nancy Mandell and Ann Duffy.

Bibliography to Introduction

Brickman, Julie, and John Briere.
1984   "Incidence of Rape and Sexual Assault in an Urban Canadian Population". *International Journal of Women's Studies* 7 (May/June): 195-206.

Armstrong, Pat.
1984   *Labour Pains: Women's Work in Crisis.* Toronto: Women's Press.

Brodie, Janine.
1985   *Women and Politics in Canada.* Toronto: McGraw-Hill Ryerson Limited.

Gee, Ellen, and Meredith M. Kimball.
1987   *Women and Aging.* Toronto: Butterworths.

Hall, M. Ann, and Dorothy A. Richardson.
1982   *Fair Ball—Towards Sex Equality in Canadian Sport.* Ottawa: Canadian Advisory Council on the Status of Women.

Jaggar, Alison M., and Paula Rothenberg Struhl.
1978   *Feminist Frameworks Alternative Theoretical Accounts of the Relations between Women and Men.* New York: McGraw-Hill Book Company.

Lerner, Gerda.
1986   *The Creation of Patriarchy.* New York: Oxford University Press.

MacLeod, Linda.
1987   *Battered But Not Beaten . . . Preventing Wife Battering in Canada.* Ottawa: Canadian Advisory Council on the Status of Women.

Rowbotham, Sheila.
1973   *Hidden from History.* London: Pluto Press.

Smith, Dorothy.
1979   "A Sociology for Women". In *The Prism of Sex Essays in the Sociology of Knowledge,* edited by Julia A. Sherman and Evelyn Torton Beck, 135-187. Madison, Wisconsin: The University of Wisconsin Press.

Spender, Dale.
1982   *Women of Ideas and What Men Have Done to Them From Aphra Bem to Adrienne Rich.* London: Ark Paperbacks.

Statistics Canada
1985   *Women in Canada: A Statistical Report.* Ottawa: Minister of Supply and Services.

Weitzman, Lenore J.
1985   *The Divorce Revolution: The Unexpected Social and Economic Consequences for Women and Children in America.* New York: The Free Press.

Acknowledgements

Many people have helped us with this book and we thank them for their support and encouragement. Earlier drafts of the manuscript were read and critiqued by Gordon Darroch, Rose Hutchens, Deborah Harrison, Leslie Sanders and Dusky Lee Smith. Their helpful comments and suggestions were much appreciated. Thanks go, also, to the Women's Studies Group at York University, including Shelagh Wilkinson, Joan Gibson, Anne-Marie Ambert and Alice Propper, for their ideas and encouragement. We also appreciate the support provided by Butterworths' editor, Janet Turner. It was her continued enthusiasm and encouragement which made the project a possibility. Thanks to our families—Lionel and the boys, Jeremy, Ben and Adam; and Dusky Lee and Hermana—who managed the inconvenience and general preoccupation to which they were, from time to time, subjected. Finally, thanks to each other for keeping one another going when the work seemed overwhelming and there was no time to do it.

Contributors

PAT ARMSTRONG

An activist in women's issues since the 1960's, Pat Armstrong co-parents two teenage daughters and teaches Sociology at York University. Her research and writing focus on women's work, family and health. Co-author with Hugh Armstrong of *The Double Ghetto: Canadian Women and Their Segregated Work* and *A Working Majority: What Women Must Do For Pay*. Author of *Labour Pains: Women's Work in Crisis,* her current research uses a hospital setting as a means of exploring how the economic recession is influencing women's work and family life.

HUGH ARMSTRONG

Hugh Armstrong is Associate Dean of General Studies at Centennial College in Toronto. In addition to the books and articles he has written with Pat Armstrong, he is author of several articles on employment and on the state and is an editor of *Studies in Political Economy.*

MONICA BOYD

Monica Boyd is a Professor of Sociology at Carleton University. She has written numerous articles, chapters and books which focus on immigrant women, gender inequality in the labour force, changing Canadian attitudes towards women, popular opinion on abortion, and changing patterns of marriage and divorce in Canada. A past member of the federal Canadian Advisory Council on the Status of Women, she currently is a member of the OECD Monitoring Panel on Migrant Women. She also is a member of the federal National Statistics Council, founding chair of the Advisory Committee on Social Conditions for Statistics Canada and the president-elect of the Canadian Population Society.

ANN DUFFY

Ann Duffy teaches sociology at Brock University in St. Catherines, Ontario. Active in the women's movement since the early 1970's, she was for several years a member of the Board of Directors of the Hamilton Rape Crisis Centre. Her research and writing interests centre on women and power, the social construction of sexuality and women's participation in paid employment.

ROBERTA HAMILTON

Roberta Hamilton is Coordinator of Women Studies at Queen's University where she teaches in the Department of Sociology.
She is the author of *The Liberation of Women* and co-editor with Michele Barrett of *The Politics of Diversity*.

NANCY MANDELL

Nancy Mandell currently teaches Sociology and Women's Studies at York University, Toronto. Her interest in children's history, development and daycare has led to a number of articles on these subjects. She is currently involved in qualitative studies on the effects of employment on family life and family practices in reproducing class and gender relations.

SUSAN McDANIEL

Susan A. McDaniel is an Associate Professor of Sociology at the University of Waterloo where she has taught since 1976, after completing her Ph.D. at the University of Alberta. She is the author of two books, *Social Problems Through Conflict and Order*, with Ben Agger (1982, Addison Wesley) and *Canada's Aging Population* (1986, Butterworths). As the recipient of Canada's first Therese Casgrain Research Fellowship, for 1987-88, she is completing work on a book tentatively titled *Childbearing in Change*. She is the author of some 40 articles and book chapters on fertility, contraception, abortion, adoption, sexual assault, women's health, gender and women inventors. She also is frequently invited to speak to groups and associations across Canada on various women's issues and comments often on these issues in the media. In 1981, she was awarded the University of Waterloo's Distinguished Teacher Award for continued excellence in teaching.

NORENE PUPO

After working for a number of years for the Alcohol and Drug Addiction Research Foundation of Ontario, Norene Pupo became an Assistant Professor of Sociology at the University of Toronto in 1984. Active in community concerns, she has for several years been a member of the Social Planning Council of Metropolitan Toronto. These responsibilities are balanced off with her role as the co-parent of a very active two-year-old. Her research and writing interests are in women's work choices, Canadian political economy and higher education in Canada. She is currently completing a major study of women in the part-time labour force.

ROBERT STEBBINS

Robert A. Stebbins is Professor of Sociology at the University of Calgary. His research interests lie in social psychology, deviance, the arts, and work and leisure. He is the author of *Commitment to Deviance* (1971), *The Disorderly Classroom* (1974), *Teachers and Meaning* (1975), *Amateurs* (1979), *The Magician* (1984), *Sociology: The Study of Society* (1987), *Canadian Football* (1987), and *Deviance: Tolerable Differences* (1987). He is also co-editor of two anthologies: *Fieldwork Experience* (1980) and *The Sociology of Deviance* (1982), as well as author of numerous journal articles and book chapters.

CONTENTS

PART I

The Participants in Modern Family Life

CHAPTER I

Women, Wives and Mothers

Roberta Hamilton

In the last 20 years, the feminist movement has challenged every aspect of social life in Canada, as it has throughout the world. No arena has been too public, too intimate, or too scholarly to remain untouched by this latest and most widespread resurrection of the centuries-old struggle for sexual equality. Juliet Mitchell called this struggle "The Longest Revolution" (1984). As in earlier periods, though never so profoundly, this struggle threatens the interests and unleashes the anxieties of so many people in so many ways that the backlash it has provoked could be called "The Longest Counter-Revolution".

This chapter explores the relationship between this struggle and the family. Families, in a capitalist society, comprise a changing set of relationships which take their shape from and exert influence upon that society. The argument here is that the particular nature of the contemporary family, as it emerged as part of the developing relations of capitalist society, provided the important preconditions for the women's movement. This movement produced, as a central part of its analysis, a critique of the relationships between men, women and children within the family. At the same time, the women's movement exposed the dialectical interplay between social institutions. This textbook, a feminist text on the family, results from and contributes to that critique.

Most feminist anthropologists now argue that the relationship between men and women (throughout almost all of human history) has been one of domination and subordination of women (Reiter 1975). If that is so, the question then arises, Why have there been mass movements of women to fight against oppression only during the last 125 years? The question is not, Why do we have a women's movement now? but, Why did we not have such movements very much earlier in history? The second question is, Why has the struggle for women's liberation encountered such resistance from large numbers of men, and women too?

These questions direct our attention to the family and household: its location within the broader social structure, on the one hand, and the relationships between men, women and children within the family, on the other. For wherever else women have been, historically and in the present, they are centrally located within family households. What they do there, how they do it, and how all this relates to the rest of the society varies enormously. But if we are to understand why women have behaved as they did, why they have accepted or resisted their subordinate position, and why that position has been challenged so pervasively in the last 20 years, we must begin with the family.

Yet, as feminists have emphasized, families both take their shape from and in turn condition economic, political and social relationships. Family structures, functions and roles emerge from a dynamic interchange among individuals and social forces. In the end, consequently, the society as a whole must be taken on as a dynamic set of processes. To understand what we have become, or more precisely, what we are becoming, we must understand from where we have come. This is the task of historical sociology.

We are born into relationships which are so systematic and pervasive that they appear unalterable. We talk about the family, the economic system, the government, almost without believing that it is men and women, in relationship with each other, who create and reproduce them. The new social history calls these "inevitable" relationships into question (Abrams 1982; Tilly and Scott 1978; Stone 1977; Phillips forthcoming; Parr 1982; Trofimenkoff and Prentice 1977).

This historical approach is especially useful in understanding those areas of human life that appear natural, or pregiven. For we experience ourselves as male or female so profoundly that to be told that this too, this male and female identity, is also socially constructed, in time and space, can be quite astounding, if not threatening. The anxieties unleashed by what appears to be an attack on the natural family and the natural relations between men and women have led many to contribute to the backlash against the women's movement.

Until the development of feminist theory, philosophers, sociologists and historians tended to accept the relations between the sexes as given—part of the natural order of things. Those who questioned the conventional wisdom were pretty much ignored (de Beauvoir 1949; Myrdal 1944; Hacker 1951).

Sociology students learned that the nuclear family and its sex-based division of labour was functional to society. Talcott Parsons, the most influential of these functionalist sociologists, explained that men played the instrumental role within the family—that is, they went out to work "to bring home the bacon"—and women played the affective role—that is, they cooked it (all the while running emotional interference between father and children to ensure some modicum of peace). Such a division of labour, Parsons argued, was necessary in a highly mobile, competitive society to permit the family to behave as a unit, so that husband and wife would complement each other, not compete. Yet Parsons (1959) was sufficiently astute to point out that these arrangements could be quite constricting for women.

As a description, particularly of white, middle-class American families in the 1950s, this formulation had some plausibility. Students who read this work but came from families that did not conform to the model assumed either that sociology was irrelevant for understanding social life, or that their particular family/household was deviant or at least idiosyncratic. So even though the model did not describe what their families were really like, it described what they thought they *should* be like. Functionalism was more like normative philosophy than sociology.

How then, less than 20 years later, could there appear a feminist textbook on the family, a text that argues systematically that relations between men and women within the family, as elsewhere, are socially constructed, and that the family is a prime site for the reproduction of the relations of domination and subordination between the sexes? This question leads us back to the women's movement. For the feminist critique of the family developed within this social movement, not within the learned academies or within the established disciplines.

The impetus to examine and change oppressive conditions hardly can be expected to come from those who are privileged by those conditions, from those who are part of the dominant or established order. If your mother has always washed your clothes, cooked your meals, and generally cleaned up after you, do you think it likely that one day you would throw up your hands in horror and insist on developing a more equitable division of labour? We should not be surprised that the motivation for examining these practices came not from men, but from women. It was not male sociologists teaching and writing in the universities (who, after all, were also fathers, husbands—and sons), but women, many of them young, who felt dismayed that their education was leading directly to two full time jobs: low-paid waged work and unrelieved domestic labour (Armstrong, this text; Report 1970; Women Unite! 1972). The women's movement provided the social basis for initiating a critique of the dominant sociological paradigms. This critique, against considerable resistance, eventually became incorporated into the university curriculum.

It is clear, therefore, that many reasons exist to prompt a most important question: if societies have been patriarchal since time out of mind, as pre-industrial people would say, why are the movements of women for social, economic, and political justice such recent historical developments?

Asking this question does not suggest that patriarchal relations are ahistorical. Indeed, the variety of ways in which sexual inequality occurs boggles the mind. Patriarchal relations are constructed historically, as are those of race and class. Yet the concept of "patriarchy" draws our attention to the systematic, sustained and pervasive production and reproduction of inequality between men and women. This does not mean that all men have had a better time of it than do all women. As the late feminist historian Joan Kelly (1984, 4) explained: we must look at the *relation* between men and women *within* any particular society if we are to understand whether and how history has dealt uneven hands to women and men. In comparison with the majority of men, women and children living today, for example, most of us in Canada, certainly those of us at university, in one capacity or another, are enormously privileged. Sexual inequality, like other socially constructed hierarchies, however, is alive and well within our own milieu.

History is constantly in the making. Yet some historical changes have been so dramatic that they transformed the social landscape. To really understand the peculiarities of our own environment, we must return to these periods. This kind of history requires what Raymond Williams (1977, 121) has called "epochal analysis" because we concentrate upon "dominant and definitive lineaments and features". Here we sacrifice important variations and exceptions for broad contours. In a certain way we compare two photographs, instead of running a moving picture. This kind of history has two advantages: it provides us with distance from our common-sense world-view, and it highlights the interrelatedness of our current social practices. The last great transition in human history—some would say the greatest there has ever been—was the transition from feudalism to capitalism (Giddens 1981) which began in England at the end of the sixteenth century. A new set of economic relations was emerging on the world stage, and with them, as an intrinsic part, new forms of the family, and new kinds of relations between men and women (Dobb 1963; Hilton 1986; Brenner 1986; Hamilton 1978).

THE FEUDAL FAMILY

At the end of the sixteenth century, the majority of people in Europe lived in small households on land which they possessed, but did not own outright. They yielded a living from this land, at least in years when there were good harvests, with some people doing better than others. There were several ways people enhanced their chances of survival: by sending children out as servants to better-off neighbours, thus leaving more food for family members; by selling surplus produce at local markets, thus producing some income; by gathering wood for fuel from the common land to which they had access; and by wage-labouring for small businessmen.

These particular property arrangements had important consequences for the relations between the sexes, or more especially for relations between husband and wife. For marriage was as necessary for men as for women. Husband and wife required the labour of the other to survive and to feed their children who also contributed once they turned four or five. As a result, widowers, after what we might consider an indecently short period of mourning, remarried. "To thrive the yeoman must wive" wrote a practical poet of the time, and most did, some several times (Tusser 1557). Historian Eileen Power (1965, 410) argued that the interdependence of husband and wife produced a kind of rough and ready equality between them. In addition, a fair amount of physical abuse was directed from husband to wife. The main point here is that the labour of each was interrelated and embedded within the network of relations between them and their children.

The family was an economic unit, predicated on what Marx (1973) called "a unity of capital and labour". That is, the essential components needed for survival—land, tools and labour—were present within each household. The enormous relevance of this relationship between kinship, capital and labour becomes clear when we compare it with the situation of men and women in our society. Here there is not "unity" between labour and capital. All that most people own is their labour power—that is, their ability to labour. This they must sell for a wage in order to provide a living for themselves and their children. Indeed, the desperation of the unemployed is directly attributable to this historically particular and very peculiar arrangement in capitalist society. Willingness to labour is not enough. There is nothing to labour upon unless someone gives you a job: a job which he or she, but almost always he, can take away because s/he owns or controls the resources necessary for the "realization of labour" (Marx 1973, 471). When a pulp and paper mill closes down, or an insurance company or university buys some fancy new machines, people are thrown out of work and back onto the labour market. Understanding the unity of labour and capital is crucial for understanding feudal society, its particular form of the family/household, and how it differed from our own.

The implications of these arrangements can best be understood by comparing them with what came later, with what we ourselves are familiar. Production and consumption were not two radically separate processes. We must go twice into the labour market. First we sell our labour, as any other commodity would be sold, in order to acquire a wage. Then we must take this money back to the marketplace to purchase what we need, and can afford, to get us by until the next paycheque

(Luxton 1980, 124–28; Secombe 1980, 71). In feudal society, however, work and home were coterminous. The distinction between "real" work and housework was meaningless. Perhaps most surprising for us, only the glimmerings of a split between public and private life had developed. Today we go to such lengths to protect our privacy. Our houses, for example, are divided into rooms clearly demarcating different kinds of activity. We believe that children should be protected from witnessing expressions of adult sexuality. Our feudal forebearers did not share these delicate inhibitions. Peasant hovels, like overcrowded slums today, did not provide the space for carefully constructed retreats—we call them bedrooms—away from children. Even kings and queens in palaces did not believe that their sexual activities should be beyond the gaze of others, as Philippe Ariès showed in his path-breaking book, *Centuries of Childhood*.

As social life became divided into producing commodities and buying them, into work and home, as labour was divided into wage labour and housework, and as society settled into public and private realms, it is striking that women became associated with the second of these pairs of concepts, and men with the first (Hamilton 1978, 24–28). It is assumed that men produce things; women buy things. Hence women are extravagant: how many Dagwood and Blondie comics have been a poke at Blondie, the wacky spendthrift? How many jokes have you heard husbands make about wives spending all *their* money? (See Luxton 1980, 168–73 for some very unfunny examples.) Also, men go to work; women stay home—or should stay home. These ideas persist even in the face of much contrary evidence. Women are the staple of private life. They not only do the housework, they protect the private realm, family life, intimacy, personal feelings, even morality (Hamilton 1978, 96).

We accept all these categories as providing accurate descriptions of our life. They seem natural. All these aspects of life, however, were embedded within the feudal household. The dependent interrelations between men and women, the production and reproduction to meet daily needs and the needs of the next generation, were part of the same web of life. Men and women were unified within the family, which encompassed a mutual set of obligations and privileges. This also held true for the wives of craftsmen and tradesmen who were partners in their husbands' businesses, and for noblewomen who ran the large, multifaceted manors (Clark 1919; Charles and Duffin 1985).

A second point also relates to this idea of embeddedness in the feudal family. The peasant households possessed but did not own their land. Their tenure of the land was well protected in law, until the bourgeoisie gained power after the English Revolution and began changing property laws to suit its own interests (Hill 1969, 147; Manning 1978; Neeson 1984). Even in feudal times, however, tenure was not absolute. People were obliged to turn over a certain amount (an amount which varied historically) of money, goods or labour to the lord, to the church and, in some places, with the rise of absolutism, to the state (Goubert 1973; Mousnier 1979; Bloch 1966; Hilton 1986). The laws of the society, backed by military force, ensured that peasants, however reluctantly, handed over some of the fruits of their labour to others. This was how the dominant class, the nobility, siphoned off the surplus that the rest of the people produced; indeed, this is how the elite secured and sustained its dominance. This served to make the lord, priest or tax collector quite unpopular, as the long history of peasant resistance attests (Ladurie 1974, 201; Brenner 1986).

All ruling classes must have a means of appropriating the surplus produced by the majority, whether they be peasants or wage labourers. Without this appropriation they would cease to be a ruling class. In our society, for example, most people are paid a wage. For Marx this wage represented a subsistence which ensured that workers had enough to keep body and soul together in order that they could continue to work. The amount of subsistence varies historically and depends upon many factors: the ratio of labourers to jobs; the sex, education, and bargaining power of workers; the mobility and alternative investment opportunities for capital. What workers produce, but do not get paid for producing, is this surplus which goes to the owners as both overhead and profit. If students work at Burger King in the summer, the profits from all the hamburgers that they make but do not get paid for producing go to Mr. Burger King, so that he can add yet another Burger King to the blighted cityscape. This surplus then contributes to putting some little corner restaurant out of business (Reiter 1986).

In capitalist society, surplus accumulates through economic, not legal coercion. The relationship with employers is purely contractual: workers agree to work and employers agree to pay them until they quit or are fired. Beyond the working contract they have no responsibilities or obligations to each other. If a woman goes into labour, her boss will not send his wife over to supervise the delivery as a feudal lord might have done. More likely, if a boss can get away with it, he will fire her as soon as he knows she is pregnant. On the other hand, if he needs some help in his garden he will not expect her to send her husband or son over at the weekend to help, as might have happened on a feudal manor. The relationship between peasant and lord, between household and lordship, was embedded in a set of shifting obligations and privileges. If peasants did not much like their lords, they could not go shopping for new ones, and if nobles did not like their peasants they could not select others. The nobles, however, had ways of bringing recalcitrant subjects to heel.

So the peasants were tied to their land, as the surest guarantee of subsistence, with the greatest risks to survival being bad harvests and rapacious landlords. Husband and wife were tied to each other through their mutual need for each other's labour. Peasant and lord were tied through sets of obligations which, in general, went from the bottom up, although lords might earn a bad name if they proved inhospitable or lacking in properly paternalistic behaviour. The exploitative relations between peasants and lords were interwoven into a complex network of interdependencies. Challenging the lords' right to a surplus could jeopardize an entire family's fragile package of survival strategies, including the right to shelter and land. Furthermore, members of each household worked their own plot of land. This isolating work experience—unlike work in a modern factory or office—did not provide the collective work experience that can bind together those in the same circumstances while, at the same time, separating them from those above.

Similarly, most men and most women found it impossible to survive without marriage and household. Certainly, the interdependence of husband and wife was crafted within a society that never doubted the inferiority of women. The laws of church, state, and manor sustained and counselled the subordination of women to men, and wives to husbands (Middleton 1983; Rogers 1966). Some women did challenge their husbands' authority, particularly when the latter violated community standards (Davis 1982). The penalties for resistance, however, were high in a society that provided only one location for work and home, and no alternative ways to piece together a living. These feudal arrangements obviously did not provide fertile ground for either a labour movement or a women's movement. Their entrance onto the world stage awaited the development of capitalism, with its own particular form of patriarchy.

THE TRANSITION TO CAPITALISM

A great deal has been written about how capitalist relations developed in the very heart of feudal society (Marx 1973; Dobb 1963; Hilton 1976; Hill 1969; Brenner 1986). In simplest terms, however, people had to lose their means of subsistence, namely the land, before they could be free to sell their labour power in the marketplace. At the same time there had to be those who owned and controlled capital with which to purchase the newly freed labour power. Surplus capital and surplus labour, therefore, can be seen as two sides of the same coin. The gradually accumulating capital derived from the surplus produced by the workers. This surplus capital then was reinvested in further capitalist (at first primarily agrarian capitalist) development. This capital accumulation underwrote the Industrial Revolution and, in a more general sense, the availability of capital and labour provided the preconditions for the Industrial Revolution (George 1971; Hamilton 1978, 15–17). The spiralling growth of capital and labour involved a snowballing and mutually reinforcing set of processes.

In general, during the transition to capitalism, people were forced or persuaded to leave the land: common lands were enclosed, rents were raised, and the parliament that emerged after the half-finished English Revolution confirmed the process through abolishing feudal tenures and instituting the contemporary system of buying and selling land. In this process some grew richer, but many more took to the roads, embarking upon new lives of vagabondage and crime. Many others went to work for their better-off neighbours (Hill 1969, 147; McMullan 1984).

This process created not only wage labourers, but also consumers (Appleby 1978). For landless people have to buy everything they need (that is, what they can afford) in the marketplace. By the end of the seventeenth century expanding markets were being created, not just in England but in America (Davis 1973; George 1971). These markets helped to make the already rich even richer, while creating the newly rich. These expanding markets have reached an illogical zenith today. Capitalism requires the continuing creation of new needs. People must be persuaded to spend their money in new and spectacular ways, preferably on things requiring frequent replacement. The importance of the isolated nuclear family to capitalist expansion is clear. Every household needs its own everything: washing machines, stoves, cars, cottages, videos, microwaves, blenders, all of which lie idle most of the time (Zaretsky 1976; Hayden 1981; Cowan 1983).

This transition to capitalism encompassed more than the origins of contemporary economic relations. Challenges to political relationships accompanied the shift to contractual relations in the economic sphere. Kings and nobles had been compared to fathers. Their subjects owed them obedience and deference. In return, rulers were expected, at least in theory, to look after their subjects, according to their station in life. The authority of kings and other rulers was held to be divinely inspired, natural and unlimited. When the feudal world came asunder and new classes and new relations between classes developed, so too did new political ideas expressing these new economic realities (Manning 1978).

The rising class of bourgeois capitalists no longer depended upon the pleasure of the court or on traditional property arrangements for their livelihood. The ideology of the self-made man finds its origins here. Self-made men made their money from agriculture, trade and colonization, or through providing services to those who did. Thus we find an expanding professional class of doctors, lawyers, and bankers, who shared in the new interests and lifestyles of the bourgeoisie. These men hired others to work for them on a contractual basis. Ideas about the divine right of kings held little sway for the new "self-made" men. Radical ideas (i.e., rulers only ruled because of a contract between them and the ruled) gained adherents, and men of property began insisting upon parliaments that would protect their interests. The door to universal suffrage creaked open. At the same time, religious reformers insisted upon a personal, unmediated relationship between the individual and God. In lay hands the Bible proved a controversial document. If still believed to be divinely inspired, it was now being humanly interpreted in a myriad of ways. Contracts between ruler and ruled, individuals and God, and employers and employees became the order of the new day. But wait a minute! Not between husband and wife.

As much as the economic, political and religious theorists insisted upon contractual relationships in the public world they continued to build this new world upon the indissoluble unit of husband and wife. Marriage was a property relationship, and the wife was still clearly part of the husband's property. The relationships between ruler and ruled, employer and employee, even individual and God, were becoming questions of personal choice, requiring constant renewal, part of the world seen to be humanly wrought. The family remained part of the natural order of things, with the woman as its linchpin (Eisenstein 1981).

Contradictions were already developing around the position of women in this new society. These contradictions were experienced in very deep and significant ways for many women. To understand them we must explore how the family/household itself was changing during this transition to capitalism, how the role of women and the relationship between husband and wife were transformed, and how these changes had very different implications for the emerging bourgeoisie and the burgeoning proletariat.

To begin, peasants were becoming wage-earners. The split between work and home meant that women no longer could perform their reproductive tasks of bearing and rearing children in the *same* location as their other work. They were confronted with the necessity of making a living for their families and at the same time ensuring that their children did not die of neglect. The conventional division of labour between husbands and wives cast men in the role of economic providers. But this was little more than a cruel joke because the wages a man could command (certainly in early capitalism) barely covered his own food and drink. The family wage was a fantasy. It still is, except for the highest paid union workers who, at times, have been able, through the collective bargaining process, to earn sufficient money to support a family (Secombe 1986; Barrett and McIntosh 1980; 1982; Armstrong 1984). The economic interdependence between men and women broke down. Women and children became a burden—for many men an insupportable burden. This "Second Humble Address" from the Poor Weavers provides an example:

That the Poor's Rates are doubled and in some places trebled by the multitude of Poor Perishing and Starving Women and Children being come to the Parishes, while their Husbands and Fathers not able to bear the cries which they could not relieve are fled into France . . . to seek their Bread (Quoted in Clark 1919, 118).

The family as economic unit encountered some perilous days, which have grown into decades and centuries. The number of children today with sole-support and poverty-stricken mothers indicates that this was a long-term consequence of the development of capitalist relations (Armstrong, this text).

In the growing bourgeoisie, women also lost their productive role. As the former busy, hospitable, and many-faceted manor gave way to private homes with separate spaces for servants, children, and parents, and as work took men more and more away from home, women were increasingly relegated to and immersed in the privatized, isolated world of the newly constituted nuclear family. At the same time as their husbands, fathers and sons were remaking the world in their masculine image, wives ceased to be business partners and became instead the 'Angel in the House' (Rowbotham 1972, 29). Mary Astell lamented this change. She pleaded, "Can you be in Love with servitude and folly? Can you dote on a mean, ignorant and ignoble Life?" (1701, 52).

A new ideology was in the making, however. First a few, but then many, began to argue that a life in this newly constituted family was the pinnacle to which women should aspire. The home of the "honest, upright Englishman" was described as the "sweetest and purest thing on earth" (Flynn 1920, 75). In time it was realized that women's special qualities—purity, chastity, patience, gentleness—would be bruised in contact with the raucous world that capitalists were creating outside their doors. This world included a growing class of desperately poor women in many areas of the city, as well as servants occupying the least favoured parts of the bourgeois home. Many of these working-class women supplemented their meagre wages by sexually servicing the men of the bourgeoisie who found the homes they created with their pure and protected wives to be too confining. What struck many observers at that time was the presence of two classes of women: one poor, one affluent; one overworked, the other bored; one sexual, the other chaste; one independent by necessity, the other dependent in every sense on a husband or father.

The new ideology, "the cult of true womanhood" (Reuther 1973) proved enormously powerful. As sections of the working class organized and commanded better wages, the ideology that good husbands supported their wives, and good wives were full-time home-makers was also spreading, and would receive, much later, a properly academic stamp in the sociology of Talcott Parsons (1959). As the economic interdependence of husband and wife became unravelled, new ways—ideological, political and economic—emerged to tie women to the family. But it was a very different sort of family than in feudal times.

Perhaps the most effective of these new ways was the development of a most novel idea: that love and marriage not only went together, but indeed *had* to go together (Sarsby 1983). As long as marriage had been primarily an economic arrangement, as it was throughout the feudal era, there was no special belief that husband and wife had to love each other—certainly not in our sense of falling in love with each other. Passions such as this were known to exist, but their instability was well recognized and, therefore, better left to less permanent liaisons than marriage. Furthermore, the Catholic Church in the Middle Ages revered celibacy as an adult life course.

The Protestant reformers thought no better of lust and sexual passion that did the clergy of the Church of Rome, but they rejected celibacy as a means to achieve personal holiness, and argued that a godly life could be pursued best by those in other stations and callings. They promoted marriage and believed that man and woman should love each other even as they loved God. Even conjugal sex was blessed, providing that passion was kept well in check (Hamilton 1978, Ch. 3).

What the Protestants did not (and could not) know was that the world was changing. They had intended the marital partnership to be embedded in the feudal life of economic interdependence between husband and wife, each working with and for each other, and collectively for their children. That kind of life, as we have seen, was disappearing. The emerging bourgeois family, stripped of its economic functions, became the site of a married couple, brought together by mutual love and admiration, enough—as it had to be—to last a lifetime. Protestants were as adamantly opposed to divorce as Catholics, and they even closed the annulment option. The ideology of romantic love had found a vacuum, and the early Protestants would have undoubtedly expressed horror by its elevation to the modern foundation of marriage.

The women of the bourgeoisie became almost totally dependent upon their husbands. Other than governessing, there were few jobs open to, and suitable for, women of the middle and upper-middle classes (Peterson 1972). The legitimating ideology for this life of dependence is still familiar: ideas about romantic love, idealization of family life, separate spheres for women and men, and the needs of children.

THE FIRST WOMEN'S MOVEMENT

The main focus for feminists at the turn of the twentieth century was neither women's location in the family, nor the inequality and oppression their position produced. Given the dependence of most women and their children upon husbands and fathers, a frontal critique of the family would have been individually and collectively impossible. For, as Jeffrey Weeks (1981, 163) put it, "in the absence of alternative avenues for middle-class women, their actual survival often depended upon a secure legal marriage". A critique of the family awaited the new conditions of the 1960s that ushered in the contemporary women's movement. So what, then, was this first movement about?

Primarily, it challenged the limitations on women's activities in the public sphere. The men of the rising bourgeoisie had been challenging their own subordinate place in the aristocratic order for some two centuries. This challenge constituted the small "l" liberal assault upon the aristocratic order. It was accomplished in the name of the rights of man, of individual worth, expression and achievement. It insisted that contracts between subject and rulers be negotiated through elections. This liberal attack included demands for the freedom of worship, freedom of speech, freedom of the press, and equality of opportunity.

As so often happens historically, when a particular group or class insists upon certain rights for itself, others, who hear the rhetoric which often is cast in universal terms, believe that it means them too. Men of property, for example, only intended the vote for men of property. Increasingly, however, working-class men insisted upon inclusion. They fought and struggled and won the right to vote (Thompson 1984). Sooner or later women would insist upon these same rights for themselves. Mary Wollstonecraft in *A Vindication of the Rights of Women* had provided the argument in 1792. Women, she pointed out, also were rational beings. If they did not behave rationally, it was a result of limited upbringing and education, not innate "feminine" qualities.

As time passed, women challenged their enclosure in the limiting and limited private sphere. They took over rhetoric (never intended by men to apply to women), insisted upon their right to participate equally in public. They demanded the right to vote, to own property, to enter professions and to receive an education. These were radical demands. True to their liberal roots, they were demands for equality of opportunity. They did not address squarely questions about equality of condition, although women's unequal starting place in the race of life, created by their reproductive tasks and their place in the family, was sometimes perceived. Women challenged their denial of property rights and the legal power of husbands over wives and children; they insisted upon their legal right to child custody when marriages dissolved, and their right to divorce abusive husbands. Yet they did not question the validity and underpinnings of the family itself.

These women of the bourgeoisie railed against the double standard which permitted their husbands to have sexual relations with other women, women who might have been working full- or part-time as prostitutes to supplement meagre wages. From the vantage point of bourgeois women—some of whom did comprehend the double exploitation/oppression of their working class sisters—their husbands' sexual activities were threatening: certainly they feared venereal disease. They wanted the vote, among other things, to clean up the world, including their husbands' behaviour; they sought to impose a single standard of sexual behaviour on the sexes (Gordon 1984). As one famous slogan went, "Votes for Women! Chastity for Men!" Could it have been otherwise in a world without, for example, safe and trustworthy methods of birth control, antibiotics, opportunities for economic independence, or access to child support from state or husbands?

These feminists emphasized that they wanted the vote and education to become better mothers. They argued that women's special role in the family equipped them to play an important role in humanizing the brutal public world. That world, with the participation of women, could become as clean as their own kitchens. Perhaps, at times, they phrased their demands in these socially acceptable ways to ward off criticism, to try to alleviate the monumental anxieties their demands had unleashed. But most often they must have been sincere.

Today their demands form part of the conservative status quo (Eisenstein 1981, Ch. 10). Even Phyllis Shlafly and R.E.A.L. Women do not argue that women should not have the right to vote. (Dubinsky 1984; Eisenstein 1981). Their quarrel is with feminists who have uncovered the limitations of equality in the public sphere, and the inadequacy of such demands given the unequal social locations of men and women.

For it was one thing for women, like men, to be free to make and break contracts in public arenas: to vote in elections, to change their minds and vote for others in the next election, to take and leave employment, to prepare for that employment. But as second-wave feminists began to point out, there were several catches for women. This time feminists occupied a better position to criticize the family, that institution so revered by their predecessors. The nuclear family—based as it was on monogamy and compulsory heterosexuality (Rich 1980), on men's breadwinning role and women's domestic role, and on the institution of motherhood (all of this confirmed in law)—constituted the primary site for the constitution and perpetuation of male domination and female subordination. Or so, in the 1970s, feminists began to argue (Mitchell 1971; Chodorow 1978; Dinnerstein 1976; Maroney 1986). This argument encompassed many aspects, and more appeared with each layer that was uncovered.

Before looking more closely at this developing perspective on the family, let us look at why these feminists were in a position, as no women before them, to place the family itself under critical scrutiny. The earlier struggles for education and entrance to professions, together with the enormous expansion of service industries and state bureaucracies, had brought hundreds of thousands of women into the labour force and, therefore, towards new possibilities for economic independence. A marriage licence was no longer the only meal ticket in town: now some women could earn enough money to support themselves and their children. In particular, however, young university-educated women, unmarried and childless, were in a position to confront the assumptions and practices of the conventional nuclear family.

These new possibilities for economic independence also carried with them new possibilities for structured sex inequality. The development of poorly paid job ghettoes and the double day of labour provide two major examples. These new forms for perpetuating patriarchy encouraged the feminist critiques of the economic, political, legal, social and sexual assumptions underlying the monogamous, nuclear family. Private troubles—wife battery, marital rape, disproportionate poverty of women (especially sole support mothers and older women), incest, isolation, unwanted pregnancy—were transformed into public issues (Mills 1959). In calling the so-called natural world of the family into question, feminists insisted that this institution was socially constructed, and like the rest of society, thoroughly structured by sexual inequality.

For the new wave of feminists, nothing remained sacred. Even romantic love was examined as an historical development, carrying with it a dark underside for women (Firestone 1970, Ch. 7). Most people who married, both men and women, did so because they were in love. In the absence of economic interdependence, the ideology proclaimed that love should both provoke and maintain marriages. But falling in love was played out very differently by men and women. The poet who wrote

Man's love is of man's life a thing apart,
'Tis woman's whole existence (Lord Byron)

was still not far off the mark. It is women who still choose marriage over education and career, and put aside both to start a family. When marriages break up because one or both partners are no longer in love, women are left with half-finished educations and few marketable skills for supporting themselves and, usually, their children. Their departed husbands, with their superior education and wage-earning potential, can fall in love again, and begin anew. The disproportionate number of women-led families below the poverty line provides grim confirmation of what otherwise might appear as a cynical interpretation. Furthermore, what stands between most middle-class women and poverty is a husband's or ex-husband's salary, and how he chooses to use it.

The same set of capitalist social relations that provided the preconditions for the contemporary women's movement also gave rise to the unreciprocated economic dependence of women upon men, and in their absence, upon the state. How can this apparent contradiction be explained? This is a difficult puzzle to untangle, and there are no easy answers. But the contractual relations of capitalism release men and women, in theory, to sell their labour power in the marketplace. That 'freedom' has produced a new kind of tyranny. Karl Polanyi (1944, 163–64) argued that

> the individual in primitive society is not threatened by starvation unless the community as a whole is in a like predicament . . . The principle of freedom from want was equally acknowledged under almost every and any type of social organization up to about the beginning of sixteenth-century Europe.

Polanyi's point is true to the extent that the relations between people had not been parcelled out into a set of contracts. However devastating this new freedom—the freedom to sell your labour power or to starve—has been for men, its consequences for women and their children have been far more devastating. Women's lives are simply not divided up as easily as men's. It is dehumanizing for men to be reduced to wage-earning machines, and to have their labour power reduced to a commodity which may or may not be marketable. But how are women to sell their labour power in the marketplace if they are pregnant, or nursing infants? Furthermore, one must explain why there have been so many acts of commission and ommission that make it even more difficult for women to organize their lives for waged work. Laws against birth control and abortion; the lack of maternity and paternity leave; the refusal to spend societal resources on daycare and nightcare: all this stands in the way of women entering into the "gender neutral" contracts of the capitalist marketplace.

Explaining the enormous societal resistance to making the capitalist marketplace a truly non-gendered marketplace, that is, an arena that thoroughly takes account of the exigencies of women's and men's lives, constitutes a tall order. The nature of capitalism, the social and psychological dynamics of patriarchal relations, and especially the intertwining of the two, must all be taken into account. The capitalist quest to maximize profit will never offer the resources required for women and men to enter its marketplace and its corridors of power on an equal footing. Only the struggle of women and men for new ways to allocate resources and make decisions can alter that reality. Their joint struggle for the welfare state in its broad sense, a state that puts the welfare of its citizenry at the top of its agenda, reveals this clearly. Many of the existing priorities of the state in the social arena that have been struggled for and won (that women now risk losing) stand as confirmation that women and their needs are particularly ill-served in capitalist society. Women alone with children are over-represented on welfare rolls, while a great variety of social services attest to the particular dilemmas that confront women in an unreconstructed capitalist society.

Women have found themselves fighting alone on many issues, fighting not only the state, but most men, and many women as well. For the demands of feminists for a whole world that includes women produce great anxiety for many people. Men may not need women economically, but they have needed them as sources of emotional support, domestic labour, nurturing for themselves and their children, and for their sexual lives. Feminists have challenged the gendered division of labour which underwrites all of these needs. Feminists struggle for a world that maximizes the possibilities for the economic independence of women from men; a world that does not privilege one kind of sexual arrangement—monogamous heterosexuality—over others; a social and political environment that makes it possible for women to raise children alone, with other women, or, if they choose, with men; a vision that pushes us not always gently toward economic and psychological restructuring.

Paradoxically, the contractual relations of capitalism make possible the articulation of these alternatives while at the same time denying their full realization. It is not an historical accident that we live in the midst of the greatest mobilization of women that the world has witnessed. Women sense the possibilities of freedom that the contractual relations of capitalism reveal. They no longer are tied inescapably to households and husbands for their very survival and the survival of their children.

Some women with education, economic resources and well honed juggling skills have more choices than those in any generation before them. Yet much evidence shows that if room exists for token women in the bastions of male power, new ways for preventing their collective inclusion are in the making. Breaking down the misogynist practices and feelings of men, and women, may prove a very long, and not always edifying, historical task (Horowitz 1977; Hamilton 1986; Burstyn 1983; Bashevkin 1985; Kaufman 1987).

Today there are right-wing conservative governments in England, the United States, and in some Canadian provinces, most notably British Columbia and Saskatchewan. The federal Conservatives tried to de-index old age pensions, promised to reintroduce capital punishment and have responded to the crying need for universal daycare with a half-baked proposal for direct payment to parents. Much of the success of right-wing governments, particularly in the United States, rests upon the way they have managed to exploit people's legitimate anxieties about growing unemployment, reduced state services, and the threat of global annihilation. Their call is for a return to a time when "mothers were mothers and fathers were fathers" (Eisenstein 1984). In other words, they advocate reinforcing the patriarchal family with a breadwinner father and a mother at home. They paint a nostalgic and harmonious picture of family/household life in the past that has little to do with the experience of most of the people, as we see from the historical interpretation presented in this chapter. At times they insist that all of society's problems, from the threat of nuclear war through youth unemployment and drug use, could be solved if only women returned to their god-given role in the family. In this scenario, working women, homosexuals, lesbians and feminists become the scapegoats for deep economic, political and social problems. At its worst, it has become a campaign of hate. Although the feminist movement has never had so many adherents and supporters, it has also never had so many virulent and outspoken opponents.

Historical study can help in challenging these powerful myths about the past. But it can also help us differentiate the real options before us from those which rest on little more than anxiety, fear and misogyny.

Women have always had to support their families. In feudal society they toiled without respite to support themselves and their children. In capitalist society they have had to supplement their husbands' incomes through work done at home, through seeking waged work and making whatever arrangements they could for their children, or by fighting for a subsistence income from the state. Because of death, sickness, desertion, or unemployment, many have been sole supporters of their children. The particular contingencies of women's lives today emerged on the world stage with the transition to capitalism three hundred years ago. That world was also a patriarchal world, and the relations of patriarchy took on their own special form in the new society.

It is very clear then that the road to women's emancipation does not lie in the re-creation of a non-existent past but in the struggle for a society that takes account of and tries to resolve the contradictions with which women are confronted in contemporary society. Juliet Mitchell undoubtedly spoke better than she knew when she first coined the phrase "the longest revolution" in 1966. At times it seems that it has just begun.

Bibliography

Abrams, Philip.
1982   *Historical Sociology*. Somerset: Open Books.
Appleby, Joyce Oldham.
1978   *Economic Thought and Ideology in Seventeenth-Century England*.
            Princeton: Princeton University Press.
Ariès, Philippe.
1962   *Centuries of Childhood*. New York: Random House.
Armstrong, Pat, and Hugh Armstrong.
1984   *The Double Ghetto*. Toronto: McClelland & Stewart.
Astell, Mary.
1701   *A Serious Proposal to the Ladies for the Advancement of Their
            True and Greatest Interest*. 4th ed. London: printed by J.R.
            for R. Wilken.
Barrett, Michèle, and Mary McIntosh.
1980   "The Family Wage: Some Problems for Socialists and Fem-
            inists". *Capital and Class* 11 (Summer): 51–72.
1982   *The Anti-Social Family*. London: Verso.
Bashevkin, Sylvia.
1985   *Toeing the Lines: Women and Party Politics in English Canada*.
            Toronto: University of Toronto Press.
Bloch, Marc.
1966   *French Rural Society*. Berkeley: University of California Press.
Brenner, Robert.
1986   "Agrarian Class Structure and Economic Development in
            Pre-Industrial Europe" and "The Agrarian Roots of Eu-
            ropean Capitalism". In *The Brenner Debate: Agrarian Class
            Structure and Economic Development in Pre-Industrial Europe*,
            edited by T.H. Aston and C.H.E. Philpin, 10–63 and
            213–328. Cambridge: Cambridge University Press.
Burstyn, Varda.
1983   "Masculine Dominance and the State". *The Socialist Register*:
            45–89.
Charles, Lindsey, and Lorna Duffin, eds.
1985   *Women and Work in Pre-Industrial England*. London: Croom
            Helm.

Chodorow, Nancy.
1978   *The Reproduction of Mothering: Psychoanalysis and the Sociology of Gender*. Berkeley: University of California Press.
Clark, Alice.
[1919]   *Working Life of Women in the Seventeenth Century*. London: G. Routledge; reissued 1982, Routledge and Kegan Paul.
Cowan, Ruth Schwartz.
1983   *More Work for Mother: The Ironies of Household Technology from the Open Hearth to the Microwave*. New York: Basic Books.
Davis, Natalie Zemon.
1982   "Women on Top". In *Society and Culture in Early Modern France*. Stanford: Stanford University Press.
Davis, Ralph.
1973   *The Rise of the Atlantic Economies*. London: Weidenfeld and Nicholson.
de Beauvoir, Simone.
[1949]   *The Second Sex*. 1972. Harmondsworth: Penguin Books.
Dinnerstein, Dorothy.
1976   *The Mermaid and the Minotaur: Sexual Arrangements and Human Malaise*. New York: Harper and Row.
Dobb, Maurice.
1963   *Studies in the Development of Capitalism*. New York: International Publishers.
Dubinsky, Karen.
1984   "Lament for a 'Patriarchy Lost'—Anti-feminism, Anti-abortion, and R.E.A.L. Women in Canada". Ottawa: Canadian Research Institute for the Advancement of Women: Feminist Perspectives N. 1.
Eisenstein, Zillah.
1984   *Feminism and Sexual Equality*. New York: Monthly Review Press.
1981   *The Radical Future of Liberal Feminism*. Boston: Northeastern University Press.
Firestone, Shulamith.
1970   *The Dialectic of Sex*. New York: Morrow.
Flynn, John.
1920   *The Influence of Puritanism*. Port Washington: Kennikat Press.
George, C.H.
1971   "The Making of the English Bourgeoisie, 1500–1750". *Science and Society* 35: 385–414.
Giddens, Anthony.
1981   *A Contemporary Critique of Historical Materialism*. London: Macmillan.

Gordon, Linda, and Ellen Dubois.
1984   "Seeking Ecstasy on the Battlefield: Danger and Pleasure in
            Nineteenth Century Feminist Sexual Thought". In *Pleasure
            and Danger: Exploring Female Sexuality*, edited by Carole S.
            Vance, 31–49. Boston: Routledge and Kegan Paul.

Goubert, Pierre.
1973   *The Ancient Regime: French Society 1600–1750*. New York:
            Harper & Row.

Hacker, Helen.
1951   "Women as a Minority Group". In *Social Forces* 30(1): 60–
            69.

Hamilton, Roberta.
1978   *The Liberation of Women*. London: Allen & Unwin.
1986   "The Collusion with Patriarchy: A Psychoanalytic Account".
            In *The Politics of Diversity: Feminism, Marxism and Nationalism*,
            edited by Roberta Hamilton and Michèle Barrett. London:
            Verso.
1987   "Does Misogyny Matter?". *Studies in Political Economy* 23:
            123–39.

Hayden, Dolores.
1981   *The Grand Domestic Revolution: A History of Feminist Designs
            for American Homes, Neighbourhoods and Cities*. Cambridge,
            Mass: Harvard University Press.

Hill, Christopher.
1969   *Reformation to Industrial Revolution*. Hardmondsworth: Pen-
            guin Books.

Hilton, Rodney.
1976   *The Transition from Feudalism to Capitalism*. London: New Left
            Books.
1986   "A Crisis of Feudalism". *The Brenner Debate: Agrarian Class
            Structure and Economic Development in Pre-Industrial Europe*,
            edited by T.H. Aston and C.H.E. Philpin, Cambridge: Cam-
            bridge University press.

Horowitz, Gad.
1977   *Repression: Basic and Surplus Repression in Psychoanalytic The-
            ory*. Toronto: University of Toronto Press.

Kaufman, Michael.
1987   *Beyond Patriarchy: Essays by Men on Pleasure, Power and Change*.
            Toronto: Oxford University Press.

Kelly, Joan.
1984   *Women, History and Theory: The Essays of Joan Kelly*. (Women
            in Culture & Society Ser.) Chicago: University of Chicago
            Press.

Ladurie, Emmanuel Le Roy.
1974   *The Peasants of Languedoc.* Trans., with an introduction by John Day. Chicago: University of Illinois Press.
Luxton, Meg.
1980   *More than a Labour of Love.* Toronto: The Women's Press.
Manning, Brian.
1978   *The English People and the English Revolution.* Harmondsworth: Penguin.
Maroney, Heather Jon.
1986   "Embracing Motherhood: New Feminist Theory". *The Politics of Diversity: Feminism, Marxism, and Nationalism,* edited by Roberta Hamilton and Michèle Barrett, 398–423. London: Verso.
Marx, Karl.
1973   *The Grundrisse.* Harmondsworth: Penguin Books.
McMullan, John.
1984   *The Canting Crew: London's Criminal Underworld, 1550–1700.* New Brunswick: New Jersey: Rutgers University Press.
Middleton, Christopher.
1983   "Patriarchal Exploitation and the Rise of English Capitalism". In *Gender, Class and Work,* edited by Eva Garmanikow et al., 11–27. London: Heinemann.
Mills, C. Wright.
1959   *The Sociological Imagination.* New York: Oxford University Press.
Mitchell, Juliet.
[1966]   "The Longest Revolution", *New Left Review.* Reprinted in *The Longest Revolution* by Juliet Mitchell, 1984. New York: Pantheon Books.
Mousnier, Roland.
1979   *The Institutions of France under the Absolute Monarchy: Society and State.* Chicago: University of Chicago Press.
Myrdal, Gunnar.
[1944]   "Appendix 5. A Parallel to the Negro Problem". In *An American Dilemma.* 1962. New York: Harper & Row.
Neeson, J.M.
1984   "The Opponents of Enclosure in Eighteenth-Century Northamptonshire". *Past and Present* 105: 114–139.
Parr, Joy, ed.
1982   *Childhood and Family in Canadian History.* Toronto: McClelland & Stewart.
Parsons, Talcott.
1959   "The Social Structure of the Family". In *The Family: Its Func-*

tion and Destiny, edited by R.N. Anshen, 241–274. New York: Hayner.

Peterson, M. Jeanne.
1972   "The Victorian governess: status incongruence in family and society". In *Suffer and Be Still*, edited by Martha Vicinus, 3–19. Bloomington, Ill.: Indiana University Press.

Phillips, Roderick.
1988   (forthcoming) *Putting Asunder: A History of Divorce in Western Society*. Cambridge: Cambridge University Press.

Polanyi, Karl.
1944   *The Great Transformation*. Boston: Beacon.

Power, Eileen.
1965   "The Position of Women". In *The Legacy of the Middle Ages*, edited by C.G. Crump, 401–433. Oxford: Clarendon Press.

Reiter, Ester.
1986   "Life in a Fast-Food Factory". In *On the Job*, edited by Craig Heron and Robert Storey, Kingston: McGill-Queen's University Press.

Reiter, Rayna.
1975   *Toward an Anthropology of Women*. New York: Monthly Review Press.

Report of The Royal Commission on the Status of Women. Ottawa:
1970   Information Canada.

Reuther, Rosemary.
1973   "The cult of true womanhood". *Commonweal* (November 9): 127–32.

Rich, Adrienne.
1980   "Compulsory Heterosexuality and Lesbian Experience". *Signs* 5(4): 631–660.

Rogers, Katherine.
1966   *The Troublesome Helpmate, A History of Misogyny in Literature*. Seattle: Washington Paperbacks.

Rowbotham, Sheila.
1972   *Women, Resistance and Revolution*. New York: Vintage Books.

Sarsby, Jacqueline.
1983   *Romantic Love and Society*. Harmondsworth: Penguin.

Secombe, Wally.
1980   "Domestic Labour and the Working-Class Household". In *Hidden in the Household*, edited by Bonnie Fox, 25–99. Toronto: The Women's Press.

1986   "Patriarchy stabilized: the construction of the male breadwinner wage norm in nineteenth-century Britain". *Social History* 11(2) (January): 53–76.

Stone, Lawrence.
1977   *The Family, Sex and Marriage in England 1500–1800.* London: Weidenfeld & Nicholson.
Thompson, Dorothy.
1984   *The Chartists: Popular Politics in the Industrial Revolution.* London: Temple Smith.
Tilly, Louise A., and Joan W. Scott.
1978   *Women, Work and Family.* New York: Holt, Rinehart & Winston.
Trofimenkoff, Susan Mann and Alison Prentice, eds.
1977   *The Neglected Majority: Essays in Canadian Women's History.* Toronto: McClelland and Stewart.
Tusser, Thomas.
1557   *Five Hundred Points of Good Husbandry.* Quoted in Mildred Campbell, *The English Yeoman*, p. 255. New York: Barnes & Noble, 1942.
Weeks, Jeffrey.
1981   *Sex, Politics and Society: The regulation of sexuality since 1800.* London: Longman.
Williams, Raymond.
1977   *Marxism and Literature.* Oxford: Oxford University Press.
1972   *Women Unite!* Toronto: Canadian Women's Education Press.
Wollstonecraft, Mary.
1792   *A Vindication of the Rights of Women.* London. Printed for J. Johnson.
Zaretsky, Eli.
1976   *Capitalism, Family and Personal Life.* New York: Harper & Row.

CHAPTER 2

Men, Husbands, and Fathers: Beyond Patriarchal Relations

Robert A. Stebbins

The nuclear family of husband, wife, and their children and the household they form and maintain is an ancient ideal. Homer described that ideal in *The Odyssey* (Book VI, p. 180) in a statement made by Ulysses to the queen:

> May the gods grant you all things which your heart desires, and may they give you a husband and a home and gracious concord, for there is nothing greater and better than this—when a husband and wife keep a household in oneness of mind, a great woe to their enemies and joy to their friends, and win high renown.

Ulysses' ideal (and presumably that of the queen as well) is alive and well in twentieth century Canada. As evidence, consider the increasing number of female university graduates who, despite their plans to pursue a work career outside the home, also plan to marry and have children (Lopata 1971, 48; Ambert 1976, 98–99; *Calgary Herald* (Saturday, February 12) 1983: B7, 137).

Despite the myth that men resist marriage, and hence the ideal of which Homer wrote, there is considerable evidence that they, too, want to marry. Nordstrom (1986, 31–32), in a summary of previous research, concludes that a greater proportion of men than women eventually find matrimony. Moreover, husbands more often report being happier with marriage than wives, perhaps for the practical reason that they enjoy more health benefits from the marital relationship. In harmony with these findings is the observation that men initiate divorce less often than women. In the study conducted by Nordstrom (1986), few of the men in his sample felt pressure to marry or said that they had drifted into marriage. Most of them actively sought this relationship.

All this, it would appear, is grounds for eternal family harmony and bliss. Both husband and wife agree on the benefits of marriage and "keeping a household in oneness of mind". Yet, today both have other interests and obligations, some of which are as powerful as the interests and obligations that they share with reference to the household. Somehow both must co-operate and compromise with each other from time to time in a way that keeps the household in operation, while balancing the demands of their external interests and obligations. The amount of give and take here is rarely perceived by both members of the couple to be equal. In this chapter we explore the male view of this process, keeping in mind the observation that, whatever their other interests and obligations, men generally want family involvements of some kind.

MEN IN FAMILIES

For most married men, the family is an important hub of their daily activities. When viewed from the perspective of this family hub, which includes wife and/or children (if any), these activities fall into two broad categories: interests and obligations. Although they are sometimes interesting and enjoyable, *obligations* have as their main quality the fact that they impose a significant degree of constraint on us. Obligations exist at home and at work. *Interests* lack a significant sense of obligation; they are forms of leisure. Leisure interests may be pursued within or outside the family circle, or they may be pursued simultaneously in both domains.

Men, including married men, fulfill their obligations and pursue their interests, in part, according to the *male gender role*. Of course, maleness is by no means always uppermost or even consciously on a man's mind when he is at work, at home, or at play. Yet, thinking and behaving as he has learned to and is expected to think and behave is a frequent consideration at some level of awareness and intensity when doing what he is obliged to do or is interested in doing. We learn to think and behave in gender appropriate ways.

Against this background of being male, pursuing interests, and fulfilling obligations, married men interact with other members of their families. To the extent that their interests and obligations are not shared with those members, they experience special patterns of rewards, costs, tensions, accommodations, and the like that are different from those of members of his family. The question is, how different is his life and in what ways does it differ?

OBLIGATIONS

That there is a sense of involuntariness about obligations is not necessarily bad. People enjoy fulfilling certain obligations, even though they perceive that they have little reasonable choice but to do so. A father might feel strongly obligated to attend either a hockey game in which his son is playing, or the graduation from high school of his daughter, and might look forward with pleasure to both events. We shall consider three main family-oriented obligations that face men in their roles as husbands and fathers: their occupation, their participation in domestic chores, and their parenting.

Occupation

One typical family issue that falls under the heading of occupation is the amount of time that the husband and father of the family spends at work. Research has tended to center on excessive amounts of work time (beyond the conventional 35-to-40 hours per week), as manifested in overtime, multiple jobs (moonlighting), and commitment to a line of work that has no clear limits, for example, running a store or practising a profession. Perhaps the most careful study in this area is that of Staines and Pleck (1983), which is based on a national sample in the United States. They found that excessive work did not lead to a reduction in the amount of time spent on household chores when compared with the average work week of 35 to 40 hours. How much time men in general actually spend doing household chores is discussed in the next section.

Staines and Pleck did demonstrate, however, that working beyond the conventional number of weekly hours is a source of family strain. Similar findings were obtained by Keith and Schafer (1980) and Mortimer (1980). The former examined the levels of strain generated by husbands who held two jobs; the latter studied the effects of the long hours put in by professionals and managers.

Work that requires the husband and father to work all or part of each weekend results in less time devoted to housework and to interaction with children (Staines and Pleck). Not so with shift work, which these investigators found to increase significantly the amount of time that male workers spend on domestic chores. This pattern may result, in part, from the fact that many shift workers have time on their hands during periods of the evening and morning when there is little else to do than housework. Shift work, however, does create strain over the scheduling of family activities (Tasto *et al.* 1978; House 1980).

The four-day or compressed work week is still another way in which the amount and organization of time devoted to work affects family life. In the four-day week, the typical number of hours worked (35 to 40) is compressed into four days. Research by Maklan (1977a; 1977b) suggests that, when compared with the conventional workweek, the four-day modification results in more time being spent with children and allocated to family chores.

Work as a central life interest

A *central life interest* is a segment of an individual's life in which a substantial emotional investment has been made (Dubin 1979, 419). Although more than one segment of our lives can become central in this way, limitations on time and money preclude us from developing many of them. Many family men consider work a central life interest and regard household chores and child-rearing as secondary to it (Berger and Wright 1978).

The extreme expression of work as a central life interest is *workaholism*, and those who suffer from it are known as *workaholics*. Workaholics are those "whose desire to work long and hard is intrinsic and whose work habits almost always exceed the prescriptions of the job they do and the expectations of the people with whom or for whom they work" (Machlowitz 1980, 11). The workaholics can and do work anytime and anywhere and that they prefer work to leisure (Machlowitz 1980, 29–30), surely relegates family life to a sort of residual category. Although the addiction to work knows no social-class boundaries, the intrinsic rewards of the work to which they are addicted indicates that this condition is more typical of highly involved occupations. These include managers, professionals, craftsmen, and proprietors.

Such people clearly work long hours, the effects of which we have already considered. The same is true of another kind of male for whom work is a central life interest: the man who frequently works overtime or who works at multiple jobs. While it is possible that some in this category also find their work to be intrinsically rewarding, the majority appear to work excessively because they want the money. Their work is extrinsically rewarding.

But recent evidence indicates that the principle of work as primary and family as secondary is beginning to fade. For instance Campbell, Converse, and Rogers (1976), in their study of the quality of American life, found that many younger men are reversing the two priorities. However, we shall see when we reach the discussion of interests that there is another interpretation to work's recent decline as life's number one priority for men. The question raised there is whether the shift of allegiance away from work has been toward the family or toward an external leisure interest or toward both.

Family chores

The family chores that face the married couple are many and varied. Brubaker and Ade-Ridder (1986), in a comparative study of the expected division of gender-specific family responsibilities in a retirement community and the wider community, found that the husbands classified these chores in the following way: Both groups of husbands expected their wives to cook meals and wash the clothes. Both groups accepted the responsibility for yard work, automobile maintenance, earning money, and household repairs. They expected the responsibility to be shared equally for such matters as shopping, washing dishes, cleaning house, writing letters, scheduling family social events, and making family decisions. Despite their expectations, however, the retired husbands in this study tended to share tasks with or perform tasks customarily assigned to wives more often than the husbands in the larger community.

The traditional division of household labour is now showing signs of change. At first, when the proportion of wives working outside the home began to increase, (see Chapter 4), several studies revealed that the husbands of these wives did little or nothing to offset their loss of time for household chores by assuming some of them themselves.

Pat and Hugh Armstrong (1984) pointed out that working wives hold two jobs: the paying job outside the home and the job of housework inside the home. Luxton (1981) found that when their wives started paid work, the working-class husbands helped them (on weekends) an average of a half-hour more than previously. The middle-class husbands actually reduced their domestic work. These are Canadian studies, the findings of which parallel those of various American studies of the same problem (e.g., Sanik 1981; Pleck 1981).

But the most recent research in the United States suggests that men may now be starting to share more than previously in the running of the household. The reasons for this change are not yet clearly understood. McHenry et al. (1986) hypothesize that some husbands may be touched by a sense of guilt, obligation, and unfairness upon realizing that their wives are contributing to a traditional male function, namely, breadwinning, while they are not reciprocating by contributing to any of the traditional female functions, namely, doing household chores.

Further, the ways in which husbands are helping to run the household have still not been sharply identified. Is it possible that they are helping more with washing the dishes, cleaning the house, and transporting their children from place to place than with cooking meals, cleaning or ironing clothes? The latter three are more demanding in the sense that they are daily or near-daily responsibilities that require a significant degree of skill and knowledge. As such they are more difficult to delegate. Where a wife could use help most, her husband, in the typical case, is least able to offer it.

All this suggests that in the past and, to some extent, in the present, the issue of who does which family household chores can generate an uncomfortable amount of tension. Emily Nett (1980, 73), in summarizing several pertinent Canadian and American studies, concluded that, in general husbands do suffer a significant degree of tension as a result of their wives' employment outside the home. But, even here, there is contradictory evidence. Booth's (1977) research in Toronto and that of Lupri and Frideres (1981) in Calgary found no such tension.

Parenting

Coincident and congruent with what has been said so far about the decline of work as a central life interest for men and their assumption of some of the chores around the house, is their increased involvement in parenting, or child-rearing (Lips 1983). It is not that men were heretofore uninvolved in child-rearing in their families, but that their earlier comparatively minor involvement has increased in recent years, particularly among younger men. Such involvement includes playing with their children, disciplining them, helping solve their problems, working with them on their schoolwork, interpreting the social and physical world, and the like. Parenting for fathers is beginning to amount to something more substantial and profound than changing diapers or baby-sitting.

Russell (1983) reports that fathers who help with child-rearing in the ways just mentioned are highly satisfied with the experience. Indeed, for some, the attraction of this sort of interaction with their children is at the root of their declining interest in work or in their desire to limit their work so as to have sufficient time for their children. Additionally, fathering is another way in which the husband can shoulder family responsibilities that would otherwise fall to the mother who, more often than not these days, has less time for them owing to her employment outside the home.

It may be that such experiences are favorably evaluated because most fathers are able, following traditional sex-role models, to keep work and family as discrete spheres of their lives (Miller and Garrison 1982, 256). Even when household chores and child-rearing duties are more or less equitably shared, the wife and mother often seems to hold the ultimate responsibility for internal family and household operations. Given her own childhood socialization, she finds it difficult, if not impossible, to compartmentalize work and family demands, no matter how absorbing the former. Men, on the whole, do not face this problem. Socialized to look toward the outside, extrafamilial world as they have been, they can separate and more smoothly rank their commitments of time to the various activities in their lives, where they are used to keeping work, leisure, and family as distinct spheres. Thus, the parenting father may still be, as Backett (1982, 228) puts it, a peripheral father:

> In saying this I am not denying that there has been *some* change in the amount of participation by men in childcare activities. However, I feel that

it is more realistic to view this, not as any considerable real change in degree of task allocation, but rather as a relaxation in traditional social prejudices about the kinds of childrearing behaviour considered "appropriate" for a man and for a woman.

One category of father who is not allowed this luxury, however, is he who is a single parent. Fathers as single parents who acquire custody of their children through divorce, separation, or, much more rarely, widowerhood, also acquire the main responsibility for child-rearing. In 1981 more than 17 percent of single-parent families in Canada were headed by men (Statistics Canada, 1984). If the American pattern may be generalized to Canada, about one-third of these fathers have custody of girls of all ages (Orthner and Lewis 1979).

In a comparative study of single mothers and fathers, Ambert (1982) found that the fathers reported better child behavior toward them than did the mothers. The children also expressed more appreciation toward the fathers than toward the mothers. Not surprisingly, given these differences, the fathers reported greater satisfaction with the single-parent role than the mothers did. Ambert's study also demonstrated that men can and do fulfill the need for physical and psychological nurturance of young children, although men in this position worry about their ability to do so.

Of course, there are difficulties faced by single parents of both sexes. Chang and Deinard (1982) singled out three major problems: the opportunities to date are restricted by domestic responsibilities; the responsibilities limit advancement opportunities at work; and the demands of work and domestic chores limit time to be spent with children. Men, in particular, indicate that they have difficulties in the areas of lifestyle and sex education with respect to their girls. Moreover, raising children brings with it demands for occasional displays of affection and sympathy, emotional behavior that is foreign to the traditional male gender role.

RELATIONSHIPS

The two main forms of relationships considered here are the marital bond and extrafamilial friendship. Other forms certainly exist. Less intense, rather casual ties with other people on the order of acquaintanceships and work relationships are two examples. Although they may be considerable, the effects of these on family life are unknown.

The marital bond

We have already noted that men usually value the marital bond and gain a great deal from being in it. It should be noted in passing that a number of feminists take exactly the opposite stand; namely, that men place a low value on marriage. These two positions are reviewed by Salt

(1986). He espouses the first, as does Nordstrom (1986), who interviewed a sample of 71 men, some of whom had more traditional views of marriage and some of whom had less traditional views.

The more traditional men in particular stressed that they had reached a stage in their lives where getting married seemed reasonable and important. Nordstrom (1986, 33) summarizes their views: "Rather, it could almost be said that they wanted what they felt marriage would bring, and *then* sought women to marry." These men were often more eager to marry than their wives were.

Both categories married for two main reasons: companionship and security. A man finds companionship in marriage when he finds a woman in whom he can confide his emotions and his troubles. This woman—his wife—is, in most cases, the only such person in his life. For many of Nordstrom's sample, companionship, as described here, is what love is all about. Love is not the romantic and emotional feelings that some of them felt at the time of marriage, which for them now is less intense.

Being accepted and emotionally supported engendered a sense of security for these husbands. The man can relax at the end of the day with his wife and companion, with someone who will listen to him and whom he can trust. Home and wife are seen as a refuge from the uncertain and impersonal world outside.

A variety of additional considerations also made marriage special for men. Nordstrom (1986) points out that it has an instrumental value for more traditional men. They can become family men, they can re-create the kind of family in which they grew up or repair the weaknesses of that family. Some traditional men value highly the services of their mate in the areas of cooking, cleaning, and child-rearing. Less traditional men said that through marriage they achieved the enjoyment of their wives as distinct and interesting persons who are enjoyable to be with.

Friendships

There is a rapidly growing scientific literature on friendship, which centers on a range of issues only some of which bear on the present chapter. Duck and Perlman (1985) review some of the conceptual and measurement problems that continue to confound research in this area. What is reported in this chapter must therefore be considered tentative, given that much refinement remains to be done.

One of the consistent research findings in this area that bears on men in families is the tendency for men to have larger networks of moderately close friends when compared with women who have smaller networks composed of very close friends (Fisher and Oliker 1980; Granovetter 1973). That is, intimacy and expressiveness are sacrificed to some extent in the wider sweep of friendly relationships maintained by the typical man. Despite this difference, Maccoby and Jacklin (1974) found that boys and girls reported no consistent differences in their needs for affiliation.

Peter Stein (1986) notes that men not only have fewer close friends, but they also have more difficulty in forming friendships when compared with women. Several factors bearing on this difference have been identified. One, men are frequently competitive with one another. Two, they lack role models from which to learn the skills of developing and maintaining intimate relationships. Three, men (at least those in North America) are reluctant to show such emotions as affection and tenderness. Fourth, many men feel a need to demonstrate their control, which includes a reluctance to share intimate experiences and feelings.

The male friendship network nevertheless abruptly declines in size upon marriage, and does not start to expand again until middle age (Farrell and Rosenberg 1981). Family demands and those of work cut into the time formerly available for friendly relations. Although probably truer for the less traditional than for the more traditional husbands, wives also replace substantially the companionship of former male friends. Farrell and Rosenberg (1981) indicate that the male friendship network expands as occupational retirement approaches and work by Ross-Franklin (1983) shows that this expansion continues into the retirement years. It appears that some men develop a number of close friendships in old age following the deaths of their wives (Petrowsky 1976). Loneliness, however, is a problem for others in the same situation.

Farrell (1986) concludes after his review of the literature on the subject, that the relatively superficial nature of men's friendships may render their friends less effective as buffers against stress when compared with the deeper friendships of women. This observation squares with one made earlier in this chapter, which is that many men seek emotional support from their wives. It appears that this level of support is, in general, unavailable elsewhere in their social world.

INTERESTS

The leisure interests of men, as they bear on this chapter, fall into two categories. There are *familial* leisure interests, or those conducted with a man's wife, his children, or both. There are also *non-familial* interests, interests that, by and large, are pursued independently of a man's family.

Interests, whether familial or non-familial, whether male or female, can be casual or serious (Stebbins 1982). *Serious* leisure is an activity that its practitioners can identify with. It is also an activity in which they can have a career based on growing skill, knowledge, and training. At times there is a need to persevere at acquiring and/or expressing these qualities, which, however, leads to such durable benefits as self-actualization, self-enrichment, self-expression, and enhanced self-image. *Casual* leisure has none of these qualities. It is engaged in for the direct and immediate, often hedonistic, gratification that it can bring the participant.

Familial interests

There are many forms of casual leisure in which some or all members of Canadian families participate. Camping is a popular family activity, as are picknicking, hiking, watching television, dining out, visiting the local zoo, and playing games at home. A father reading a story to his children, as opposed to reading the newspaper strictly for personal enjoyment, is engaging in a common form of casual family leisure. Family gatherings with relatives or close family friends also fall here. Still, a father who drives one of his children to hockey practice or a nearby cinema would probably define these services as chores or family obligations instead of leisure.

Forms of serious family leisure are less common than forms of casual family leisure, a ratio that is also found in the wider society (Stebbins 1982). One of the reasons for this discrepancy is that serious leisure, as noted already, requires a significant degree of perseverance and effort. Many adults and children have little inclination to commit themselves this deeply to any form of leisure.

Nonetheless, members of families, even entire families, do sometimes become absorbed in some sort of serious leisure. As such it becomes a central life interest for those who participate. This happens with music, skiing, bowling, tennis, fishing, and hunting, to mention but a few. Possibly even more common is the blending of casual and serious forms, such as when the family turns out to watch (as casual leisure) one or more of its members perform a piece of music at a public concert or compete in a local tennis tournament (as serious leisure). An illustration of this mixture comes from those fathers, and occasionally mothers, who pursue amateur archaeology. Those family members who are not archaeologists sometimes accompany those who are on excavations lasting a day, a week, or even two weeks. For the former the outing is an occasion for camping, fishing, hiking, and the like, while for the latter it is an occasion to engage in a serious avocation (Stebbins 1979).

Although it is well established that most leisure takes place in the home, not all home-centered leisure involves other members. A man might pursue the serious hobby of woodworking alone in his basement or work on his stamp collection in the solitude of his study. However, the most common of all leisure activities in many Western nations is watching television at home, a form of casual entertainment that is frequently consumed in the company of other family members (Roberts 1978, 95–96).

As Kelly (1982, 175) points out, just because home-centered leisure is the most common and frequent of all leisure, does not necessarily mean that it is the most satisfying. Mothers and fathers may participate in certain forms of recreation because, for example, the family members who participate with them are handy. They may participate on the strength of the belief that it is good for family cohesiveness or child development to engage in shared leisure, even though they might prefer to do something else. Here is one point where leisure activities and family obligations become difficult to distinguish empirically, even though we can define them separately as sociological concepts.

Non-familial interests

Recent evidence indicates that husbands, when compared with wives, especially those with children, participate significantly more in leisure outside the home (Horna, in press). Indeed, most husbands have more time for leisure than their wives. Wives, like their husbands, may engage in non-familial leisure in the home, but their smaller social networks tend to limit the range of their external leisure involvements. This pattern is particularly true for working-class wives vis-à-vis their husbands (Roberts 1978, 97).

The non-familial leisure of husbands may be either casual or serious. Typical casual leisure includes attending a hockey or football game, drinking with friends at a tavern, snowmobiling on a Saturday afternoon, reading a novel, or going for a walk. A wide range of hobbies, amateur pursuits, and career volunteer activities serve as serious leisure for some men. Although few of these activities inherently exclude wives (women do many of them), amateur and hobbyist pursuits in particular are expressions of personal interest. People engage, for example, in amateur science or sport, or seriously collect paintings, or tinker with old cars, because they have developed an interest in doing so (Stebbins 1982). Members of their families or even their friends are not an essential part of these undertakings.

Self-fulfillment

Non-familial interests, be they casual or serious, are at the root of a recent change in orientation among many workers in Britain and North America. A number of impressionistic and descriptive studies (see Stebbins 1982 for a review) indicate that, more and more, people are working primarily because they need the money to sustain their leisure interests (after physical survival). Moreover, these interests are consuming a growing proportion of their working hours. In short, work is becoming less and less a central life interest.

This change in orientation is not exclusively limited to men. It is, however, most prominent in those workers who have organized their adult lives around an occupational career, which, historically, has included a much larger proportion of men than women. Wives who have started paid work for the first time or returned to such work after many years of raising children, and who do so primarily for the purpose of supplementing the family budget, have not had this change in orientation. Work for them is not, and in many cases never was, a central life interest.

By this reasoning, then, the desire to cut back on the emotional involvement in, and time devoted to, paid work is presently more often found in the modern husband-father than in the modern wife-mother. In place of work these men (and less frequently women) hope to find *self-fulfillment* in their leisure, a benefit that work cannot provide in significant degree. They see in their work as demanding *self-denial*, as working to enhance or further someone else's interests, principally those of the boss or their family or both.

The pursuit of self-fulfillment is the pursuit of the development of oneself as a distinct person. Leisure, instead of paid work, is increasingly seen as providing the opportunity to do this. While a small segment of the population will always be committed to their work, perhaps even to the extent of becoming workaholics, the question raised earlier may now be readdressed: is the shift in allegiance among those who are searching for self-fulfillment in their leisure toward familial leisure or non-familial leisure?

Unfortunately, no research has been conducted that directly bears on this question. There are hints, however, that men as husbands and fathers are particularly given to seeking their self-fulfillment in non-familial leisure, with the serious form being most likely to lead them to that fulfillment. Married men, who have been traditionally more oriented away from the home than married women, fit better the following observations made by Daniel Yankelovich (1981, 10) on the many Americans who are searching for self-fulfillment away from the job:

> But now tens of millions of Americans have grown wary of demands for further sacrifices they believe no longer be warranted. They want to modify the giving/getting compact in every one of its dimensions—family life, career, leisure, the meaning of success, relationships with other people and relations with themselves.
>
> On traditional demands for material well-being, seekers of self-fulfillment now impose new demands for intangibles—creativity, leisure, autonomy, pleasure, participation, community, adventure, vitality, stimulation, tender loving care. To the efficiency of technological society they wish to add joy of living. They seek to satisfy both the body *and* the spirit.

Yankelovich goes on to note that most of the people he interviewed who were devoted to the ideal of self-fulfillment were having trouble with their marriages. Collette Carisse (1975) pointed to the same problem in the Canadian family when she argued that married couples may drift beyond the range of the partner's tolerance of a certain leisure lifestyle, leading to family malfunctioning, discomfort, and even pathogenic behavior. John Kelley (1983, 144), in looking into the future of leisure and the family, predicts that "failing to meet expectations for leisure sharing in marriage will become more frequently a basis for divorce even when the breadwinner, homemaker, sexual and parental roles are being fulfilled adequately."

ROLE CONFLICTS

The modern husband and father thus faces a number of strains in his everyday life, several of which have been hinted at in the foregoing discussion.

1. There is the conflict of marriage and family versus leisure. Men frequently want to get married and often want to have children, but they also increasingly value non-familial leisure, which is likely to take them away from home.

2. There is also the conflict of marriage and family versus career. A number of men who want to get married and perhaps to have children also want to succeed in a complicated, absorbing, fulfilling line of work.

3. Related to number 2 is the conflict of marriage and family versus financial need, where there is a drive to make money through moonlighting and overtime.

4. More specifically, some men confront the conflict of family obligations versus leisure. Here they wrestle with the dilemma of either helping their wives with routine household tasks or seeking interesting leisure. There is rarely enough time for both.

5. Built into number 4 is the conflict for some men of women's work versus men's work. The traditional male often defines washing dishes or preparing meals as unmasculine, possibly as work for sissies.

6. On a related note is the conflict of the dual breadwinner versus single breadwinner, a conflict that is pervading more and more households. Again from the traditional male's point of view, it is an indignity to have to rely on one's wife to garner enough money to run "his" household at a respectable level.

7. The conflict of the marital relationship versus friendships refers

to the difficulty many family men face in allocating enough time to all their important relationships.

8. Finally, there is the conflict of familial leisure versus non-familial leisure. With only so much time available for leisure of any kind, how much is to be spent with family, and how much at activities that exclude them?

"If only there were enough hours in a day", the typical husband and father might lament, "then I could do all these things and experience no tension." Although limited time is a common problem fueling all eight conflicts, it is not the only problem. In an era of rapid change in the institutions of family, work, and leisure, many men are caught in the need to restructure their hierarchy of values. The allocation of time to various activities is made easier when their relative priorities are clear.

Unfortunately, those priorities cannot be established, at least for the present. The value of work, as we have just seen, is undergoing change. The amount of work in the future in a variety of areas will be less (see Jenkins and Sherman 1979). In the meantime leisure, once a supplementary form of relaxation between sessions of work, is now becoming a central, if not the central life interest of many men. All this is happening while marriage rates and family size are decreasing and divorce rates are rising. The core values concerning marriage and children appear to be up for reconsideration as to their ultimate importance.

As a consequence of these conflicts, the sturdy, always-in-control, unflappable adult male of yesteryear is possibly becoming a phenomenon of the past. Or at least he is becoming a distinct rarity in the present. True, the number of well adjusted, invincible men has no doubt been greatly overestimated both in the past and in the present, just as the number of women who possess the opposite characteristics has undoubtedly been overestimated. But today's role conflicts in the spheres of family, work, and leisure will certainly do little to bring myth in line with reality.

To the extent that these role conflicts remain unresolved in the mind of today's husband and father, the possibility of a forceful resolution to the tension they cause is always there. This is one important point in family life where the man's awareness of his masculinity is likely to be acute. If his conception of himself as a man is challenged in selecting or constructing a solution to a family conflict, the solution selected or constructed could be one favoring his understanding of "the masculine thing to do" in such circumstances. The masculine thing to do could include the use of power and possibly violence, if they are seen as necessary, justifiable, maybe even proper, in his attempt to reduce the conflict he feels.

The resolution of the conflict results in the man's psychological peace, but it is produced by a process that is profoundly sociological: "masculinities are constructed not just by power relations but by their interplay with a division of labor and with patterns of emotional attachment" (Carrigan, Connell, and Lee 1987, 178). A powerful and perhaps violent resolution is possible to the extent that men in our society still hold *hegemonic* positions. That is, they hold positions of power and wealth that are legitimated and perpetrated by the institutional structure of the society (Carrigan, Connell, and Lee 1987, 177–182).

SUMMARY

Ulysses' ideal of a husband and wife keeping a household with oneness of mind is still being sought in the twentieth century. Myth to the contrary, even the modern man wants to marry, and often he wants to have children. Yet, both partners frequently have obligations and interests that threaten the smooth running of the household they share. The amount of give and take in pursuing these and in sharing in the demands of the household is rarely perceived by both members of the couple to be equal.

For most married men, the family is the hub of their daily activities. However, familial interests and obligations compete for time and allegiance with external interests and obligations. Men fulfill these obligations and pursue their interests within the expectations of the male gender role.

Work, domestic chores, and parenting are among the main family related obligations facing the modern man. Although work beyond the conventional 35-to-40 hour work week does not lead to a reduction in the amount of time spent on household chores, excess work is a source of family strain. The same may be said for shift work. Weekend work reduces the amount of time a man spends with his children and the amount he devotes to housework. The compressed work week, however, produces more time for both.

Work is the central life's interest for many men. In its extreme form it may become workaholism, where work has a high intrinsic value. For some men, however, work is of central importance because it provides them with money. Work here is of extrinsic value. Recent evidence indicates that the principle of work as primary, therefore family as secondary, is beginning to fade.

One study indicates that husbands classify family chores as men's work or women's work in the following way: Wives are expected to do the cooking of meals and the washing of clothes. The husbands feel that they are expected to do yard work, maintain the car, earn money, and repair household items. They expect to share equally with their wives in such matters as shopping, washing dishes, cleaning house, writing letters, scheduling family social events, and making family decisions.

For many years this division of labour has remained much the same, even though many wives now also work in the labour market. Recent research in the United States suggests that the situation may be starting to change. The wife and mother, however, still may be saddled with the most demanding of all household chores—the cooking of meals and the washing the ironing of clothes, all being difficult tasks to delegate. Family tension sometimes results from disagreement about who shall do what at home.

There is also evidence of increased involvement by fathers in parenting, an experience they report being highly satisfied with. Men, however, appear to be more able than women to keep family and work spheres psychologically separate, and to rank the importance of these spheres with greater clarity. They may thus be subject to less tension about where to draw the line between family and work than their working wives.

Fathers as single parents suffer many of the same problems that working wives suffer. Domestic chores limit time with children, while chores and children limit advancement opportunities at work. Yet research indicates that single fathers are greatly satisfied with their parental role, a sentiment that is shared by their children.

Both more traditional and less traditional men seek marriage for two main reasons: companionship and security. In a companionship a man finds a woman in whom he can confide his emotions and troubles; in the latter kind of marriage he finds someone who can accept and support him psychologically. Some traditional men value highly the services of their wives, whereas less traditional men stress the importance of their wives as interesting persons to be with.

Men tend to have large networks of moderately close friends compared with the medium-sized networks of very close friends of women. This difference is partly accounted for by the fact that men have more difficulty in forming friendships than women do. Male friendship networks decline abruptly with marriage and only start to expand around middle age, a process that continues into retirement from employment. Men's relatively superficial friendships may help explain why they seek emotional support from their wives.

Interests of husbands and fathers may be familial or non-familial and serious or casual. Most family interests are casual, whereas the individual interests of the male head are somewhat more likely to be serious, and considerably more likely to be oriented away from the family. Nor is family leisure necessarily the most satisfying leisure for either fathers or mothers.

Although there is evidence that paid work is becoming less and less a central life interest for many men, there is evidence too that they are at least as attracted to self-fulfilling leisure as they are to family interests and relationships. The pursuit of self-fulfillment is the pursuit of the development of oneself as a distinct person. Leisure, especially in its serious form, is increasingly seen as an opportunity for accomplishing this. However, such leisure is individualistic and is not nearly as conducive to involvement by all or most of the family as is casual leisure.

Thus, the modern husband and father faces a number of strains in everyday life. Eight conflicts were identified: marriage and family versus leisure, marriage and family versus occupational career, marriage and family versus financial need, family obligation versus leisure, women's work versus men's work, dual breadwinner versus single breadwinner, marital relationship versus friendships, and familial leisure versus non-familial leisure. The solid, Rock-of-Gibralter husband and father, if he was ever very common, is, in the face of these tests, certainly likely to become less so today. In resolving family-related personal conflicts, he may draw on his hegemonic position in the community by asserting his power, and possibly by resorting to violence.

Bibliography

Ambert, A.M.

1976   *Sex structure.* 2d ed. Don Mills, Ont.: Longmans Canada.

1982   "Differences in children's behavior toward custodial mothers and custodial fathers". *Journal of Marriage and the Family* 44:73–86.

Armstrong, P., and H. Armstrong.

1984   *The double ghetto: Canadian women and their segregated work.* Toronto: McClelland & Stewart.

Backett, K.C.

1982   *Mothers and fathers: A study of the development and negotiation of parental behaviour.* London: Macmillan.

Berger, M., and L. Wright.

1978   "Divided allegiance: Men, work, and family life". *Counseling Psychologist* 4:50–53.

Booth, A.

1977   "Wife's employment and husband's's stress: A replication and refutation". *Journal of Marriage and the Family* 39:645–650.

Brubaker, T.H., and L. Ade-Ridder.
1986   "Husband's responsibility for household tasks in older marriages. In *Men in families*", edited by P.A. Lewis and R.E. Salt, 85–96. Beverly Hills, CA: Sage Publications.

Campbell, A., P. Converse, and W. Rodgers.
1976   *The quality of American life.* New York: Russell Sage.

Carisse, C.B.
1975   "Family and leisure: A set of contradictions". *The Family Coordinator* 24:191–197.

Carrigan, T., B. Connell, and J. Lee.
1987   "Hard and heavy: Toward a new sociology of masculinity". In *Beyond patriarchy*, edited by M. Kaufman, 139–194. Toronto: Oxford University Press.

Chang, P., and A. Deinard.
1982   "Single father caretakers: Demographic characteristics and adjustment process". *American Journal of Orthopsychiatry* 52:236–243.

Duck, S., and D. Perlman.
1985   "The thousand islands of personal relationships: A prescriptive analysis for future explorations". In *Understanding personal relationships*, edited by S. Duck and D. Perlman. Beverly Hills, CA: Sage Publications.

Dubin, Robert.
1979   "Central life interests". *Pacific Sociological Review* 22:405–426.

Farrell, M.P.
1986   "Friendship between men". In *Men's changing roles in the family*, edited by R.A. Lewis and M.B. Sussman, 163–198. New York: Haworth.

Farrell, M.P., and S.D. Rosenberg.
1981   *Men at midlife.* Boston: Auburn House.

Fisher, C.S., and S.J. Oliker.
1980   *Friendship, sex and the life cycle.* Institute of Urban and Regional Development, Working Paper no. 318. Berkeley, CA: University of California.

Granovetter, M.S.
1973   "The strength of weak ties". *American Journal of Sociology* 78:1360–1380.

Horna, Jarmila L.A.
in press   "Family and leisure". In *The family and marriage*, edited by K. Ishwaran. Toronto: Wall and Thompson.

House, J.S.
1980   *Occupational stress and the mental and physical health of factory workers.* Ann Arbor, MI: Institute for Social Research.
Jenkins, C., and B. Sherman.
1979   *The collapse of work.* London: Eyre Methuen.
Keith, P.M., and R.B. Schafer.
1980   "Role strain and depression in two-job families". *Family Relations* 29: 483–488.
Kelly, J.R.
1982   *Leisure.* Englewood Cliffs, NJ: Prentice-Hall.
1983   *Leisure identities and interactions.* London: George Allen & Unwin.
Lips, H.M.
1983   "Attitudes toward childbearing among women and men expecting their first child". *International Journal of Women's Studies* 6:119–129.
Lopata, H.Z.
1971   *Occupation housewife.* New York: Oxford University Press.
Lupri, E., and J. Frideres.
1981   "The quality of marriage and the passage of time". *Canadian Journal of Sociology* 6:283–305.
Luxton, M.
1981   "Taking on the double day". *Atlantis* 7:12–22.
Maccoby, E.E., and C.N. Jacklin.
1974   *The psychology of sex differences.* Stanford, CA: Stanford University Press.
Machlowitz, M.
1980   *Workaholics.* Reading, MA: Addison-Wesley.
Maklan, D.M.
1977a   *The four-day workweek: Blue-collar adjustment to a nonconventional arrangement of work and leisure time.* New York: Praeger.
1977b   "How blue-collar workers on 4-day workweeks use their time". *Monthly Labor Review* 100 (8):18–26.
McHenry, P.C., S.J. Price, P.B. Gordon and N.M. Rudd.
1986   "Characteristics of husband's family work and wives' labor force involvement". In *Men in families,* edited by R.A. Lewis and R.E. Salt, 73–84. Beverly Hills, CA: Sage Publications.
Miller, J., and H.H. Garrison.
1982   "Sex roles: The division of labor at home and in the workplace". In *Annual Review of Sociology,* edited by R.H. Turner and F. Short, Jr., 8:237–262. Palo Alto, CA: Annual Reviews Inc.
Mortimer, J.T.
1980   "Occupation-family linkages as perceived by men in the early

stages of professional and managerial careers". In *Research on the interweave of social roles*, edited by H.Z. Lopata, vol. 1. Greenwich, CT: JAI Press.

Nett, E.M.
1980   "Marriage and the family". In *Courtship, marriage, and the family*, edited by G.N. Ramu, 59–77. Toronto: Gage.

Nordstrom, B.
1986   "Why men get married: More and less traditional men compared". In *Men in families*, edited by R.A. Lewis and R.E. Salt, 31–54. Beverly Hills, CA: Sage Publications.

Orthner, D., and K. Lewis.
1979   "Evidence of single father competence in childrearing". *Family Law Quarterly* 8:27–48.

Petrowsky, M.
1976   "Marital status, sex, and the social networks of the elderly". *Journal of Marriage and the Family* 38:749–756.

Pleck, J.H.
1981   *The myth of masculinity*. Cambridge, MA: MIT Press.

Roberts, K.
1978   *Contemporary society and the growth of leisure*. London: Longman.

Ross-Franklin, J.
1983   Ph.D. dissertation. "The impact of retirement on marital dyad members". Buffalo, NY: State University of New York at Buffalo.

Russell, G.
1983   *The changing role of fathers*. Milton Keynes, Eng.: Open University Press.

Salt, R.E.
1986   "Introduction: What men get out of marriage and parenthood". In *Men in families*, edited by R.A. Lewis and R.E. Salt, 11–30. Beverly Hills, CA: Sage Publications.

Sanik, M.M.
1981   "Division of household work: A decade of comparison, 1967–1977". *Home Economics Research Journal* 10:175–180.

Staines, G.L., and J.H. Pleck.
1983   *The impact of work schedules on the family*. Ann Arbor, MI: Institute for Social Research.

Statistics Canada
1984   *Canada's lone-parent families*, Cat. 99–933. Ottawa.

Stebbins, R.A.
1979   *Amateurs: On the margin between work and leisure*. Beverly Hills, CA: Sage Publications.
1982   "Serious leisure. A conceptual statement". *Pacific Sociological Review* 25:251–272.

Stein, P.J.
1986   "Men and their friendships". In *Men in families*, edited by
            R.A. Lewis and R.E. Salt, 261–270. Beverly Hills, CA: Sage
            Publications.
Tasto, D.L., M.J. Colligan, E.W. Skjei, and S.J. Polly.
1978   *Health consequences of shift work*. SRI Project URU-4426.
Yankelovich, D.
1981   *New rules: Searching for self-fulfillment in a world turned upside
            down*. New York: Random House.

CHAPTER 3

The Child Question: Links Between Women and Children in the Family

Nancy Mandell

INTRODUCTION

Children are central to feminist analyses of the family. Two opposing themes are evident. On the one hand, children are seen as the source of women's oppression by restricting their activities in the public arena. It has been demonstrated that because women choose marriage and motherhood, they invest less in education and job training and often seek low-paid, part-time work near home (Lewis 1986). By making the biological bearers of children socially, legally and ideologically responsible for their upbringing, women are contained in the home and constrained in the work world. Biology, it seems, makes the domestic domain the natural world of women. On the other hand, children are seen as the source of women's power and connection to the public realm. Women's unique capacities for nurture and succor give women intense pleasure and interpersonal power, and serve as an ideological rationale for women's entry into the world of work as moral reformers, supervisors and teachers of children.

These two rival approaches—the philosophy of constraint and the philosophy of empowerment—suggest divergent solutions to women's relationships with children. Constraint philosophers question the conflation of biological and social reproduction, the naturalness of the domestic sexual division of labour. They urge women to reject these roles altogether. Empowerment philosophers idealize the power of maternity and accept the ideology of motherhood which prescribes that the bearing and nurturing of children should exist at the center of women's lives while men are exonerated from fathering in any authentic sense (Levine

1983). They suggest women continue to bear and raise children in addition to assuming responsibility for home and work.

Both positions recognize that the fates of women and children under patriarchy are intertwined. Women's relationship to reproduction and children represents the material basis on which patriarchy rests. Men have dominated women by controlling their reproductive and labour power. Children are the products of women's labour. As long as the bearing and rearing of children represents a crucial task in perpetuating patriarchy, the economic and social fate of children will parallel that of women.

This chapter traces historical variations in the status of children and demonstrates how changes in family structure, ideology, roles and relationships affect ideas about children and women's relationships with children. Childhood is examined as a social construction, notions of which have varied enormously in different eras. Class, gender and cultural variations in expectations about children's capacities for work and independence allow us to question our own ideology of motherhood and reflect on alternative ways of incorporating children into family life.

THE INTERCONNECTIONS OF WOMEN AND CHILDREN

Historical images of childhood have changed as women's roles and responsibilities have altered. In this way, the fate of children reflects women's experiences. Children's status can be seen as moving through three distinct phases. The first stage, *indifference toward childhood*, reflects European society before the 1500s when children were considered economically productive but emotionally disposable. Gross distinctions were drawn only between helpless infants and potentially helpful dependent children. Children were introduced to adult activities early in life and expected to participate in a productive fashion. Women's roles as producers and consumers within their homes reflected the emphasis on marriage as a business transaction, and on family as a kin relationship, rather than a love relationship. Children were not conceptualized as special creatures requiring a mother's exclusive attention, nor was motherhood intermingled with definitions of femaleness. Once past infancy, children were seen as economically dependent and physically limited, but not socially or intellectually inferior to adults.

Beginning around the late 1500s and early 1600s, ideas of childhood as a distinct ontological state developed. This second phase, the *emergence of childhood*, is characterized as a transitory one in which economic and cultural changes, and changes in the structure and roles of the family, contributed to the modern distinction of childhood as a state of passivity, helplessness and dependency, conducive to moral training. Women's roles within the modern family also altered during this period.

The third period, *the ascendancy of childhood*, has lasted from the mid-1800s to today. During this time, the cult of childhood has been at its height. Children have been valued as emotional, not economic, assets. Child-rearing experts have emerged in the form of child psychologists, social workers and teachers. A body of literature has developed about children, that provides advice and models of child development to parents. Children's books and educational devices also abound. The emergence of the cult of domesticity corresponds with the cult of childhood. Motherhood was seen as women's defining role as long as women were excluded from employment.

Today, as women increasingly assume a lifelong combination of both wage labouring and mothering, they are demanding more independent identities and lives for themselves and their children. Yet children remain subordinate. The deglorification of parenthood, the exploitation of the young, the rising economic costs of raising children, the alienation of adolescents from the family, the process of making children into adults (Postman 1982) and the significant decline in Western fertility (Greer 1984) suggest widespread cultural ambivalence toward children. Similarly, the roles of women are undergoing considerable change. We have, for example, instituted so many cultural disincentives to mothering, that antinatal policies and attitudes have depressed fertility (Greer 1984). The so-called erosion of childhood (Postman 1982) raises issues for feminists. Are the increasing institutionalization of children, society's anti-child attitude and new birth control technologies going to undermine the status of children in society and transform children into commodities? Will women's economic independence free women and children from dependence and from being treated as childlike?

These historical fluctuations accentuate certain trends in the relationships between women and children. In the first place, the fate of children and women traditionally has been tied together. Most women, in most cultures, devote most of their lives to the care and nurturing of children. Much of the lived oppression of women has been experienced through the unending and sometimes unsatisfying work of child care (Maroney 1986; Luxton 1982; Rubin 1976). Much of the enjoyment, creativity and pleasure of women also has been experienced through mothering. Because they are so central in their children's lives, women report enjoying their considerable influence on children's development (Boulton 1983).

Children mediate women's relation to the traditional, patriarchal family. Women's dependence and their subordination to men's authority in the family is rooted in women's responsibility for, and identification with, children.

The relationship between mother and child is not rooted in biology. Rather, what a child is depends on values and norms that predominate in a particular society. Historically and culturally, children vary from being seen as independent to dependent. In the Middle Ages, children were seen as replaceable; during the 1900s, children were viewed as irreplaceable.

Women's roles and responsibilities for children depend on prevailing conceptions of children. When children are seen as independent and adult-like, women have more freedom to live independent lives themselves. Conversely, when children are constructed as helpless dependents requiring constant moulding, women's responsibilities as mothers, sisters and grandmothers intensify. The burden of children has been exacerbated as women's responsibilities for children have been expanded through the influence of child-care experts and have been reinforced through ideologies of maternal instinct and mother-love. Finally, much of what a society defines as appropriate behaviour for children depends on how female adult roles are understood. Childish mannerisms, such as giggling, smiling, laughing, fidgeting and nervous habits are also characteristics stereotyped today as typically female behaviour.

All of these elements indicate that childhood is socially constructed and that the lives of women and children are intertwined. From a feminist perspective, it follows then that childhood could be constructed in such a way that women and children are freed from mutual dependence. However, women's freedom must not be gained at the cost of children's rights. Society must assess its value of children and guarantee they are not liberated from maternal care only to be exploited and controlled by non-familial agents such as day-care institutions. Reconciling constraint and empowerment philosophies constitutes the task of contemporary, feminist revisionism of children. This chapter will examine this central issue by detailing historical changes in children's status.

INDIFFERENCE TO CHILDREN: MEDIEVAL EUROPE

Historical comparisons of the status and treatment of children reveal that childhood is a cultural creation. The form and role of childhood varies enormously by social conditions and by time periods. Yet it is the function of ideology to present childhood's current form as natural, inevitable and universal.

One of the features of childhood that continually changes is the arbitrary dividing line between adult status and child status. Accounts of medieval childhood suggest that distinctions between adults and children were not as sharply drawn as they are today. Since adults and children lived a collective, public life there was no need to single children out for special protection or to develop theories about their nature. Some historians (Aries 1962; Plumb 1976; Postman 1982) have gone so far as to suggest an absence of concepts of childhood in the medieval world.

It seems, however, that even though medieval children were viewed differently than they would be two centuries later, there was a concept of childhood in medieval times. Ideas about children were quite concrete, relatively unsophisticated, undeveloped and not institutionalized by theoretical studies and reports. Certain features of medieval life have been widely reported which help to explain this material, simple and untheoretical construction of childhood in that era.

In the first place, medieval adults tended to distinguish all individuals dichotomously, in terms of whether they were economically independent or dependent. Infants were in a group by themselves since society recognized they required special protection and care. Our modern conception of childhood as an age status was not experienced in medieval times. "Child" referred not to age, but to dependency, and could include individuals aged 7 to 27. By ages 5 to 7, when most children communicated effectively, they were considered semi-independent. Economically dependent adult males, who had not yet established an income of their own sufficient to support themselves and a family, were referred to as children. Most women remained financially dependent all their lives; however, early marriage and continuous childbearing deemed the designation "child" inappropriate for women.

Second, work and family life overlapped in feudal society since the household was the basic unit of production. In this setting, women and children were expected to be productive and to contribute economically to the household.

Third, medieval children were seen as dependents who learned adult skills and values through apprenticeship and through integration into the community. Since the public world of work overlapped with the private experience of family life, children intermingled with adults in every aspect of life. By the age of 7, boys and girls of all social classes worked and played alongside adults. The majority of children left home for a period of residence with kin or masters. In England, even the rich sent their children into the houses of others in order that they might learn specific skills, manners and social customs. Education and socialization into adult culture occurred "naturally" as adults and male children attended non-age-graded schools or as young males worked as apprentices to neighbouring craftsmen.

Fourth, in both peasant and noble families, a sexual division of labour occurred. Boys imitated men's work apprenticing as labourers, servants, craftsmen or professionals. Boys, often those over the age of 10, who went to medieval Latin schools, boarded with families in the school's town. While the Middle Ages witnessed the emergence of universities (Oxford, Cambridge, University of Paris), schooling was an uncommon experience, intended initially only for male clerics. The general means for the transmission of skills and cultural knowledge for everybody was apprenticeship. While women were never educated in schools, they were apprenticed as domestics and labourers. By the age of 13 or 14, most women were married and running households.

Female childhood remained remarkably unaffected by technological or cultural changes from the Middle Ages to the seventeenth century. Even in the seventeenth century, some 10-year-old girls were already functioning as little women. Education for women seemed superfluous within such a rigidly patriarchal and gender stratified society. Young women had limited occupational opportunities throughout the Middle Ages, with the exception of their labour within the guild system. Usually single or widowed women worked as cobblers, belt and sweater makers, leather dressers, purse makers, furriers, bakers, saddlers, tanners, goldsmiths, lace makers, and embroiderers of church vestments, religious hangings and coats of arms (Adams 1980, 320). Guild records indicate that within Europe, over 200 occupations were open to women (Campbell 1893, 46, 49; Oakley 1974). When the guild system ended, women lost these economic opportunities.

Fifth, gender differences in childhood experiences paralleled the extremely patriarchal and hierarchical nature of Medieval society. Many adults were considered the property of adults of superior status, being any one of slaves, serfs or feudal liege-lords. Both high- and low-status children were dependent, obedient and deferential to male household heads. Patriarchal authority was so rigidly prescribed that some (Lee 1982; Plumb 1976) describe medieval relationships as property arrangements. Women and children were considered the chattels of the property-holding males of society. Mothers had no property rights in their own children, and often were referred to as "flirts, bawds and deceiving wives in the popular tales, saints and martyrs in the drama, unattainable objects of passionate and illicit love in the romances" (Tuchman 1978, 50–51). Similar to their mothers, children were depicted as both saints and sinners, innocents and evil forces to be controlled. All children married according to their fathers' wishes, and the iron rule of primogeniture ensured inheritance by the eldest son. Until the eighteenth century in England and the nineteenth century in Canada, men had the right to beat both their wives and their children for disobedience; such acts were frequently neither investigated nor punished. Wives and children could be and were dealt with in any manner husbands wished since " . . . there can be no injustice to one's own property" (Adams 1980, 161).

So while children were integrated into adult life, they remained totally subordinate to private patriarchy. Their status paralleled that of their mothers. Aries tells us (1962, 356) that "by sixteenth century, . . . any acts a wife performs without the authority of her husband or the law are null and void. This development strengthens the power of the husband who is firmly established as a domestic monarch". In the early Middle Ages, parents of the upper strata arranged marriages for their children. A strict code of etiquette and chivalry constrained the sexual wanderings of young girls and married ladies. Young knights and married men, however, explored romantic love and sex after marriage. Among the higher classes, arranged marriages contributed to the double standard, mistresses and high rates of illegitimacy.

Sixth, the strength of private patriarchy obviated the need for strong state measures to control the wanderings of women and children. Paternalism prevailed, was widely accepted, and was reinforced by the communal nature of family life. Medieval life was not experienced as private, separate or distinct. Rather, life was a collective, integrated and homogeneous affair. All ages and classes, peasants and feudal lords alike, shared the same information, lived for the present, and existed in the same social and intellectual world.

There was no concept of a unique, separate self or a distinct individuality that transcended the community or social group as there is today. The idea of personal identity was fused with the community's identity. Distinctions between a private family life and a public world of work and leisure were not clearly demarcated. The nuclear family and kin community were embedded in one another in terms of personnel (Adams 1980, 63). Structurally and attitudinally, the nuclear family had little existence apart from the kin-friend-neighbour milieu in which the individual functioned (Adams 1980, 63). Neither individual nor family privacy existed.

Because of community surveillance that resulted from the lack of privacy, there was little need for state intervention into family affairs. The community could be counted on to ensure the subordination of women and children. When the state did intrude, it aimed to preserve the nuclear family and patriarchal, spousal relationships. The first medieval French shelter for abandoned children, established in 1180 in Montpellier by a religious order (Fuchs 1985) was a state action designed to prevent infanticide and prop up the traditional patriarchal family. Rather than assuming direct responsibility for raising these children by placing all of them in state-run orphanages, other people's homes were used as model family units. Infants were sent to wet nurses in the countryside until age three or four. Then they returned to the church-run charity hospitals and remained there until an apprenticeship could be arranged.

Seventh, while women and children were all subject to private patriarchy, some class distinctions existed in the experience of childhood. Both aristocratic and peasant children learned through apprenticeship and service. Both classes of children experienced this "semi-autonomous" stage of residing outside of their homes at an early age, and both were firmly subordinate in status to adult men who had the right to beat them, control them and dispose of their labour (Lee 1982). Despite these similarities, feudal-peasant childhood distinctions did exist.

Childhood ended earlier for peasant boys and girls of all classes. Peasant boys were given adult rights and responsibilities around the age of 14 or 15 when they could achieve economic independence. In contrast, sons of knights were not considered to be adult until the age of 21, when they were strong enough to bear full armour and fight alongside their fathers. From the thirteenth century on, the upper-class standard became the norm for all classes, and the age of majority remained 21 until 1970 in England (Freeman 1983). Regardless of class, life for girls consisted of marriage, motherhood and family work. Once old enough to accomplish these goals, girls moved from paternal supervision to spousal supervision.

Medieval society reflected, not an absence, but an indifference to childhood as being a state of any particular social consequence. The social and cultural integration of children into adult life meant children were not regarded as sexually innocent. Since children engaged in the same leisure pastimes as adults, playing games, telling tales, singing ballads, attending plays and drinking in alehouses, they were privy to, and no doubt a part of, adult sexual behaviour from a very early age. There was no way to keep childhood separate from adult life (Lee 1982). Modern notions that people should live in clearly demarcated private spaces and should have private expressions of thought and feeling were absurd in the cramped and congested public lives of the Middle Ages. Cultural transmission and the continuation of private patriarchy occurred through apprenticeship. While children and women were economically productive, they remained financially dependent and subject to control by men through family, church and state. Historically, as long as children remained economically productive, men controlled their futures. Similarly, women's financial dependence on male earnings, through marriage and motherhood, linked women and children in subordination.

THE EMERGENCE OF CHILDHOOD: EUROPE AND CANADA FROM THE 1500s TO 1700s

Between the fifteenth and sixteenth centuries, social attitudes toward women, children and the family began to change (Aries 1962). Children were increasingly viewed as possessing a distinct, particular nature which was different from that of adults. Childhood began to be seen as a stage in the life cycle, requiring protection, nurture and parental supervision. Women became primarily responsible for the care and control of children. As with other occupations in which women predominated, the concentration of women as primary caretakers led, over time, to a decrease in the prestige and power ascribed to the parental role.

Several writers (Aries 1962; Hoyles 1979; Freeman 1983) have documented social and economic indicators of children's changing status. Drawing on the art of the times, Aries (1962) tells us that the seventeenth century was very significant in the evolution of themes of childhood. Solitary portraits of children became common, nudity became an essential convention in child portraitures, subject painting gave the child a place of honour with countless childhood scenes of a conventional character, and the family portrait centered around the children. Seventeenth century art suggests family life was becoming more child-centered.

By the 1590s, it was customary for children to wear clothing that distinguished them from adults. Children adopted the attire of boys and wore the short pants we associate with children. By 1600, each child acquired a unique name. When children died they were commemorated on parents' tombstones and in their own marked graves. Slang and jargon crept into children's speech. The practice of wet-nursing children continued but, where possible, nurses were moved into the family homes, under the mothers' supervision. With the invention of the printing press in the 1450s, mass production of children's literature became possible. In 1545, the first English book on pediatrics was published. One pediatric childcare manual, written by Thomas Raynauld, was so popular in England that it went through seven editions before 1600.

From the late 1500s on, the concept of childhood flourished due to a renewed interest in education, the transition from feudalism to capitalism, the increasing privatization of the family, and the continued domestication of married women. The emergence of childhood for children thus corresponds with the emergence of domesticity as a marital norm for women. The effects of these changes on the lives of children parallel those experienced by women.

In the first place, we see the beginning of society's tendency to associate children with all sorts of negative qualities and the eventual diffusion of these characteristics to women. Children were the initial recipients of such ignominious characteristics as weakness, irrationality, imbecility, prelogicism and primitivism (Freeman 1983). The lower classes were also treated more as children, as the idea of childhood became increasingly linked to subservience, dependence and other objectionable qualities.

Secondly, while society held some positive images of children, the negative labels provided a rationale for increased private and public control of children. The transition from medieval to pre-industrial society was a movement from being unmindful of children to containing them (Suransky 1982). For example, middle- and upper-class children were banned from gambling, licentious sexual activity and other bawdy adult entertainment. Etiquette books warned against the exposure of children to indecent, sexually explicit books and language. Children between the ages of 7 and 14 were seen now as creatures whose morality, chastity and socialization needed to be supervised and channelled. They were no longer seen as capable of regulating themselves. Children were treated and trained like animals needing to be "broken in" (Stone 1979).

Rival theories of children's needs and vulnerabilities characterize this historical period. Synnott (1983) outlines the existence of five perspectives, including the humanism of Montaigne, the repressiveness of Calvin, Wesley and the Puritans, the environmentalism of Locke, the romanticism of Rousseau, and the genetic determinism of eugenicists. These rival views of children as inherently good or evil creatures, as blank slates or genetically determined beings, as responsive to kindness or to cruelty, emphasize that within this era there existed several worlds of childhood. Each discourse related to the socio-economic function of the child within gender specific locations. Sons of nobles or merchants, middle-class boys, educated in schools and through apprenticeships, were, and still are, likely to be viewed benignly as empty vessels waiting to be filled up with socially requisite knowledge. In contrast, peasant or working-class boys, labouring and taking on adult manners early, were viewed and are viewed suspiciously as precocious, aggressive waifs who are constantly in need of strong discipline.

Yet underlying all of these rival views is the ideology of patriarchy. Legally, morally and economically, children, like their mothers, were subject to their father's wishes. For example, a father was entitled to his children's services, and he could demand that they work for him without pay. If a child worked for an outsider, that child's father was entitled to his earnings. Adams (1980) describes the child's position in the colonial American family as one dominated by the "three Rs": repression, religion and respect. Female children, like adult women, were even more subjugated since even the illusion of occupational choice was denied to them. Patriarchal, authoritarian control over children's marriages and occupations varied by class. Where the property, power and status of parents were considerable, children could be strictly controlled. Conversely, propertyless parents had no economic leverage with their children (Freeman 1983a).

The third effect of the emergence of a distinct concept of childhood was that this change affected boys more than girls, thus reflecting a more profound alteration in the working lives of fathers than of mothers. Changes in the treatment of children first began with middle-class boys, whose lives had changed materially. The movement from feudalism to merchant capitalism (Freeman 1983a) and the extension of formal schooling (Aries 1962) made it both necessary and possible for the sons of merchants, professionals and businessmen to acquire prolonged training and skills. Postman (1982) suggests that a technological revolution, the invention of the printing press, created an economic and cultural transformation of society. the availability of books enabled adults to be distinguished from one another on the basis of literacy. Maps, business books, pediatric childcare manuals, fiction, astronomy, geology and medicine codified and systematized knowledge in a way previously unknown. Knowledge, its mastery and its exchange, became a source of power available to the literate.

Economic changes created a need for men to acquire more education and training that would enable them to master more complex socio-economic arrangements. Burgeoning fields of commerce, agriculture and science required literacy from its youthful apprentices before their economic enterprises could be secured and expanded. Once wealth was acquired, it required an orderly transmission to the next generation so that it would be used purposefully. For these reasons, the concept of childhood affected boys more than girls; it affected the middle ranks more than the landowning nobility. Childhood emerged first as a male, middle-class phenomenon.

While Canadian historical work on children is sparse, it appears that childhood, as a unique preserve, emerged first among middle-class merchants and professionals. Prolonged schooling was first encountered by the sons of lawyers, clergymen and moralists. Among the middle and upper classes in New France, secondary education was reserved for males between the ages of 9 and 15. It functioned as training for the administrative, judicial and military elite of New France (Moogk 1982). Even though the *idea* of free, basic elementary education was widespread in New France in the 1700s, it rarely occurred. As a result, rural illiteracy was high. In 1741, nearly 60% of Montreal householders surveyed could not write their names. Few school masters existed, leaving the burden of education with overworked parish and missionary priests. Eventually education filtered down to the lower classes, but even then, girls were more likely than boys to find formal elementary education helpful. Nuns taught girls, who were generally better educated than their male peers.

A further effect of the emergence of childhood was the introduction of class differences in children's familial and educational instruction, and the use of the family and the school system as instruments of class reproduction. Throughout the 1700s, parents, tutors and master craftsmen taught more children than were instructed in schools. Manual trades, as well as the professions of notary, surgeon and merchant were learned by father-son contact or through apprenticeship. In this way, the class system reproduced itself through the family.

The typical Canadian family, at this time, was an economically self-sufficient unit. Trade centers existed where individuals could take their surpluses and exchange them for what they lacked. Certain specialties, such as blacksmiths and apothecaries, flourished. But work, hence education, was essentially home-based. For girls of all classes, education involved training in home-making and motherhood. Boys were expected to learn farm work or apprentice in a trade. Since Canadian life was largely rural, children were valued for their contributions to their family's welfare. On farms, children helped with housework, childcare, gardening, gathering firewood and herding animals.

Where craft apprenticeship occurred, boys benefited more than girls (Moogk 1982). Only one in one hundred girls apprenticed, and they became seamstresses. Unless they joined a religious order, young girls were expected to make marriage their career. In the United States, throughout the 1700s, a grade-school education was deemed unnecessary for young girls destined for marriage. From 1620 to 1776 in colonial America, there were almost no female wage-earners except those in domestic service. A few women did engage in home-based spinning and weaving and other types of work associated with textiles and clothing production (Scanzoni and Scanzoni 1981). A content analysis of magazine articles between 1750 and 1800 reports on a few female attorneys and women in business. Yet, a woman's usual lot was domestic labour, reproduction and the socialization of children.

The transition from pre-industrial, rural living to an urban, industrialized nation affected the education of boys and girls. In England, the separation of the home from the workplace began much earlier than it did in Canada. By the mid-1600s, as many as half a million English peasants were already propertyless as a result of enclosure laws, conversion of the land from tillage to pasture and the abolition of feudal tenure. Once evicted from the land, the economic basis of the peasant family ceased. Husbands and wives were forced to sell their labour power to survive. Dependent wives and children became economic burdens for the landless. Children were valued only for their ability to supplement their father's grossly inadequate wage. Conversely, middle- and upper-class boys remained in school for longer periods of time.

In Canada, the pre-industrial era dominated until the nineteenth century (Armstrong and Armstrong, this volume). Almost all productive acts took place in the home. Production was small scale, labour intensive and sex-stratified. Until the late 1880s, most Canadians lived on farms and engaged in agriculture or they fished or worked in lumbering and the fur trade (Gaffield 1984).

As childhood emerged, motherhood was redefined. The cult of domesticity, which conflated femaleness with motherhood, began to be articulated at the same time as the concept of childhood. Changes in the structure of family life altered parent-child relationships, especially those between mothers and children. As historians (Shorter 1975; Stone 1979; Trumbach 1978) have indicated, family relationships, the ways family members treat one another, altered long before infant mortality decreased. This ideology of familialism, ideas about the meaning of family relationships, altered between the 1600s and 1700s. Emerging first with the bourgeoisie and squirarchy, the new familial ideology emphasized romantic love as an essential ingredient in marriage, idealized the companionship and spiritual partnership between husband and wife, and accentuated the warm and sentimental bond between mothers and children (Harris 1976). The cult of domesticity developed side by side with new ideas about childhood. Harris (1976) credits the Puritans, at the turn of the seventeenth century, with providing institutional credibility to attacks on arranged marriages and the double standards of courtly love. As a group, Puritans idealized the Christian marriage founded on affection and spiritual compatibility. Their emphasis on the voluntary and emotional potential of marriage spawned renewed interest in childrearing.

Stone (1979) labels this emergent philosophy the emergence of affective individualism. This refers to the development of self-introspection and the demand for personal autonomy. Individual family members demanded privacy and self-expression. Privacy meant the increasing separation of the family from the community, and family members from one another. This separation was accomplished by the glorification of family life, the rise of childhood, the cult of motherhood and the furthering of the belief that marriage was a sacrament.

These cultural values, today taken for granted within marriage, radically altered familial relations. Interestingly, this ideology developed among the bourgeoisie and the squirarchy, the first class to educate boys and the first class to adopt new child-rearing methods. Their maternal, affectionate and permissive child-rearing behaviour developed from their recognition of children as a special status group within the private family. Children experienced greater freedom and warmer affective relations with their parents. These new attitudes did not, initially, affect either the aristocracy or the artisan and cottager classes. The former were thought to remain indifferent to their children, while the latter continued to exploit their children's labour and treat them brutally (Freeman and Lyon 1983).

The transformation of family relationships within the merchant, professional, and commercial classes was a response to improved material conditions brought on by market capitalism. Children signified different burdens and opportunities for parents in different classes. Well into the seventeenth century, the word "child" referred to dependency and subservience. Among the bourgeoisie, "child" began to take on its modern connotation of age. In seventeenth century Massachusetts, "child" referred to a dependent less than 7 years old who could still sleep with siblings and servants. "Youths" included semi-independent persons between the ages of 12 and 25. "Adults" referred to autonomous individuals above the age of 25. Between 1700 and 1725, the legal age of majority in Canada's New France became 25.

Not only the treatment, but also the status of women and children varied, roughly inversely to wealth and social standing (Gies & Gies 1980). As Gies & Gies (1980) suggest, peasant and artisan women and children shared work and responsibility with husbands and brothers on a nearly equal basis. Life varied little for adults and children in this group for a long time. Conversely, noble women, at the top of the hierarchy, were less valued for their productive accomplishments than for the indirect access they provided to property and wealth. In the middle classes, women managed households, raised children, and assisted husbands in their businesses when required. The concentration of literacy in this class ensured that more men than women could read and write. Conventions for middle-class girls included learning cooking, baking, weaving, bedmaking, spinning, embroidery and basic literacy (Gies and Gies 1980). An ideology of gender, which predated capitalism, drew rigid lines between masculine and feminine responsibilities. The care of young children and the apprenticeship and teaching of girls was left to women, while young boys were moved into the masculine world of apprenticeship and formal education at the age of 7.

The final effect of the emergence of childhood concerns its development within a patriarchal ideology. Modern notions of child behaviour and child-rearing became embedded in the private, middle- and upper-class patriarchal family form. Eventually domestic paternalism represented the dominant familial ideology. The ideas that children required special protection before joining adult society fitted neatly with the idea of a privatized, nuclear family providing this special form of treatment. Puritan ideas of democracy and equality were not applied to the propertyless, thus they excluded women, children and the lower class. In turn, this unequal application of the new liberalism strengthened the patriarchal family, since the rule of the father was substituted for the rule of kings (Rowbotham 1974). Women were seen as helpmates of men. Children were viewed as fathers' economic possessions and mothers' moral responsibilities. Women were to train children to take their place within society.

In time, this private, patriarchal, familial ideology invaded the community, assuming a form of public patriarchy through state involvement. The 1600s saw the beginnings of what Foucault (1973) calls the "Great Confinement"—a movement to withdraw the undesirables from society and to use institutions as effective apparatuses for the control and isolation of its deviant members (Fuchs 1984). Deviant children were those not assuming their place within middle-class families. The state also defined infanticide as a capital crime in Canada in the 1700s, and from

1706 on, the government arranged for illegitimate children to be fostered by individual families or religious institutions. Similarly, in colonial New England, close ties existed between the family and the local government. The family was responsible for the care of the poor, the widowed and the disabled, the education and apprenticeship of children (Zaretsky 1982). These familial protectionist principles, enshrined in the poor law, the law of *parens patriae*, have remained the legal basis of an ever-expanding series of state interventions designed to prop up the nuclear, patriarchal family (Zaretsky 1982).

By the end of the 1700s, a number of themes associated with the emergence of childhood had developed. The experiences of children varied significantly by class and gender. In general, women's status declined as commercial capitalism, the privatized nuclear family, the cult of domesticity and the bureaucratized government eroded women's role in politics and the economy (Gies and Gies 1980). Children's fates mirrored their parents', with girls occupying less prestigious and powerful positions than boys.

THE ASCENDANCY OF CHILDHOOD: 1800s TO TODAY

The 1800s marked the transition of North America from a pre-industrial to an industrial society. Between 1849 and 1896, Canada experienced its Industrial Revolution and became a mature, industrial, capitalist society. Both functionalist (Parsons and Bales 1955) and materialist (Marx 1954) interpretations agree that the separation of the workplace from the home altered familial roles and responsibilities. Women became responsible for domestic and affective labour, while men assumed the instrumental and wage labour chores. Industrialization did not create these gender divisions. Rather, economic changes created a set of social relations in which pre-existing divisions were not only reproduced but solidified into different relations in the wage-labour system (Freeman and Lyon 1983). Alice Clark's "Working Life of Women in the Seventeenth Century" (1919) demonstrates that even in pre-industrial times, when goods were being produced in the household, there was a sexual division of labour which antedates capitalism. Women's productive work was valued and recognized, but women were considered morally, economically, legally and socially adjunct and secondary to men. It is not that industrialization rendered women more subservient. Rather middle-class women's productive work was relegated to the home where it was invisible and wageless, hence deemed worthless by society. Throughout all stages of industrialization, working-class women were forced to find wage and non-wage ways to supplement and stretch the family income. When women did work outside the home, "wage rates reflected the expectation that they would rely on men as providers" (Cott 1977, 21–22).

Differential class and gender socialization of working- and middle-class children throughout the 1800s mirrors the fates of their mothers. The Victorian era was one of harsh repression and brutality for working-class children, and a century of increased protection, surveillance and nurture for middle-class children.

These class distinctions in childhood experiences were reflected in two competing discourses. The middle-class process of making children sacred conceptualized children as economically useless but emotionally priceless (Zelizer 1985). The working-class, instrumental discourse constructed children as valuable economic contributors to the family income. These two competing discourses paralleled the ideologies of domesticity that defined middle- and working-class women. Middle-class women were seen as economically unproductive but emotionally and morally superior in child-rearing. Working-class women remained economically productive, either directly, through wage remuneration, or indirectly by extending the family income. They were viewed as negligent and thoughtless mothers in need of scientific guidance. By the 1920s, the gradual expulsion of children from the cash nexus was complete, and the middle-class process of making children sacred triumphed. The cult of childhood spread as rapidly as the middle-class cult of domesticity.

Throughout the 1800s and the early 1900s, working-class women and children continued to contribute to the family income. Canadian data on children demonstrate that their earnings on farms and in factories were essential to family survival. As Paar (1980, 82–83) tells us, all Canadian farm children worked.

> Young boys of 8 fetched wood and water, gathered eggs, fed and herded animals. As they grew older, boys chopped wood, hoed potatoes, dug turnips and helped with the haying. Fourteen year old boys worked like men, ploughing in the spring and fall, threshing and husking corn in the winter, cutting wood. . . . Girls from age 6 on, participated in the household chores of babysitting, cleaning, cooking and sewing and they helped the men outdoors. Their responsibilities increased as they grew older. Hired girls between 14 and 18 did more heavy housework and helped in the cash-earning dairy and poultry enterprises on the farm.

Working-class women and children laboured in factories as well as on farms. Youth were vital to capitalist development. Katz and Davey (1978) in their classic study of adolescents in Hamilton, Ontario, during the mid-1800s, demonstrate that adolescents had a place in society, prior to industrialization, as servants and apprentices. These positions allowed adolescents a measure of autonomy. Hamilton's idle and under-employed youths provided a labour pool to fill the factories and industries.

While life was clearly brutal, industrialization made it possible for children to find work close to home. Capitalism undermined apprenticeship since it was incompatible with a wage system of labour. In the eighteenth and early nineteenth centuries, rural parents routinely sent their children off to work. Eleven- and twelve-year-olds were placed out as maids, servants, plowboys and helpers. In Peel County, Ontario, Parr (1980, 85) reports that between 1841 and 1871, 41% of households included boarders, servants, labourers, apprentices or orphaned children. Only industrialization altered this pattern. In a study of changes in Hamilton, Ontario, Katz and Davey (1978) demonstrate that in 1851, approximately 40% of all young men between 17 and 25 years of age lived as boarders. Children in the new industrial society were living at home for longer periods of time. This meant they were increasingly under parental surveillance.

According to Kealey (1979, 4), in the late nineteenth century, women and children constituted one-third of the total labour force in urban centres. Between 1861 and 1871, the proportion of women and children employed in Montreal's shoemaking and clothing industries increased 50 to 80% respectively (Palmer 1983). In 1871, one in seven workers in Ontario's three leading boot and shoe production centers was under 16, and one in three was a woman. Children worked in bakeries, in tobacco manufacturing, and in sewing and machine factories. In 1891, women and children constituted 33% of the industrial workforce in Toronto and 42% in Montreal (Palmer 1983). By 1871, in Montreal, one in every four boys aged 11 to 15 was engaged in wage labour.

Gender distinctions in women and children's work hardened. Industrialization had more effect on the work of single young women than on men, since economic changes allowed women to leave domestic service and enter industrial work as dressmakers, milliners, tailors and teachers (Katz and Davey 1978). By the 1880s, single women had become a vital component of the labour force. They represented about 15% of the workforce in North America. However, the 1889 Royal Commission revealed that female workers comprised a low-paid stratum that worked in cotton textiles, shoe factories, domestic service, garment production, the tobacco industry and teaching. Their wages were one-third that of their male counterparts and they could be "counted on to work for small wages, to submit to exasperating exactions and to work uncomplainingly for long hours" (Palmer 1983).

Many women also sewed at home under a piece-work system. Daughters joined their mothers, sisters, and aunts at the kitchen table, hemming skirts, embroidering pin cushions, stemming artificial flowers or sorting nuts (Nasow 1985). Young girls minded younger siblings and helped their mothers with the extra work generated by taking in boarders and laundry. Unlike their male counterparts, the girls were not paid and hence never had any spending money of their own. Parents were not embarrassed by their expectation that children would hand over most of their earnings to them. Parents expected deference and obedient service from their children, and felt they had the right to ask children to contribute to the household in ways that would lighten their own burden (Lewis 1986).

The need for children's paid and unpaid contributions accounts for the drive from 1867 on for the importation of British children. Between 1869 and 1919, approximately 73,000 dependent children immigrated as labourers and servants (Sutherland 1976). Those under 9 years old were adopted. Those between 9 and 18 were put under a contract of indenture. In return for their labour, they were provided with room and board, and they were clothed and taught. Organizers like Barnardo and Rye (Parr 1980) invoked the middle-class rhetoric of domesticity to legitimize their mass importation of child labourers. Homeless British children "needed" loving and nurturing Canadian home environments. In actuality, their plight was far less sanguine. These children were " . . . more valuable as producer goods and relatively cheap as consumer goods". It cost little to feed and clothe these children whose labour at lighter household chores freed adults to complete the heavy farm tasks (Parr 1980, 87).

The work day and work week was long and arduous for both city and rural children. City children regularly worked $5^1/_2$ or 6 days, putting in approximately 60 hours per week. The 1889 Royal Commission on the Relations of Labour and Capital detailed the violent, exploitative and savage treatment of many working-class children. The Commission recorded the beating and imprisonment of children who were employed in factories. The report expressed shock and dismay at the extent of child labour, the employment of women and the grossly inadequate sanitary and safety facilities for workers. It recommended forbidding the employment of children under 14 years, especially in mills, factories and mines, since "this injures the health, stunts the growth and prevents the proper education of such children so that they cannot become healthy men and women or intelligent citizens" (Kealey 1973, 13). The Royal Commission also recorded employers' frank and blatant reasons for hiring women and children. They were an economically cheap source of labour. The women, in particular, were expected to be docile, clean, quick, cheap, sober and temporary. After marriage, women stopped working, only to be replaced by another group of young women. The turnover depressed women's wages and contributed to their being labelled as unreliable, uninterested and frivolous workers (Trofimenkoff

1982). Children were similarly typecast. A combination of children's declining economic contributions and their expanding educational opportunities gradually removed children from industry by the early 1900s.

The 1890 Royal Commission on the Prison and Reformatory System, struck to investigate child welfare and juvenile delinquency, also revealed the harsh experience of Canadian immigrant children. The hearings also heard numerous complaints about children taking work away from adults. Responding to organized labour's briefs, the committee suggested immigration be restricted, since these children were depressing adult wages, corrupting "good" Canadian children and ultimately were an expense to the taxpayer through their adolescent incarceration in reformatories, refuges and workhouses. Continual economic fluctuations like the depression of the 1870s, the moderate prosperity of the 1880s and the deep depression of the early 1890s, shook business confidence, and created an impetus to remove women and children from industry.

Gradually throughout the late nineteenth and early twentieth centuries work opportunities for children declined just as those for married women also decreased. The 1891 census reports that 13.8% of all Canadian children between the ages of 10 and 14 were gainfully employed. By 1921, this number had declined to 3.2%. In agriculture, the decline was from 11.4% in 1891 to 1.9% in 1921. Although children were a major component of the workforce in factories, shops and department stores in the 1870s, by 1900 one-third of Macy's employees were "cash" boys and girls. By 1900, they were replaced first by the pneumatic tube and then by cash registers. Only a minority of American children remained employed full-time in areas not affected by automation or by the arrival of cheap, adult immigrants. These children worked in southern textile mills, they picked berries, canned fruit, shucked oysters, tended machines in sweatshops, and helped adults with their jobs in tenement flats.

A combination of restrictive child labour laws, compulsory education acts and declining employment opportunities for children eventually pushed them out of wage labour. Yet, schooling and working were not viewed as mutually exclusive activities. Education acts in force around 1890 stipulated that children between the ages of 7 and 13 had to attend school for 100 days a year. Child labour laws reduced the employment possibilities of children who were under 14 years. By the turn of the century, predominantly male city children performed certain types of dead-end and often part-time jobs. Working-class children, mostly boys, assumed part-time jobs selling newspapers, shining shoes, making deliveries for tradesmen, carrying messages for businessmen and doing odd jobs for shopkeepers. Those too young to earn steady wages helped stretch the family income by scavenging food from outdoor markets and collecting coal and wood from the railroad tracks and streets (Nasow

1985). According to the instrumental discourse, children were expected to contribute to the family's income in any way they could.

Throughout the early nineteenth century, work and school experiences for middle-class children were vastly different from those of their working-class peers. Middle-class parents entered into a new economic contract with their children, whereby parents relinquished children's wages and instead subsidized their spending habits (Zelizer 1985). By 1893, doling out children's allowance was a standard middle-class practice. Since both boys and girls spent less of their time as producers and more as pupils, it was also a necessity. The sons and daughters of skilled artisans and craftsmen, public, commercial and business employees and professionals including preachers, lawyers, doctors, dentists and high school teachers lived mostly in towns and were largely unemployed. Characteristically, middle-class boys were the first to prolong their schooling, since most girls married, and married women were absent from wage labour.

Before 1850, many poor Canadian children received no education. Of those who did, economic exigencies determined their school attendance. The majority of children received some schooling, but attendance was seasonal and brief. Working-class boys learned most of what they needed to know in apprenticeship programs at work, while girls acquired skills at home. Those who attended school in the early nineteenth century had a choice between a mixture of private school education run by religious and non-denominational groups, and government-aided common schools and public school education run by charitable organizations (Lennards 1986). In the mid-1800s, Katz and Davey (1978) report, working-class Hamilton children attended school less regularly and for shorter periods of time than did their middle-class peers. By 1871, with the introduction of compulsory education, schooling between the ages of 7 and 12 became nearly universal in Canada. School was no longer voluntary, but compulsory for a minimum period of time every year. Yet, few working-class boys attended longer than necessary, and few were found in the higher grades. It was not until employment opportunities decreased for children that enforcement of labour and education laws tightened, and school leaving ages were consistently raised from 10 to 16. A greater number of children attended school more regularly, for longer periods, and were taught by better-educated teachers (Sutherland 1976). Between 1891 and 1923, the total enrolment in public elementary and secondary schools nearly doubled. By 1920, the number of 14- to 17-year-old Americans in high school was 600% what it had been 30 years earlier (Nasow 1985). Children stayed in school longer and thus began work two to five years later than they had in the 1890s.

Child labour and schooling laws reveal society's vacillation between viewing children instrumentally and viewing them sentimentally. State agencies recognized class differences in the value of children. In 1899, for example, more than one half of the American states issued poverty permits to children allowing them to work if their earnings were necessary to support themselves, disabled fathers or widowed mothers (Zelizer 1985). Similarly, in the early 1900s, the Toronto Board of Education authorized early school leaving for children whose wages were deemed essential for family survival. As students and workers, working-class children lived in two worlds (Nasow 1985). They were dependents at school and home but quasi-adult workers and consumers in the streets. In contrast, middle-class children came to occupy only one world as sentimentalized and idealized dependents. These positions corresponded to those filled by their mothers in society.

The early twentieth century is remembered as a period of intense competition between two discourses. The preservation of the moral child was pitted against the image of the useful, wage-earning child. This competition introduced what Zelizer (1985) calls a new cultural equation: if children were useful and produced money, they were not being properly loved. Middle-class reformers campaigned vigorously against child labour. Children under 14 years were constructed as unfit and ill-prepared to assume adult roles and responsibilities, including part-time, after school jobs. Child psychologists buttressed their claims. They prophesied that children forced into the workplace before they had been adequately prepared would be physically, morally and intellectually stunted (Nasow 1985). Psychology, aided by the rise of domesticity, constituted the child as a special creature, an emotional investment to be admired, cuddled, cared for and protected from evil. Not only were children not to work, but they also were to be excluded from adult leisure activities. Adult work sites, like the streets, movie theatres, vaudeville halls, amusement parks, penny arcades and candy shops, were sources of sexual corruption, hence off limits to children. As the century wore on, the idealization rhetoric dominated and became diffused to all classes.

Interestingly, it was middle-class feminists who pushed most vigorously for the segregation of children from adults. Early nineteenth-century feminists accepted women's responsibilities for home and children and believed that women's moral purity and spiritual genius would purge society of its corrupting, male influences (Morrison 1976). When women sought to move into the public arena, their efforts were directed at improving the welfare of children. Thus, when women explored emancipatory possibilities for themselves, they accomplished the same for their children (Morrison 1976).

Middle-class women ventured from the home as social reformers, as redeemers of a new family life for children, especially working-class ones. Working-class mothers, for example, were condemned for their "fecklessness" and "carelessness". Educating these women was touted as a solution to infant mortality, juvenile delinquency, school absence and street gangs. Middle-class women glorified the roles of family and mother as essential socialization agents. Women's natural, maternal instinct was the basis for their superiority as parents. In 1871, Darwin advanced the "maternal instinct theory" of behaviour as an explanation for women's limited intellect, emotionality, childlike behaviour and physical resemblance to children. This instinct was seen as accounting for women's piety, purity, submissiveness, intuition and sensitivity, characteristics which made her perfectly suited to child-rearing and ill-suited to wage labour.

Women of that time internalized this ideology about mothering since it corresponded with their social reality. Women were stuck in the home and ventured into public settings only by acting as agents for children. Women actively practised traditional mothering roles in social contexts by establishing a host of charitable, educational and welfare groups, including the hospital for poor children in 1887, called The Hospital for Sick Children, the Y.W.C.A. and the Women's Christian Temperance Union. In 1894, the National Council of Women of Canada became an institutional representation of maternal feminist beliefs about the connection between mothering, family life and social reform.

Numerous messages were contained in the middle-class process of making children sacred, a discourse which gradually became diffused to include all children. Relying on the social sciences, it normalized the ideal child. Children required the care of a full-time mother. "Exalting the child went hand in hand with exalting the domestic role of women." (Zelizer 1985). Women were felt to be pious, gentle, loving, pure and devout and thus ideal as social housekeepers and moral watchdogs of the hearth and community (Contratto 1983). By providing the correct environment for child development, mothers undertook the moral regulation of children. The house became an enclosed space, set apart from the outside world, in which this synthetic and controlled environment was created.

The cult of child psychology produced an explosion of books, pamphlets and magazine articles directed at first-time mothers concerned with infants and pre-schoolers' development (Urwin 1984). They advocated the use of manipulative, rather than coercive, child-rearing tactics. Middle-class mothers were seen as examples of the "soft" socialization techniques while working-class mothers were disdained for their unsophisticated use of more harsh methods. The effects were supposedly reproduced in their children's behaviour.

The scrutiny of psychology was bolstered by the medical-hygienist pole (Donzelot 1979). Pediatricians, public health nurses and social workers institutionalized a norm of "normal" child development by routinizing infant testing, regular check-ups and intelligence testing. Through these medical, familial and educational scrutinization practices, "good" children were increasingly differentiated from "bad" ones. Bad children resulted from bad mothering and included virtually all who exhibited anti-social manifestations, including delinquency, drug abuse, school failure and mental illness. The "time bomb" message (Contratto 1983) was clear: what mothers did with small children, however seemingly unconnected with them, might have serious, permanent effects later on. This logical, irrefutable, expert assertion persists today as a key element of the sacred-child discourse. The overall effect of creating and policing this discourse in school, crime and labour laws has been to narrow the definition of acceptable childlike behaviour. Individuals and social organizations collude. For example, the self-righteous "Mothers' Movement" of the early twentieth century advocated issuing licences for "professional mothers". Similarly, large scale organizations, including reform Christians and the new professionals of the child study, kindergarten and juvenile reform movements, and Canadian politicians, enlisted in the moral campaign to improve the welfare of children (Sutherland 1976). For example, the 1913 Royal Commission on Industrial Training and Technical Education advocated the introduction of domestic science because of the direct and continuous influence of the home on children. Good homes ministered to the welfare of the people "by ensuring conditions under which the children may be healthy, wholesome and happy" (Sutherland 1976, 190).

The growth of state agencies in the twentieth century represents a shift from government by families to government through families (Donzelot 1979). As mentioned earlier, this change began in the 1600s with the privatization of family life. The state sought to remove undesirables from society and to use its tutelary complex of hospitals, prisons, foster families and reform schools to control and isolate deviant children (Foucault 1977). Technological, medical and scientific advances lent credibility to professional expertise. By the end of the 1700s, social reformers of the enlightenment had come to believe that the state, the community writ at large, had a collective responsibility to care for undesirables (Fuchs 1984). Direct precursors of the modern welfare state are found in the institutions constructed between the 1820s and 1840s for the orphaned, dependent poor, sick, and insane (Zaretsky 1982).

The 1850s is generally regarded as the beginning of both the child-saving and the children's rights movements. Society's concern for children revolved around the child's usefulness to society (Freeman 1983a). Poor, delinquent or illiterate children were a drain on society. The child rescue or saving movement assumed the state had a parental responsibility to help those children who could not care for or protect themselves. Liberal, paternalistic rhetoric took for granted that parents, hence the state, had the power to interfere with children's lives, restrict their actions and coerce them in order to ensure society's well-being. Children were viewed as objects of intervention rather than as legal subjects (Freeman 1983a).

The origins of the juvenile delinquency system and the movement for compulsory education, for example, were seen as state solutions to the crime and delinquency of children. Schools functioned as a cheap form of moral police (Prentice 1977, 132), controlling children's behaviour, monitoring their parents' actions, and promoting appropriate adult-child relationships. In all of these areas affecting children, middle-class women, in their roles as caretakers, teachers, social workers and psychologists, acted as moral supervisors, mediating between private and public domains.

Canadian child-saving followed patterns established in the United States and Britain. Originally, children were institutionalized along with the aged, infirm and insane in orphan asylums that included notorious ones in Kingston, London, Montreal and Toronto (Rooke and Schnell 1981). By the twentieth century, dependency was so specialized that the prison, the lunatic asylum, the industrial school, the almshouse, the rescue house, the Children's Aid Society, and the orphanage all met special needs. By the 1920s, most provinces no longer housed orphans in poor asylums.

One of the main ways the state has justified its involvement with children has been on the basis of science. Scientific advances in the understanding and measurement of childhood have been widely used as an argument to reassert women's quintessential maternal function (Mitchell 1973). The early women's movement coalesced around the notion that only women can effectively bring up children. Proper management of children in the home was bolstered by child-rearing experts in the schools. Child training became a scientific, professional undertaking dependent on an ever-expanding body of mostly psychological research and the professionalization of child care. Between 1923 and 1929, the Laura Spelman Rockefeller Foundation spent more than $7 million dollars in Canada and the United States to establish research institutes and parent education centers. The University of Toronto's Institute for Child Study was an example of the attempts to standardize and control expert child raising (Ehrenreich and English 1979). These institutes became a structure from which to diffuse expert advice to mothers.

This rapid professionalization of child training was part of Canada's overall commitment in the 1930s and 1940s to professionalize child care as a whole. Rooke and Schnell (1981) tells us how the energetic Charlotte Whitton, the first head of the Canadian Council on Child Welfare, sought to extend social welfare to include every aspect of children's lives. Originally interested in hygiene, employment, education and recreation, this national body eventually examined movie censorship, school attendance laws, youth employment, mental hygiene, "social" diseases, unwed parenthood, mothers' and family allowances, child legislation, delinquency, moral reform, drug and liquor traffic, birth control, immigration, playgrounds, housing, handicapped persons and divorce. The council acted as a moral watchdog over all aspects of children's lives (Rooke and Schnell 1981).

Academics disagree as to the consequences of child rescue programs. Groups like the National Council of Women in Canada, for example, in the early 1900s stated that children whose mothers lack material or cognitive resources are at a disadvantage. Thus the state has a collective duty to limit such inequalities by redistributing economic support or services like child health and education. The National Council of Women in Canada advocated improvements for children including reform of children's courts, factory inspection, urban sanitation, temperance, improved care for neglected children, and improvement in the working conditions of women and children. These demands were made to improve the material welfare of women and children.

Other assessments of child-rescue actions are more cynical, suggesting that measures like intelligence testing and juvenile courts, which are designed to protect children, are a cloak to control a "problem population", hence their mothers. Rather than being a means to redistribute wealth or opportunity, the child saving movement was a punitive, romantic and intrusive effort to control the lives of urban, lower-class adolescents and to maintain their dependent status (Freeman 1983).

Adherents of this latter position describe the twentieth century as the growth of the therapeutic state (Lasch 1977). This increased state intervention represents an intrusive middle-class effort to impose an alien moral code on working-class children. The state promotes middle-class interests by continually expanding its definitions of how children can best be protected, from what and from whom. The juvenile reform movement (Platt 1974; West 1984), the schooling movement (Prentice 1977) the charity and public health movements (Zaretsky 1982; Fuchs 1984) all reveal similar consequences: the expanded surveillance of childhood and the increased proletarianization of parenthood. By working through intermediaries—doctors, teachers, psychologists, social workers, juvenile judges, legislators—the state consolidates its therapeutic apparatus and gradually assumes more of the education and supervision of children and their families.

This ever-expanding state intervention is largely invisible. Never before have children been so covertly monitored and regulated while maintaining the illusion of freedom and self-control. The primary school, for example, represents an important site in which the state, through teachers, constructs individual free will, all the while observing, checking and monitoring individual children (Walkerdine 1985). Ironically, women, themselves highly regulated, have assumed the moral guardianship of children in their roles as nurses, teachers and social workers. These "caring" professionals become facilitators, instructors, and monitors, as they morally regulate children through the provision of an appropriate environment.

CONCLUSION

In this twentieth "century of the child", we have witnessed the expulsion of children from wage labour, the diffusion of the middle-class "children as sacred" discourse, and the expansion of the state's power to intervene in the lives of children and their families. As women's lives alter, conceptions of and actions toward children also change.

Women and children are subordinated to patriarchy in both their public and private lives. The very role of mother is one increasingly at risk of being deprived of civil liberties (Freeman 1984). Having the power to remove children from poor physical, moral or emotional conditions, the state suggests it is acting in the best interests of society by defining children as too valuable a future commodity to be left exclusively to parents. Women are constituted as untrustworthy, as mothers in need of constant supervision by the helping professionals, who are predominately female labourers controlled by white, middle-class males. By reproducing social situations, such as current parent-child relationships, in which people feel unable to provide for their own needs without the supervision of trained experts, the therapeutic state guarantees the continued oppression of women. Also, as long as children remain materially connected to women, they will be objects of surveillance.

An ideology of mother-blaming emerged from the close surveillance of women and children. A deprived home environment was, and still is, often a pseudonym for maternal deprivation. Maternal deprivation theory suggests that mothers are responsible for the individual outcome of their children and for the general quality of family life. It suggests children need full-time mothers at home, mothers who exclusively care for all their emotional and physical needs, especially during the preschool years. Early separation of children from mothers is deemed harmful to children's future development. This powerful ideology is built into the theory and practice of the helping professions. Mothers are held responsible for conditions as diverse as mental retardation, schizophrenia, delinquency, depression, incest, violent crime, slums and prostitution (Levine 1983).

The state-as-family has contributed to the change in rhetoric about children. In the early 1900s, government agents emphasized punitive responses to recalcitrant children. As the century wore on, prevention and close surveillance were substituted for punishment. Fifteen years ago, the juvenile system talked about "children in trouble". By treating children's deviations increasingly as environmental, professional agents legitimated the removal of children from homes. Now we have moved again beyond this all-encompassing environmental excuse and begun to differentiate between delinquent and endangered children. We call the former "young offenders".

The gradual shift from private to public patriarchy sparked the children's rights movement. From the mid-1800s, reformers have argued about the necessity and consequences of replacing the father with the state. Family autonomy proponents argue for maintaining private paternalistic control over child-rearing. Self-determination advocates and equal rights advocates both advance the rescue approach of limited state intervention. However, self-determinists see children as having the same status, the same obligations and privileges of adults; egalitarians view children as subordinates requiring adults to equalize their opportunities for future advancement (Dingwall and Eekelar 1984). These ongoing arguments display the social and political constitution of children.

The children's rights movement also highlights the costly burden children have become under monopoly capital. It may be that the process of making children sacred is now an outdated luxury (Zelizer 1985). As more mothers work, the economically useless child who demands constant supervision is a tremendous burden. This may explain in part why Canadian fertility rates have dropped so steadily for the past 15 years. We have now institutionalized so many cultural disincentives to mothering that adults no longer understand how children fit into their lives.

The cult of motherhood now appears as a restrictive and ridiculous ideology for the majority of Canadian married women struggling to juggle their double days. It is not only that finding an acceptable, reliable, quality and affordable day-care environment is problematic (see Pupo, chapter 8), but also that fulfilling the script of ideal mother and responsible wage labourer is contradictory. Recent Canadian studies (Luxton 1980; Duffy, Mandell and Pupo 1989) detail the enormous strain, fatigue and irritability many women experience in their unending round of chores. Since combining work and family roles is now a lifelong combination for women, structural and ideological alterations will have to evolve to ease their burden. It is these changes in women's lives which will have the most dramatic effect on children.

Although Canadian data are not available, it seems likely that children's roles will alter in dual-worker families. Their role in the 1980s seems analogous to the one they assumed in pre-industrial, rural days. When children assumed the light, repetitive and non-strenuous tasks of housekeeping, and tending gardens, animals and babies, they freed their parents to complete the more demanding, physical work on the farms. Similarly, today, the routine household and childcare tasks children perform free their mothers to enter wage labour. As children's indirect financial contributions increase, they are treated less as children and more as adults.

As the cult of true womanhood lessens, the cult of pure childhood also decreases. Rather than being portrayed as frail, dependent and helpless creatures, children are socially constructed as robust, independent and helpful individuals who are more involved in family economics. Although children are still financially costly, women and men still claim that having children provides the greatest happiness, pleasure and joy in their lives. Given then that couples are likely to continue to want and to bear children, it also follows that the role of children within families will alter to minimize parents' financial costs and maximize parents' emotional gains. Just as women have taken on, once more, wage labour, children are contributing, once more, to the household.

It may be that the cults of womanhood and childhood, revealed in the late 1800s and early 1900s, are dissipating. While women are still primarily defined by their role as mothers, and while children are still protected, idealized and sentimentalized, both groups are increasingly being defined as instrumental, autonomous and self-sufficient workers. Once more, husbands and fathers are becoming increasingly interested in being parents as children's productive value increases. Once more, children are being given household responsibility and wage-earning chores (Connelly and MacDonald 1986). Rather than signalling a loss of childhood or a demise in children's innocence, these changes indicate the closer integration of children and women in a more egalitarian and interdependent family.

These movements towards an egalitarian family norm do not mean that children and women are socially, economically or culturally equal to men. In a patriarchal society, Canadian women and children suffer distinct disadvantages. By 1985, more than one million Canadian children lived below the poverty line. One out of every five children in the country is seriously economically deprived, and unemployment among youth remains at twice the rate of the general population. Moreover, a high percentage of new jobs being created are minimum-wage, part-time and temporary positions (Hunsley 1987). Thus the feminization of poverty (see Boyd, chapter 4) affects Canadian children as well. These largely economic changes in women's and children's lives suggest our ideological constructions of women and children as resilient, independent producers reflects their current integration into the public domain.

Bibliography

Adams, Bert N.
1980   *The Family*. 3d ed. Chicago: Rand McNally.
Aries, Phillippe.
1962   *Centuries of Childhood: A Social History of Family Life*. New York: Vintage.
Boulton, Mary Georgina.
1983   *On being a mother*. London: Tavistock.
Campbell, Helen.
[1893]   *Women Wage Earners*. Reprint 1972, New York: Arno Press.
Clark, Alice.
1919   *Working Life of Women in the Seventeenth Century*. London: G. Routledge.
Connelly, Patricia, and Martha MacDonald.
1986   "Women's Work: Domestic and Wage Labour in a Nova Scotia Community". In *The Politics of Diversity*, edited by Roberta Hamilton and Michele Barrett, 53-80. Montreal: Book Center Inc.
Contratto, Susan.
1983   "Psychology Views Mothers and Mothering, 1897–1980". In *Feminist re-visions: What has been and might be*, edited by Vivian Patraka and Louise A. Tilly, 149-178. Ann Arbor: University of Michigan Press.
Cott, Nancy.
1977   *The Bonds of Womanhood: "Women's Sphere in New England", 1780–1835*. New Haven, Conn.: Yale University Press.
DeMause, Lloyd.
1982   "The Evolution of Childhood". In *The Sociology of Childhood*, edited by Chris Jenks, 48-59. London: Bat Ford.
Dingwall, Robert, and John Eekelar.
1984   "Rethinking Child Protection". In *State, law and the family: Critical perspectives*, edited by M.D.A. Freeman, 93-114. London: Tavistock.
Donzelot, Jacques.
1979   *The Policing of Families*. New York: Pantheon Books.
Duffy, Ann, Nancy Mandell, and Norene Pupo.
1989   *Few Choices: Women, Work and Family*. Toronto: Garamond.

Ehrenreich, Barbara, and Deidre English.
1979   *For Her Own Good.* Garden City, N.Y.: Anchor.
Foucault, Michel.
1973   *Birth of the Clinic: An Archaeology of Medical Perception.* London: Tavistock.
Foucault, Michel.
1977   *Discipline and punish: The birth of the prison.* New York: Pantheon Books.
Freeman, M.D.A.
1983a   *The Rights and Wrongs of Children.* London: Frances Pinter.
Freeman, M.D.A., and Christina M. Lyon.
1983b   *Cohabitation Without Marriage.* Aldershot, England: Gower House.
Freeman, M.D.A. (Ed.).
1984   *State, Law and the Family: Critical Perspectives.* London: Tavistock.
Fuchs, Rachel Ginnis.
1984   *Abandoned Children: Foundlings and Child Welfare in Nineteenth-century France.* New York: Albany State University of New York Press.
Gaffield, Chad.
1984   "Wage Labour, Industrialization and the Origins of the Modern Family. In *The Family: Changing Trends in Canada,* edited by Maureen Baker, 21-34. Toronto: McGraw-Hill Ryerson.
Gies, Frances, and Joseph Gies.
1980   *Women in the Middle Ages.* New York: Barnes and Noble.
Greer, Germaine.
1984   *Sex and Destiny: The Politics of Human Fertility.* Toronto: Stoddart.
Harris, Barbara J.
1976   "Recent Work on the History of the Family: A Review Article". In *Feminist Studies* 3, no. 3/4 (Spring Summer)159-172.
Hoyles, Martin.
1979   "Childhood in Historical Perspective". In *Changing Childhood,* edited by Martin Hoyles, 16-29. London: Writers and Readers Publishing Cooperative.
Hunsley, Terrance.
           "A blueprint for providing tax reform for children". *The Globe and Mail,* Toronto, August 10, 1987.
Katz, Michael B., and Ian E. Davey.
1978   "Youth and Early Industrialization in a Canadian City". *American Journal of Sociology* 84 (Supplement): 81-119.

Kealey, Linda (Ed.).
1979   *A Not Unreasonable Claim.* Toronto: Women's Press.
Kealey, Greg (Ed.).
1973   *Canada Investigates Industrialism.* Toronto: University of Toronto Press.
Lasch, Christoper.
1977   *Haven in a Heartless World: The Family Beseiged.* New York: Basic Books.
Lee, John Alan.
1982   "Three Paradigms of Childhood". *Canadian Review of Sociology and Anthropology* 19(4): 591-608.
Lennards, Jos.
1986   "Education". In *Sociology* (3d ed.), edited by Robert Hagedorn, 451-485. Toronto: Holt, Rinehart and Winston.
Levine, Helen.
1983   "The Power Politics of Motherhood". In *Perspectives on Women in the 1980s,* edited by Joan Turner and Lois Emery, 28-40. Winnipeg, Manitoba: The University of Manitoba Press.
Lewis, Jane (Ed.).
1986   *Labour and Love: Women's Experience of Home and Family, 1850-1940.* London: Basil Blackwell.
Luxton, Meg.
1980   *More than a Labour of Love: Three Generations of Women's Work in the Home.* Toronto: The Women's Press.
Mackie, Marlene.
1984   "Socialization: Changing Views of Child-Rearing and Adolescence". In *The Family: Changing Trends in Canada,* edited by Maureen Baker, 35-62. Toronto: McGraw-Hill Ryerson.
Maroney, Heather Jon.
1986   "Embracing Motherhood: New Feminist Theory". In *The Politics of Diversity,* edited by Roberta Hamilton and Michele Barrett, 398-423. Montreal: Book Center Inc.
Marx, Karl.
1954   *Capital.* Vol. 1. Moscow: Foreign Languages Publishing House.
Mitchell, Juliet.
1973   *Women's Estate.* New York: Vintage.
Moogk, Peter N.
1982   "Les Petits Sauvages: The Children of Eighteenth Century New France". In *Childhood and Family in Canadian History,* edited by Joy Parr, 17-43. Toronto: McClelland and Stewart.
Morrison, T. R.
1976   "'Their Proper Sphere' Feminism, The Family and Child-Centered Social Reform in Ontario, 1875–1900". *Ontario History* 68:45-64.

Nasow, David.
1985   *Children of the City: At Work and at Play.* Garden City, New York: Anchor Press.
Oakley, Ann.
1974   *The Sociology of Housework.* New York: Pantheon.
Palmer, Bryan D.
1983   *Working-class Experience: The Rise and Reconstitution of Canadian Labour, 1800–1980.* Toronto: Butterworths.
Parr, Joy.
1980   *Labouring Children.* London: Croom Helm.
Parsons, Talcott, and Robert F. Bales.
1955   *Family, Socialization and Interaction Process.* Glencoe, Illinois: The Free Press.
Platt, A.
[1969]   *The Child-Savers.* Rev. ed. 1974, Chicago: University of Chicago Press.
Plumb, J.H.
1976   "The Great Change in Children". In *Rethinking Childhood: Perspectives on Development and Society,* edited by Arlene Skolnick, 205-213. Boston: Little, Brown, and Co.
Postman, Neil.
1982   *The Disappearance of Childhood.* New York: Dell.
Prentice, Alison.
1977   *The School Promoters: Education and Social-Class in Mid-nineteenth Century Upper Canada.* Toronto: McClelland and Stewart.
Rooke, Patricia T., and R.L. Schnell.
1981   "Child Welfare in English Canada, 1920–1948". *Social Service Review*: 484-506.
Rowbotham, Sheila.
1974   *Hidden from History.* London: Pluto.
Royal Commission on the Relations of Labour and Capital. Queen's Printer, Ottawa. 1889.
Royal Commission on the Prison and Reformatory System. Queen's Printer, Ottawa. 1913.
Royal Commission on Industrial Training and Technical Education King's Printer, Ottawa. 1913.
Rubin, Lillian Breslow.
1976   *Worlds of Pain: Life in the Working-class Family.* New York: Basic.
Scanzoni, Letha Dawson, and John Scanzoni.
1981   *Men, Women and Change: A Sociology of Marriage and Family.* 2nd ed. Toronto: McGraw-Hill Book Company.
Shorter, Edward.
1975   *The Making of the Modern Family.* New York: Basic Books.

Stone, Lawrence.
1979   *The Family, Sex and Marriage in England, 1500-1800.* Penguin.
Suransky, Valerie Polakow.
1982   *The Erosion of Childhood.* Chicago: The University of Chicago Press.
Sutherland, Neil.
1976   *Children in English-Canadian Society: Framing the Twentieth-Century Consensus.* Toronto: University of Toronto Press.
Synnott, Anthony.
1983   "Little Angels, Little Devils: A Sociology of Children". *Canadian Review of Sociology and Anthropology* 20(1).
Trofimenkoff, Susan.
1982   "One Hundred and Two Muffled Voices: Canada's Industrial Women in the 1880s". In *Canada's Age of Industry, 1849–1896,* edited by Michael Cross and Greg Kealey, 212-229. Toronto: McClelland and Stewart.
Trumbach, Randolph.
1978   *The Rise of the Egalitarian Family.* New York: Academic Press.
Tuchman, Barbara W.
1978   *A Distant Mirror.* New York: Alfred A. Knopf.
Urwin, Cathy.
1984   "Constructing Motherhood: The Persuasion of Normal Development". In *Language, Gender and Childhood,* Stedman (Eds.). 164-202. London, England: Routledge and Kegan Paul.
Walkerdine, Valerie.
1985   "On the regulation of speaking and silence: subjectivity, class and gender in contemporary schooling". In *Language, Gender and Childhood,* edited by Carolyn Stedman, Cathy Urwin, and Valerie Walkerdine, 203-241. London, England: Routledge and Kegan Paul.
West, W. Gordon
1984   *Young Offenders and the State: A Canadian Perspective on Delinquency.* Toronto: Butterworths.
Zaretsky, Eli.
1982   "The Place of the Family in the Origins of the Welfare State". In *Rethinking the Family: Some Feminist Questions,* edited by Barrie Thorne with Marilyn Yalom, 188-224. New York: Longman.
Zelizer, Viviana.
1985   *Pricing the Priceless Child: The Changing Social Value of Children.* New York: Basic.

PART II

The Dynamics of the Family: Perspectives on Change

CHAPTER 4

Changing Canadian Family Forms: Issues for Women

Monica Boyd

A quarter of a century ago, the term "family" did not conjure up the diversity which it does today. Then, the term connoted a husband-breadwinner, wife and children at home, all living in the same residence and having strong economically, socially, and emotionally based inter-actions. Today, the composition, structure and relationships within Canadian families are highly varied. Living alone is increasing, particularly among the young and the old; families are formed out of consensual unions, legal marriages, and as a result of divorce and death; families are smaller; more women are in the labour force; lone-parent families are increasing. Such diversity is important for two reasons. First, rather than indicating the decline and demise of Canadian families, these new family forms indicate the persistence and co-existence of family life alongside massive economic and social alterations in post-war Canadian society. Second, the imagery of families as comprised of "husband-bread-winner, wife at home" affects alternative family structures and the women in them. This chapter pursues these themes of change and persistence with respect to Canadian families. An initial section reviews the evidence for the persistence of Canadian families alongside the decline of the traditional family structure. Then new developments in family formation and changes in family composition and type are discussed and their implications for women assessed.

CHANGING CANADIAN FAMILIES: AN OVERVIEW

Any analysis of temporal change either implicitly or explicitly invokes a baseline model against which change is measured. Analyses of the family are no different. Despite growing historical evidence for the multiplicity of family arrangements in North America and Europe (Kessler-Harris 1982; Nett 1981; Tilly and Scott 1978), the tendency is to depict today's circumstances as they were in the past, when households and families were synonymous, the family unit often included two or more families representing multiple generations, and the dominant form was a wage-earner husband with a non-employed wife and young children.

Trend data for Canada reveal the growing inaccuracy of such depictions. One of the major changes in post-war Canada, for example, is the increasing percentage of non-family households. Much of this is due to the phenomenal growth in one-person households, which increased from nearly 1 in 14 households (7.4%) in 1951 to 1 in 5 (20.3%) in 1981 (Statistics Canada 1979a: Table 3.1; 1982d: Table 1). The tendency to live alone is concentrated among the young and the elderly, and it is attributed to the increased availability of housing, improved economic circumstances in which living alone becomes economically feasible, increased separation and divorce among the young, postponed marriages, and smaller family sizes which reduce the opportunities for the elderly to live with offspring (Thomas and Burch 1985; Statistics Canada 1979a: 21–22; 1981a: 43–48). The social implications of the trend toward living alone are still uncertain, although United States research proposes two likely consequences: first, that family life is less continuous, sandwiched between premarital and postmarital independence, and second, that generations may become residentially and socially segregated from each other (Kobrin, 1976a, 1976b. Also see Thomas and Burch 1985 and Statistics Canada, 1979a: 22 for additional discussion.).

The recent increases in non-family households are accompanied by declines in multiple-family households in Canada. These declines indicate the growing nuclearization of Canadian families, by which families consisting of parents and children increasingly are living without additional persons such as extended kin or lodgers (Statistics Canada 1981a: 34). In 1951, for example, nearly 7% or 1 in 15 households consisted of two or more families, compared to 1% by 1981 (Statistics Canada 1979a: Table 3.1; 1982d: Table 1). Explanations for these trends emphasize the desire of families and individuals for independence and privacy (Statistics Canada 1981a: 36–37).

These trends indicate increasing variation in living arrangements among Canadians, and they indicate that individuals are not living in families from the cradle to the grave. At the same time, such trends do not in themselves indicate the demise of family life in Canada. In fact, a growing percentage of men and women are marrying and forming families at some point in their lives. In 1911, for example, 88% of Canadian women and 86% of Canadian men were married by the age of 50, with the residual 12% and 14% never marrying up to that age (Statistics Canada 1978: Table 3). This percentage ever married steadily rose, until by the time of the 1981 census, 94% and 92% of women and men had married by the age of 50 (calculations based on Statistics Canada 1982b: Table 5).

Thus, Canadians do not appear to be avoiding the entry into families at some point in their lives. And most Canadians have in the past, and continue into the present, to live in a family. In 1981, 20.6 million people were living in censused families,[1] representing 84.6% of the total population (Statistics Canada 1982a: Table 1). This figure does not differ appreciably from the percentages of Canadians living in families in earlier years (Statistics Canada 1979a: Table 2.1).

While family living has remained the most prevalent living arrangement for Canadians, the form of such living arrangements has changed. In particular, the traditional family form, consisting of a male breadwinner, a wife who does not have paid employment, two or three dependent children and the requisite dog, today is a questionable image for several reasons. First, it is an oversimplified construct, in that it implies a monolithic family structure (Eichler 1983). Second, as a family form, it may lack historical generalizability. Even in earlier times, high mortality rates and the impoverishment of the industrial working class ensured that many families departed from the two parent, one breadwinner norm (Chapter 6; also Nett 1981, 247). Third, even if it were true at a particular time, the "husband-wife, husband only in the labour force" family no longer is the prevalent type of family arrangement. The zenith of the traditional nuclear family occurred during the 1950s, coinciding with high fertility levels (the post-war baby boom).

In 1961, however, only 6 in 10 families (63%) were of this type; in 1981, only 3 in 10 (35%) could be described as such (Dominion Bureau of Statistics 1963a: Table 72; 1963b: Table 8a; Statistics Canada 1984b: Table 12). More stringent definitions reduce the share even further. In 1981, husband-wife families with at least one child at home and a wife not in the labour force represented 24% of all families in Canada (Table 1); if a family with two children present is invoked, the percentage declines to 10% (Statistics Canada 1984b, Tables 1 and 12). The fact that the traditional family form represents only a modest fraction of all Canadian families is not surprising in light of the social and economic changes in post-war Canada which have influenced family formation patterns, the size of families, the labour force participation of women, the creation of lone-parent families and the dissolution of elderly families.

FAMILY FORMATION: EMERGING TRENDS

A common conceptualization of family formation associates the creation of a family with the marriage of a young, never-married man and woman. This conceptualization in fact describes the origins of most Ca-

Table 1:

Families by Family Structure, Presence of Children, and Labour Force Participation, Canada, 1981

Total Families, N	6,325,315
Total, Percent	100.0
Husband-Wife	
Children at Home	56.9
Wife Not in Labour Force, Husband in Labour Force	(24.0)
Wife in Labour Force, Husband in Labour Force	(28.7)
Wife Not in Labour Force, Husband Not in Labour Force	(3.2)
Wife in Labour Force, Husband Not in Labour Force	(1.0)
No Children at Home	31.8
Childless	14.6
Lone Parent	11.3
Female	9.3
Male	2.0

Source: Statistics Canada (1984b) Tables 1 and 12.

nadian families. In 1985, for example, 70% of the 184,096 marriages were marriages between never-married men and women, the majority of whom were in their twenties (Statistics Canada 1986e: Table 4). However, despite the importance of first marriages in family formation, the trend data point to increases in common-law relationships, to postponement of legal marriages (hence increases in the age at which most Canadians form their own families), and to increases in families created from remarriages of one or both partners.

The occurrence of common-law marriages is still low. The 1981 census recorded more than 350,000 marriage-like unions representing 6% of all husband-wife families (McKie 1986: 39–40). However, a 1984 national survey found that 1 in 6 Canadians between the ages of 18 and 64 had at some point in their lives lived in a marriage-like union. Experiencing a common-law marriage or having lived in one was more characteristic of young Canadians than of older Canadians. It appears that many of these marriage-like unions are a one-time event and a prelude to legal marriage (see McKie 1986: 40–41; Statistics Canada 1985a).

Three reasons exist for considering common-law marriages in any analysis of changing Canadian families. First, the phenomenon modifies the predominant conceptualization of first marriages as the outcome of a sequence in which persons move from their families of origin directly into those of reproduction, or detour slightly to live alone or with room-mates. Second, it indicates the growth of a new family form which appears to be transitional to a legal marriage. Third, to the extent that common-law marriages among young Canadians occur initially in lieu of legal marriages, they may partly contribute to the recent rise in couples' age at first (legal) marriages.

During the last 10 years, the average age of people at first marriages has increased dramatically, reversing a post-war downward drift. By 1985, the average age at first marriage was 24.6 for women and 26.7 for men, representing an increase of approximately two years in the average age at first marriage from that observed in the mid-1970s (Statistics Canada 1979c: Table 3; 1986e: Table 1). The delayed age at first marriages which is now occurring quite probably reflects a number of factors, including common-law marriages, the recent economic recession, and awareness of women's issues.

The increasing age at which people legally marry has several implications for families in Canada. The later the age at marriage, the more likely that men and women will obtain more education and/or have a longer labour force history before marriage. Higher education is associated with greater approval of sexual equality (Labour Canada 1984) and with increased labour force participation of women. Pre-nuptial labour force experience in turn may increase the probability of future female labour force involvement and decrease fertility (Stolzenberg and Waite 1977). Thus, indirectly, increases in the ages at which Canadians are marrying may accentuate even more the decline of the traditional family form.

In addition to common-law marriages and the postponement of legal marriages, the increasing numbers and percentages of remarriages also represent changes in family formation. Marriages that are remarriages for one or both partners are rising steadily. For example, fewer than 1 in 10 of all marriages (9%) in 1961 were between one-or-both previously married persons; by 1985, 3 in 10 marriages (30%) were remarriages for one or both of the partners (Dominion Bureau of Statistics 1963c: Table M6; Statistics Canada 1986e: Table 5). The increasing numbers and percentages of remarriages largely reflect a growing divorced population. The 1968 Divorce Act (and acts of Parliament for petitioners from Quebec and Newfoundland), extended the previous grounds for divorce from adultery only to include mental and physical cruelty, extended separation, drug or alcohol addiction, and a number of other grounds (see Boyd 1983). The number of divorces and the divorce rate soared thereafter (Statistics Canada 1979c: Table 11). By 1985, the rate stood at 1003.5 divorces per 100,000 married women (Statistics Canada 1986e: Table 10).

The dissolution of approximately 1 in 100 legal marriages annually elicits two comments. First, the institution of marriage does not appear to be in crisis; divorce rates in Canada are relatively low, particularly in relation to the United States (Robinson and McVey 1985; Rodgers and Whitney 1981; Statistics Canada 1986e: Table 23). Second, the effects of divorce in creating new family structures is consequential. Not all divorces involve dependent children, but when they do, lone-parent families result. And, while not all persons remarry, the numbers mean that the act of marriage is not solely the domain of young, never-married Canadians. Divorce also adds another family form to the already complex mosaic as new families are formed from previous marriages (Eichler 1983; Schlesinger 1976).

CHANGES WITHIN CANADIAN FAMILIES: FEWER CHILDREN

In addition to increased variation in family formation patterns, the composition of Canadian families has changed over time with respect to the number of children born, the labour force participation of women, the share of single-parent families and the living arrangements of elder women.

Compared to earlier times, families today include fewer children. This primarily reflects dramatic declines in the birth rate. In 1931, birth rates were such that, on the average, a young woman could expect to have slightly more than 3 children (a total fertility rate or TFR of 3.2). This figure rose during the 1950s and 1960s, caused partly by the increased survival rate of children, and partly by women's tendency to bear children at younger ages, and their increased parity following the Depression and Second World War (Statistics Canada 1984f: 13). But the level by which women could expect to have nearly 4 children at the close of their reproductive years subsequently dropped (see Statistics Canada 1983b: Table 1); by 1985 the birth rates were so low that a woman could expect to have fewer than two children (TFR = 1.6; Statistics Canada 1986a).[2]

Declines also have resulted from increasing rates of childlessness and postponement of first births. Between 1961 and 1981, the percentage of childlessness nearly doubled (from 13.5% to 22.7%) for ever married women aged 15 to 44, with the increase even more pronounced among younger age groups (Burke 1986; Grindstaff 1975: Table 4; Statistics Canada 1983a: Table 2). Although these levels of childlessness are unprecedented in Canadian society, they do not necessarily imply permanent childlessness. Rather, births increasingly are postponed, and most women will not bear large numbers of children in the fewer years of childbearing that remain after the first birth (see Grindstaff 1984; Rodgers and Witney 1981; Statistics Canada 1984f: 27; 1985b: 15).

Despite specific explanations for the rise and decline in post-war births (Easterlin 1980; Oppenheimer 1980; Statistics Canada 1984f: 71), recent trends are part of overall twentieth century reproductive declines. This decrease is linked to increased urbanization and industrialization which has increased female wage work and has rendered children economically less productive than formerly, largely because of laws which stipulate school attendance and prohibit child labour. In addition, rising education has increased the likelihood that persons will acquire roles outside the family, and develop a sense of mastery over their immediate world. This is associated with a greater knowledge and use of contraception, which, in turn, is facilitated by highly effective but controversial (see Chapter 7) birth control technology which was introduced in the early 1960s.

Declines in the number of children initially suggest that time spent on childcare is less than in earlier periods. However, the current emphasis on producing quality children implies that more, rather than less, time should be spent on parental activities by the adult members of Canadian families (Boyd, Eichler, and Hofley 1976). Also, a decline in births may not produce a shorter period over which such activities occur. Legally and socially defined ages for leaving school, leaving home, engaging in wage work, and acquiring the status of an adult all have been extended over the course of the twentieth century. Thus, there may be fewer children in today's families, but they reside with their family until their late teens or early twenties rather than leave in mid-adolescence. In fact, the 4-out-of-5 ratio of unmarried adults aged 15 to 24 who are living at home has been fairly stable between 1941 and 1981 (Statistics Canada 1979b: Table 3; Statistics Canada 1982a: Table 4; 1982b: Table 5). In the late 1970s and early 1980s, more than 8 out of 10 adolescents aged 15 to 19 were living in their parents' family; between 1975 and 1983, the proportion of 20 to 24-year-olds living with parents in fact increased, a trend attributable to declines in employment, and increases in unemployment and in school attendance (Statistics Canada 1985b: 91–92).

Postponing childbearing until the late twenties and early thirties has important implications for family life, not just because such timing has its own set of plus and minus considerations (Grindstaff 1984: 103–107), but because, in lengthening the time between generations, it creates a life cycle squeeze of care giving for the parents. Persons who become parents in their thirties, or bear their last child at that age, will engage in childcare until their late forties, or even later. At that time, their own parents will be elderly. It is likely that adults will divert their attention and resources away from their children only to experience the death of one parent and/or the increased care needs of the others. Since social norms dictate that women are the main care givers, and many women assume this role (Rosenthal 1985), the need to extend aid—either financial, emotional or social—to their elderly relations will have the greatest impact on women. This scenario, of course, assumes that all children leave home by early adulthood, and that the children no longer require emotional or financial support; in actuality, middle-aged women may find themselves extending assistance simultaneously to both the young and the old.

CHANGES WITHIN CANADIAN FAMILIES: WOMEN IN THE LABOUR FORCE

In addition to their fewer children, the increasing labour force participation of women represents a major change for many Canadian families. Probably fewer than 4% of married women were in the 1941 Canadian labour force (Dominion Bureau of Statistics 1968: 4). The higher levels of female labour force participation during the war years were not sustained after the war (Pierson 1977), although by 1951 the participation rate was 11.2%, and in 1961 it was just over 22% (Dominion Bureau of Statistics 1968: 4). By 1985, more than half (55%) of married women were in the labour force (Statistics Canada 1986c: 109). Such trends are noteworthy for two reasons. First, they represent a change in family characteristics from earlier times in which husband-wife families were characterized by a husband in the labour force and a wife in the home to a family in which both spouses are in the labour force. Second, women with young children increasingly are in the labour force (see Statistics Canada 1985c: 18). In 1985, 61% of all women in families with children under the age of 16 were in the labour force; 54% of women with at least one child under the age of 3 were in the labour force (Statistics Canada 1986c: 98).

Many factors account for this increased labour force participation of women in general and married women in particular (Phillips and Phillips 1982; Wilson 1985: Chapter 6). Among the most important are the increased demand for female workers associated with the move to a service economy during the post-war period, and the financial needs of families. Analyses of individual and family income distributions indicate that throughout the 1960s and 1970s incomes of husbands alone could not maintain the economic position of their families (Armstrong and Armstrong 1975; Pryor 1984). Increasingly, both spouses undertook paid work. By the 1980s, more than half of husband-wife families had both spouses in the labour force (Pryor 1984). On the average, the earnings of wives accounted for more than one-fifth of the family budget and shifted about half of all husband-wife families into higher income categories (Pryor 1984: 100; Statistics Canada: 1986b: 37–38).

Table 2:

Characteristics of Families with Children at Home, by Type of Family

		Lone Parent	
	Husband/Wife	Male	Female
Income			
Average government transfer payment	1,401	1,931	2,712
Average employment income	27,637	20,603	9,746
Average income from all sources	30,719	24,458	14,212
Living Arrangements (Percent)	100.0	100.0	100.0
Live in own home	79.8	64.2	42.1
Rented	20.2	35.8	57.9
(Gross rent greater than 25% of family income)	(24.4)	(31.3)	(64.0)
Percent in Labour Force			
Men	92.7	78.2	—
Women	52.2	—	53.8

Source: Statistics Canada, 1981 Census of Canada, Catalogue 92–935. Tables 4, 5, 22 and 23.

The post-war growth in the labour force participation of women with families also means that the traditional sole (male) wage-earner family is no longer the norm (Table 2). But, disjunctures between reality and the expectation that women work in the home have produced a double day for women and a crisis in childcare. A number of studies indicate that the acquisition of labour force positions by women has not meant equal assumption by men of domestic responsibilities. In a 1971 study, Meissner et al. (1975) observed that women did most of the household chores, accounting for 28 hours per week, compared to four hours' work by their husbands. When a wife entered the labour force, her spouse increased his share of housework by 6 minutes a week in families without a child under the age of 10, and by 60 minutes a week for families with a young child (Meissner et al. 1975: 436). Such inequalities persist. A 1981 study of Canadians showed that women who were in the labour force spent twice as much time on childcare as did men, nearly five times as much time on housework, and were more likely than men to do the family shopping. Men in the labour force spent more time than did women on household maintenance and home-based leisure such as watching T.V. (see Statistics Canada 1985c: 19).

The growing labour force participation of women in families accentuates the need for non-parental childcare. Even in families where the mother is not in the labour force, pre-school children are not exclusively cared for by parents; in 1981 more than one-third of these children were cared for in other arrangements (Statistics Canada 1982e: Table 9; also see Status of Women Canada 1986: 52–54). But, when the mother is in the labour force, more than three-quarters of the pre-schoolers are not cared for exclusively by parents. Much of this care is given in other homes and to a lesser extent in the women's own homes (Statistics Canada 1982e: Table 9). It may be unlicensed and unregulated by provincial standards and it may be of low quality (Johnson and Dineen 1981). Licensed daycare spaces are few. In 1984, 3447 daycare centres provided 139,201 spaces for children under the age of six (Status of Women Canada 1986: 51, 66). When matched against the potential demand generated by 963,000 preschool-age children of mothers in the labour force (Statistics Canada 1982e), not to mention those children whose mothers are not in the labour force but who are students, volunteers or otherwise have a reason to seek daycare, the supply indeed is inadequate. (For additional ways of estimating demand see: Health and Welfare Canada 1984: Tables 7–9; Status of Women Canada 1986: Table 3.4 and Chapter 4.) Further, many school-age children require supervision after hours; less than 5% of the potential population is in licensed daycare programs (Health and Welfare Canada 1984: Tables 7–9; Status of Women Canada 1986: Chapter 4).

The unmet need for non-parental quality childcare has several important consequences. First, a substantial number of children in Canada may be receiving no supervision or minimal custodial care (Johnson and Dineen 1981). Second, the economic factors behind the increased labour force participation of married women and lone-parent mothers are not likely to change. Unless women curtail reproduction even more than current low levels, the demand for non-parental childcare should increase, not diminish. Third, the emphasis placed on women as responsible for care giving causes many to resolve their childcare crises by leaving the labour force.[3] Despite evidence which suggests that younger women are leaving less frequently than are older women and for shorter periods (Boyd 1986), these exits can curtail the occupations and incomes of women by reinforcing employer stereotypes about women being intermittent employees and by causing women to suffer reduced or lost seniority-related benefits.

LONE PARENT FAMILIES: ON THE INCREASE

The increasing labour force participation of married women is a major factor in the declining percentage of husband-breadwinner, wife-homemaker families. The increasing numbers and percentages of lone-parent families since 1966 is a second factor. By 1981, more than 1 in 10 families was headed by a single parent (Table 1). The largest increase has occurred for female lone-parent families. Between 1971 and 1981, the numbers of female lone-parent families grew twice as fast as the rates observed for male lone-parent and husband-wife families (56% compared to 23% and 24% respectively; Statistics Canada 1984d).

The recent increases in the numbers and percentages of lone-parent families reflect major shifts in the causes of husband-wife family dissolution. Lone-parent families always have existed; indeed in 1931, they accounted for nearly 14% or 1 in 7 of all Canadian families (Statistics Canada 1984a: Table 1). However, their existence reflected mortality more than separation and divorce. In the 50 or more years since the early 1930s, dramatic improvements in life expectancy (Statistics Canada 1986d: Table C1) increased the probability that both parents would survive until the children had left home (Statistics Canada 1984a). In the absence of any substantial alterations in levels of marital dissolution through separation and divorce, increasing life expectancies decreased the percentage of lone-parent families throughout the 1950s and early-to-mid 1960s (Statistics Canada 1984a: Table 1). However, the number of divorces increased substantially after 1966 in response to the 1968 Divorce Act (see: Statistics Canada 1979c: 1983c). As a result, increasingly legal dissolution of marriages is caused by divorce rather than by mortality. In 1981, for example, divorce accounted for nearly half (45%) of all legal dissolutions of marriage (calculations based on Statistics Canada 1983d: Table 1; 1983e: Table 20), up from 28% in 1971, 9% in 1951 and 2% in 1931 (Robinson and McVey 1985: Table 3; Statistics Canada 1978: Table 7). Recent analyses indicate that if current divorce trends persist, more than one in three marriages is likely to end in divorce (Statistics Canada 1981b: 28).

Divorce and death represent final terminations of marriage. Separations also are a prelude to divorce as well as a mechanism for marital dissolution in the absence of divorce. According to the 1981 census, the size of the legally married-but-separated population is nearly equal to the currently divorced population at about one-half million persons (Statistics Canada 1982c: Table 3).

The growing importance of separation and divorce as mechanisms of husband-wife family dissolution increases the complexity and diversity of family forms. The concentration of divorces within the 25–44 age group means that many of the families affected have at least one child.

In 1985, for example, 59% of all the divorces granted involved at least one dependent child (Statistics Canada 1986e: Tables 1, 17). Thus, the legal dissolution of the original husband-wife unit often means the formation of a one-parent family. Separations also increase the formation of lone-parent families. In 1981, nearly one in two separated persons were lone parents (Statistics Canada 1982d: Table 3; 1984d: Table 15). While dissolution of husband-wife families through mortality, separation or divorce is the most important factor behind the growth of lone-parent families, another factor is the growth in single (never married) families. Approximately 1 in 10 lone-parent families enumerated by the 1981 census had a single (never married) parent compared to fewer than 1 in 33 lone-parent families enumerated in the 1950s and 1960s (Statistics Canada 1979a: Table 4.6; 1984b: Table 15).

In actuality, it is female lone-parent families which result from the dissolution of husband-wife families or the birth of children outside marriage. A total of 589,000 families, representing 82% of all lone parent families, were female lone parent families in 1981. Compared to male lone parents, female lone parents are younger, and they have younger children. In 1981, for example, nearly 38.7% of the female lone-parent families had at least one child under the age of six compared to one-quarter (25.2%) of male lone-parent families (Statistics Canada 1984b: Table 16; Paul 1984). These data indicate that women assume primary responsibility for childcare after marital dissolution.

The recent increases in lone-parent families have at least two consequences for family life in Canada. First, more children are being raised in a one-parent setting. In 1981, for example, nearly 1 in 8 (12.8%) children who were under the age of 24 and who were living in (census) families were in a single-parent family. One in 10 lived in a female lone-parent family (Statistics Canada 1984a: Table 3). Second, relative to male lone parents and husband-wife families, female lone parents are economically less well off. Table 2 shows that the average income from all sources for female lone parents in 1981 is $14,000 or slightly more than half (58%) of that received by male lone-parent families and slightly less than half (46%) of that received by husband-wife families with children at home. Relative to other families with children at home (Table 2), female lone-parent families are more likely to rent their accommodations, and the majority pay more than 25% of their family income in rent. Not surprisingly, poverty is more common among female lone-parent families than among other family types. In 1982, nearly 1 in 2 families (48%) with a female head under the age of 65 had incomes below the poverty line compared to 1 in 10 families with a male head under the age of 65 (National Council of Welfare 1984b: Table 13).

The lower labour force participation rates of female single parents, and the lower wages paid to women relative to men are factors accounting for the lower incomes and impoverishment of female lone-parent families. Although labour force participation rates for female lone parents are similar to the levels for wives in husband-wife families, they are lower than the rates for male single parents or husbands in families with dependent children (Table 2). These lower rates generally reflect the younger ages of children in female lone-parent families and the absence of a second adult with whom childcare responsibilities can be shared, which would facilitate labour force participation (Paul 1984: 95–100). As a result, female lone parents receive a greater share of their income from non-employment sources, particularly government transfer payments (Boyd 1977; Statistics Canada 1984d).

The historical origins of sexual inequality in wages are complex, reflecting occupational segregation (Hartmann 1976), and the persisting assumptions that women are dependent upon male wage-earning family members. However, female lone parents do not always have access to the income of a male. For separated or divorced women, awards of income-generating assets are feasible only if assets exist. Increasingly, alimony payments are not being awarded or are awarded only for limited duration, the argument being that within two or three years, the single parent should be self-supporting. Child-support payments are subject to default, and generally do not cover all the economic costs of raising a child to adulthood. Female lone parents thus are highly dependent on government transfer payments or on employment as sources of income. Yet, when they enter the labour force, they are paid low wages under the inaccurate assumption that women can depend on men for economic support (Alderson 1986; Boyd 1977).

The economic deprivation of female lone-parent families relative to other families is increasing over time. In 1980, the incomes of female lone-parent families was 52% of the average family income, down from 56% in 1970. One in five female lone-parent families had 1980 incomes of less than $5,000 compared to 1 in 32 and 1 in 13 of the respective husband-wife and male lone-parent families (Statistics Canada 1984d: Table 1). This declining economic status of female lone-parent families reflects both the increasing dependence over time on government transfer payments by these families (Statistics Canada 1984d), quite probably resulting from the labour force participation and childcare difficulties of young mothers of young children. The increased economic deprivation also may reflect the absence of a second wage-earner in female lone-parent families. As discussed earlier, during the 1970s many families maintained or enhanced their economic position by having a second wage-earner in the family. Although older children may be in the labour force, most young mothers of lone-parent families do not have a second wage-earner as an economic safety net against income erosion. Of all family types, female lone-parent families experienced the lowest rate of increase in income between 1970–1980, and families with both husband and wife in the labour force had the highest (Statistics Canada 1984d).

In combination with the other characteristics, the economic status of female lone-parent families has implications for the increasing numbers and percentages of children who are in them. Many of these children are small and are raised by young mothers who have "less than adequate" material resources (Statistics Canada 1984a). It remains to be seen what impact such economic disadvantages will have on the lives of these children, but concern exists that their educational and occupational opportunities will be curtailed (Statistics Canada 1984a). Relative to children in single-marriage, husband-wife families, these children may also experience stresses and strains associated with a marital breakup, although the overall impact is considered by some to be less than that caused by the loss of a parent through death (see Statistics Canada 1979a: 109). Any contact with the father may involve a second residential location, and if one or both parents remarry, new social relationships will emerge with step-parents, step-siblings, half-siblings, step-grandparents, aunts and uncles.

The creation of new families and new family relationships in fact is occurring, although it is difficult to determine the magnitude and the rapidity with which lone-parent families become blended families. Vital statistics data show temporal increases in marriages involving at least one previously married person. Comparing dates of first marriage for the currently married 1981 census population suggests that 1 in 10 men and women (11%) have marriages in which at least one spouse has been married before. However, such data do not indicate the existence or presence of natural or step-children and the myriad of social interactions that may or may not emerge with remarriage. The existing data on remarriages also says little about the length of time spent in various familial and marital arrangements. Estimates prepared in the late 1970s suggest that female lone-parent families in particular may be families in transition for relatively lengthy periods. These estimates showed that men had a slightly higher probability of remarrying than did divorced women (84% versus 75%) and that the average duration of divorce was approximately five years for men and 11 years for women (Statistics Canada 1981b: Table 1). In sum, the increasing dissolution of legal marriage through divorce, and the growth in female lone-parent families are paralleled by increasing remarriages and the creation of blended families. But the slightly lower probabilities of remarriage for women and the greater duration of years spent in the divorced state suggest that economic hardship for many of the lone-parent families will remain and require ameliorative action.

ELDERLY FAMILIES AND ELDERLY WOMEN

Along with families which have both spouses in the labour force, lone-parent families represent a significant departure from the traditional family form consisting of husband-breadwinner, wife-homemaker. Yet assumptions about housework, childcare, and economic dependency which derive from the traditional family form persist and affect women in these new family forms. Elderly families and women in them also are affected by the legacy of a traditional family structure. They depart from the model in that retirement curtails the breadwinning role of the husband. Like lone-parent families, elderly families experience reduced incomes, often based on government transfer payments. But, at the same time, elderly families are often traditional families grown old. The consequences of the assumed economic dependency of wives on husbands in early years becomes especially evident with the dissolution of these families.

Elderly families in which the designated head is aged 65 or older, represent about one in nine Canadian families.[4] Unlike their younger counterparts, these families are dissolved by death, rather than divorce or separation. But, because men have lower life expectancies than women (Statistics Canada 1986d), elderly men are likely to die within a husband-wife family; older women are much more likely to have such an arrangement dissolved by the death of their spouse and to remain widows. Fewer than two in five elderly women (aged 65 and older) are currently married, and the percentages decline with increasing age (National Council of Welfare 1984d: 14–15). Recent estimates conclude that fewer than 1 in 10 widows eventually remarry compared to 1 in 5 widowers. Widows also remain widowed for a much longer duration than do widowed men (Statistics Canada 1981b: 57–58).

Thus, for older women, many without children living at home, the death of the husband signals the end of living in a family. In 1981, for example, more than half of men aged 65 and older who lived in private households lived with their spouses in a two-person family; this arrangement characterized only one-third of the women aged 65 and older. Only 14% of elderly men lived alone in a one-person household compared to more than one-third of the elderly women (Statistics Canada 1984e: Table 3). Studies show that living alone is more likely for elderly women who have a high income; it is less likely for low-income women with many children, or for women of French or Jewish ethnicity (Statistics Canada 1981a: 43–48; Thomas and Wister 1984).

Not only do elderly women live alone more than do elderly men, but they also are more likely to experience poverty. Their 1980 income averaged well below $8,500 (Statistics Canada 1984e: Table 11; National Council of Welfare 1984a: 10–11). According to calculations for 1982, one-quarter of the families headed by elderly women are below officially designated poverty levels, as are 60% of elderly women not in families (National Council of Welfare 1984b: 25–26; Statistics Canada 1984e: Table 11; National Council of Welfare 1984a: 10–11).

Elderly women in Canada tend to be poor because they have low incomes in old age. However, these low incomes are tied to the imagery and practices associated with the traditional husband-provider, wife-homemaker, family structure. Women who have never been in the labour force or have earned only minimal amounts (less than $2000 in 1984) do not receive income from the Canada/Quebec pension plans. Even if they were in the labour force, they often receive less than do men from the CPP/QPP because of lower earnings and because they did not work as long or as consistently full-time as men (National Council on Welfare 1984b: 22–27). These differences are perpetuated with private pension plans. About one-third of the female labour force (but less than one-fifth of female workers in the private sector) are members in private employer plans, compared to nearly half of the male paid labour force (National Council of Welfare 1984b: 42–46; Statistics Canada 1985c: 78). If women leave the labour force for periods of time, the absence of vesting and portability in employer pension plans reduces pension benefits. Vesting refers to the right of employees, upon changing employment, to their own contributions and to part or all of the contributions made by the employer. Portability means that employees can take accrued pension credits from one employer to another (National Council of Welfare 1984b).

Many elderly women today either receive no labour force-related benefits or lower benefits than do men.[5] Instead, they rely on government income security programs such as Old Age Security (OAS), Spouses Allowance and Guaranteed Income Supplement (GIS) when age or low-income conditions are met (National Council of Welfare 1984a; 1984b; 1984c). While spouses are alive, they may have access to husbands' incomes. But upon death, that source of income is reduced to survivor benefits. However, the CPP/QPP benefits are tied to the value of the pension earned by the deceased; if pensions are low, survivor benefits will be even lower. Private pensions frequently do not offer survivor benefits. Thus, the dissolution of the family unit often means a substantial drop in income for elderly women, who lack substantial pensions of their own and who have in the past depended on the income of husbands. Calculations based on benefits in 1982 show that income generated from the Canada/Quebec pension plans, OAS and GIS for elderly surviving spouses was far below the poverty line, representing 60% of retirement income prior to the death of the spouse (National Council of Welfare 1984c: 5–13).

These circumstances have generated two major proposals for future pension reform. The position taken by labour and by major social welfare organizations (National Council on Welfare 1984a) seeks to improve the overall value of pension benefits associated with labour force participation. Such improvement would increase the level of CPP/QPP benefits in general as well as the level of survivor benefits paid to widows. In contrast, some women's organizations advocate a special pension for homemakers, the argument being that such women do real work, albeit unpaid and often unacknowledged, and that homemakers are excluded from pension benefits that are based on work outside the home. (Dulude 1981; National Council of Welfare 1984a; Status of Women Canada 1982). The different positions appear to reflect differences in time horizons, assumptions about female labour force participation and target populations. The pension for homemakers' argument addresses the immediate needs of elderly women, who more than young women have spent most of their time as homemakers (National Council of Welfare 1984b: 36–37). However, it also creates a number of anomalies, such as the non-payment to women who have participated in the labour force but who also have performed housework either as wives or as single parents (National Council of Welfare 1984a). The position adopted by labour and by social welfare agencies emphasizes the continued labour force participation of women and growing labour market equality as a mechanism for ensuring greater benefits to all the elderly, including women. It aims changes in the pension system less specifically at elderly women, although these women would receive increased pensions through higher CPP/QPP and survivor benefits.

CONCLUSION

The objectives of this chapter are twofold: first, to document changes in Canadian families during the past 25 to 50 years; and second, to examine some implications of these changes for Canadian women. That change has occurred is obvious. Although still created primarily by the legal marriage of single young adults, family formation is occurring later. Families today also are formed by common-law marriages and by remarriages; they are dissolved by death in later years but more by divorce and separation in youth and in middle age. Compared to the traditional husband-breadwinner, wife-homemaker, family structure of the 1950s and 1960s, families increasingly are characterized by fewer children and by women in the labour force. The recent growth in lone-parent families, and the existence of childless and elderly families all point to the multiplicity of family forms in Canada.

Yet, the past influences the present. The imagery associated with the husband-breadwinner, wife-homemaker family assumes a highly bifurcated sexual division of labour in which women are responsible for household and childcare tasks. Such imagery handicaps women in those Canadian families that depart from this traditional family form. If the family acts as a self-balancing system, the increased labour force participation of women should elicit a greater sharing by husbands in domestic responsibilities (Meissner et al., 1975: 425). This has not occurred to a significant extent. Husbands appear to help rather than to act as equals in undertaking domestic labour and childcare. In failing to initiate, fund, or otherwise support a system of childcare which meets the needs of Canadian women, the state also perpetuates the assumption that childcare is the sole responsibility of women. This legacy of the traditional family model means that women in families today often experience the double burden of combining domestic and paid work; they absorb the difficulties of obtaining quality and reliable childcare arrangements by leaving the labour force. Postponing childbearing does not resolve these dilemmas. Moreover, it creates a possible care giver squeeze for middle-aged women in that they may have dependent children and aging parents.

The assumption that families consist of male breadwinners and wives who are economically dependent on husband-generated income also affects alternative family forms and the women in them. Lower incomes for women in the labour force reflect the past argument that women need less because they are supported by male wage-earners in the family. The recent growth in female lone-parent families raises considerable concern inasmuch as a second wage-earner is less likely to exist; the parent is less likely to be in the labour force, may earn less than a male, and part of the family income may be comprised of government transfer payments. Yet, with some modification, these characteristics are also true for elderly husband-wife families and for the survivors of these families. Female lone parents and elderly widows experience a double burden of not having a male wage-earner and receiving lower wages and pension benefits if they are in the labour force. As a result, female lone-parent families subsist on lower incomes than other families, and elderly women frequently find themselves living on incomes below the poverty line when their provider dies. The result is the feminization of poverty in Canada. Such strictures remain unresolved. Policies concerning equal pay for work of equal value, childcare, and pensions are needed as is increased social and economic assistance to lone-parent families. The increased diversity in family form both accompanies and requires greater sexual equality in the home and throughout Canadian society.

NOTES

1. Statistics Canada collects much of the basic demographic data on Canadian families, mostly in the quinquential censuses of population, but sometimes through special topic surveys. Statistics Canada employs two different definitions of the term "family", to reflect the multiple dimensions and meanings of the term. The *census family* refers to a husband and a wife (with or without children who have never married regardless of age) or a lone parent (with one or more children who have never married regardless of age) living in the same dwelling. An *economic family* consists of a group of two or more persons who are related to each other by blood, marriage or adoption, and who live in the same dwelling. In both definitions, persons living in a common-law type of arrangement are considered now as married, regardless of their legal status, and they are treated as husband-wife families. The definition of the economic family is more inclusive than that of the census family (Statistics Canada 1984c: viii–ix and Table 4).

2. The total fertility rate is the hypothetical number of children a woman would have at the end of her reproductive life if she bore children at the age-specific fertility rates which characterize a given year.

3. Three national surveys of Canadians in the early 1980s reveal that marriage and family-related responsibilities are the most frequent reasons given by women for leaving the labour force. In one of these surveys, nearly half of the respondents in the labour force who had previously left for at least a year indicated that family or household responsibilities had required their departure (Boyd 1986: Tables 4 and 6; Statistics Canada 1985a).

4. This figure is based on trend data up to 1971 (Statistics Canada 1979a: Table 4.7). In the 1981 census publications no breakdowns are available for census families over the age of 65.

5. In the early 1980s, the number of CPP/QPP female beneficiaries represented a little more than one-quarter of the female population aged 25 and older; the number of male beneficiaries represented more than three-quarters of the elderly male population (Statistics Canada 1985c: 77).

Bibliography

Alderson, Gina.

1986   Rights Versus Needs: Dependency and Inequality in Divorce Policy. Master's Thesis. Ottawa: Carleton University, Department of Sociology and Anthropology.

Armstrong, Hugh, and Pat Armstrong.

1975   "Women in the Canadian Labour Force, 1941–1971".

Canadian Review of Sociology and Anthropology 12 (November, Part 1): 370–384.

Boyd, Monica.
1977   The Forgotten Minority: The Socioeconomic Status of Divorced and Separated Women. In *The Working Sexes*, edited by Pat Marchak, 46–71. Vancouver: Institute of Industrial Relations, University of British Columbia.
1983   The Social Demography of Divorce in Canada. In *Marriage and Divorce in Canada*, edited by K. Ishwaran, 248–296. Toronto: Methuen Publications Ltd.
1986   Revising the Stereotypes: Variation in Female Labour Force Interruptions. Departmental Working Paper 86–9. Ottawa: Carleton University Department of Sociology and Anthropology.

Boyd, Monica, Margaret Eichler, and John Hofley.
1976   Family: Functions, Formation and Fertility. In *Opportunity for Choice*, edited by Gail C. A. Cook, 13–52. Ottawa: Information Canada.

Burke, Mary Ann.
1986   Families: Diversity the New Norm. *Canadian Social Trends*. (Statistics Canada Catalogue 11–008E) Summer.

Dominion Bureau of Statistics.
1963a   *1961 Census of Canada. Families by Marital Status and Age of Head*. Catalogue 93–520. Ottawa: Minister of Trade and Commerce.
1963b   *1961 Census of Canada. Households and Families: Husband-Wife Families*. Catalogue 93–520. Ottawa: Minister of Trade and Commerce.
1963c   *Vital Statistics 1961*. Catalogue 84–202. Ottawa: Minister of Trade and Commerce.
1968   *The Female Worker in Canada* (by Sylvia Ostry). Catalogue CS99–553/1968. Ottawa: Minister of Trade and Commerce.

Dulude, Louise.
1981   *Pension Reform with Women in Mind*. Ottawa: Canadian Advisory Council on the Status of Women.

Easterlin, Richard.
1980   *Birth and Fortune*. New York: Basic Books.

Eichler, Margrit.
1983   *Families in Canada Today*. Toronto: Gage Publishing Ltd.

Grindstaff, Carl.
1975   The Baby Bust: Changes in Fertility Patterns in Canada. *Canadian Studies in Population* 2:15–22.
1984   "Catching Up: The Fertility of Women over 30 Years of

Age, Canada in the 1970s and early 1980s." *Canadian Studies in Population* 11:95–110.

Health and Welfare Canada.
1984 *Status of Daycare in Canada, 1984*. Ottawa: Health and Welfare.

Hartman, Heidi.
1976 Capitalism, Patriarchy and Job Segregation by Sex. In *Women and the Workplace*, edited by Martha Blaxall and Barbara Reagan, 137–169. Chicago: University of Chicago Press.

Johnson, Laura, and Janice Dineen.
1981 *The Kin Trade: The Day Care Crisis in Canada*. Toronto: McGraw Hill-Ryerson.

Kessler-Harris, Alice.
1982 *Out to Work*. New York: Oxford University Press.

Kobrin, Fran.
1976a "The Fall of Household Size and the Rise of the Primary Individual in the United States". *Demography* 18 (February): 127–138.
1976b "The Primary Individual and the Family: Changes in Living Arrangements in the United States since 1940." *Journal of Marriage and the Family* 38: 233–239.

Labour Canada. Women's Bureau.
1984 *Canadian Attitudes Toward Women: Thirty Years of Change* (by Monica Boyd). Catalogue No. L 38–38/1984. Ottawa: Minister of Supply and Services Canada.

McKie, Craig.
1986 Common-Law: Living Together as Husband and Wife Without Marriage. In *Canadian Social Trends*, 39–41. Catalogue 11–008E. Autumn. Ottawa: Statistics Canada.

Meissner, Martin, Elizabeth W. Humphreys, Scott M. Meis, and William J. Scheu.
1975 "No Exit for Wives: Sexual Division of Labour". *Canadian Review of Sociology and Anthropology* 12 (November, Part 1): 424–439.

National Council of Welfare
1984a *Better Pensions for Homemakers*. Catalogue H68–14/1984-E. Ottawa: Minister of Supply and Services Canada.
1984b *A Pension Primer*. Catalogue H68–12/1984-E. Ottawa: Minister of Supply and Services Canada.
1984c *Pension Reform*. Catalogue H68–13/1984–E. Ottawa: Minister of Supply and Services Canada.
1984d *Sixty-Five and Older*. Catalogue H68–11/1984–E. Ottawa: Minister of Supply and Services Canada.

Nett, Emily.
1981   "Canadian Families in Social Historical Perspective".
            Canadian Journal of Sociology 6: 239–260.
Oppenheimer, Valerie K.
1980   *Work and the Family: A Study in Social Demography*. New York:
            Academic Press.
Pierson, Ruth.
1977   "Women's Emancipation and the Recruitment of Women
            into the Labour Force in World War II." In *The Neglected
            Majority*, edited by Susan Mann Trofimenkoff and Alison
            Prentice, 125–145. Toronto: McClelland and Stewart.
Paul, Betty Clayton.
1984   Lone Parents. In *The Labour Force*, 93–103. Catalogue
            71–001. July. Ottawa: Statistics Canada.
Phillips, Paul, and Erin Phillips.
1983   *Women and Work*. Toronto: James Lorimer and Company.
Pryor, Edward T.
1984   "Canadian Husband-Wife Families: Labour Force Partici-
            pation and Income Trends 1971–1981". In *The Labour Force*,
            93–108. Catalogue 71–001. May. Ottawa: Minister of Supply
            and Services: Canada.
Robinson, Barrie, and Wayne W. McVey, Jr.
1985   "The Relative Contributions of Death and Divorce to Marital
            Dissolution in Canada and the United States". *Journal of
            Comparative Family Studies* 16 (Spring): 93–109.
Rodgers, Roy H., and Gail Witney.
1981   "The Family Cycle in Twentieth Century Canada". *Journal
            of Marriage and the Family* 43 (August): 727–740.
Rosenthal, Carolyn.
1985   "Kinkeeping in the Familial Division of Labor". *Journal of
            Marriage and the Family* 47 (November): 965–984.
Schlesinger, Benjamin.
1976   Remarriage as Family Reorganization for Divorced Persons.
            In *The Canadian Family Revised*, edited by K. Ishwaran, 460–
            478. Toronto: Holt, Rinehart and Winston of Canada Ltd.
Statistics Canada
1978   *1971 Census of Canada. Profile Studies. Marital Status and
            Nuptiality in Canada*. Catalogue 99–704. Ottawa: Minister of
            Supply and Services Canada.
1979a   *Canadian Households and Families: Recent Demographic Trends*
            (by Sylvia T. Wargon). Catalogue 99–753E. Ottawa: Min-
            ister of Supply and Services Canada.
1979b   *Children in Canadian Families* (by Sylvia T. Wargon). Cata-

logue 98–810. Ottawa: Minister of Supply and Services, Canada.

1979c   *Vital Statistics. Volume II. Marriages and Divorces, 1977.* Ottawa: Information Canada.

1981a   *Living Alone in Canada: Demographic and Economic Perspectives.* 1951–1976 (by Brian Harrison). Catalogue 98–811. Ottawa: Minister of Supply and Services Canada.

1981b   *Marriage, Divorce and Mortality: A Life Table Analysis for Canada* (by O.B. Adams and D.N. Nagnur). Catalogue 84–536. Ottawa: Minister of Supply and Services Canada.

1982a   *1981 Census of Canada. Census Families in Private Households.* Catalogue 92–905. Ottawa: Minister of Supply and Services Canada.

1982b   *1981 Census of Canada. Occupied Private Dwellings: Type and Tenure.* Catalogue 92–903. Ottawa: Minister of Supply and Services Canada.

1982c   *1982 Census of Canada. Population. Age, Sex and Marital Status.* Catalogue 92–901. Ottawa: Minister of Supply and Services Canada.

1982d   *1981 Census of Canada. Private Households. Type, number of Persons, composition.* Catalogue 92–904. September. Ottawa: Minister of Supply and Services Canada.

1982e   Initial Results from the 1981 Survey of Childcare Arrangements. *The Labour Force.* Catalogue 72–001. August. Ottawa: Statistics Canada.

1983a   *1981 Census of Canada. Population. Nuptiality and Fertility.* Catalogue 92–906. Ottawa: Minister of Supply and Services Canada.

1983b   *Demographic Aspects of Vital Statistics: Fertility.* Catalogue 84–X–501E. Ottawa: Statistics Canada.

1983c   *Divorce: Law and the Family in Canada* (by D.C. McKie, B. Prentice, and P. Reed). Catalogue 89–502E. Ottawa: Minister of Supply and Services Canada.

1983d   *Vital Statistics. Volume II. Marriage and Divorces.* Ottawa: Minister of Supply and Services Canada.

1983e   *Vital Statistics. Volume III. Mortality.* Ottawa: Minister of Supply and Services Canada.

1984a   *Canada's Lone Parent Families.* Catalogue 99–933. Ottawa: Minister of Supply and Services Canada.

1984b   *1981 Census of Canada. Census Families in Private Households. Selected Characteristics.* Catalogue 92–935. Ottawa: Minister of Supply and Services Canada.

1984c   *1981 Census of Canada. Economic Families in Private House-*

holds. Income and Selected Characteristics. Catalogue 92–937. Ottawa: Minister of Supply and Services Canada.

1984d   *Changes in Income in Canada: 1970–1980.* Catalogue 99–941. Ottawa: Minister of Supply and Services Canada.

1984e   *The Elderly in Canada.* Catalogue 99–932. Ottawa: Minister of Supply and Services Canada.

1984f   *Fertility in Canada: From Baby-Boom to Baby-Bust* (by A. Romanic). Catalogue 91–524E. Ottawa: Minister of Supply and Services Canada.

1985a   *Family History Survey: Preliminary Findings* (by Thomas Burch). Catalogue 99–955. Ottawa: Minister of Supply and Services Canada.

1985b   "Observation: Youth Living at Home". Pp. 91–92 in *The Labour Force.* Catalogue 71–001. Ottawa: Minister of Supply and Services Canada.

1985c   *Women in Canada.* Catalogue 89–503E. Ottawa: Minister of Supply and Services Canada.

1986a   *Births and Deaths. Vital Statistics Volume I 1985.* Catalogue 84–204. Annual. Ottawa: Minister of Supply and Services Canada.

1986b   *Characteristics of High Income Families* (by A. Rashid). Catalogue 13–584. Ottawa: Minister of Supply and Services Canada.

1986c   *The Labour Force.* Catalogue 71–001. May. Ottawa: Minister of Supply and Services Canada.

1986d   *Longevity and Historical Life Tables* (by Dhruva Nagnur). Catalogue 89–506. Ottawa: Minister of Supply and Services Canada.

1986e   Vital Statistics, Volume II. *Marriages and Divorces*, 1985. Catalogue 84–205. Ottawa: Minister of Supply and Services Canada.

Status of Women Canada

1982   "Canadian Feminist Debate: Pension for Homemakers". *Status of Women News.* Spring: 7–10.

1986   *Report of the Task Force on Childcare.* Catalogue SW41–1/1986E. Ottawa: Minister of Supply and Services Canada.

Stolzenberg, Ross M., and Linda J. Waite.

1977   "Age, Fertility Expectations and Plans for Employment". *American Sociological Review* 43 (October): 769–782.

Thomas, Kausar, and Andrew Wister.

1984   "Living Arrangements of Older Women: The Ethnic Dimension". *Journal of Marriage and the Family* 46 (May): 301–331.

Thomas, Kausar, and Thomas K. Burch.

1985   "Household Formation in Canada and the United States:

Trends and Regional Differentials". *Canadian Studies in Population* 12: 159–182.

Tilly, Louise A., and Joan W. Scott.
1978   *Women, Work and Family.* New York: Holt, Rinehart and Winston.

Wilson, Susan.
1986   *Women, the Family and the Economy.* 2d ed. Toronto: McGraw-Hill Ryerson Ltd.

CHAPTER 5

Struggling with Power: Feminist Critiques of Family Inequality

Ann Doris Duffy

INTRODUCTION

This chapter focuses on the problem of power in the modern Canadian family. Despite popular media images of the family as a cozy, happy refuge from the cold impersonal world, real family life is frequently plagued by conflict and dissatisfaction. Inequalities between husband and wife and child and parent interfere with the possibilities for intimacy and affection. While family life may provide the happiness and sense of belonging portrayed on *The Cosby Show* and *Family Ties*, it may also be a source of unhappiness, loneliness and frustration.

For many years, mainstream sociologists adopted the *Happy Days* approach and ignored these harsher realities of family relations. Feminists challenged this complacent view as an ideological construct built upon the erroneous notions that

1. the nuclear family along with the unequal roles of husband and wife are 'natural';
2. romantic love is a woman's only great adventure;
3. all 'real' women want to be mothers.

Pushed into marriage and parenthood by these powerful ideologies many women found themselves buried by domestic and childcare responsibilities. They never had the opportunity or freedom to create their own destinies.

Today, research on power in the family reveals that power inequality continues to plague many families. With surprising frequency this inequality erupts in violence and abuse. More often, family power conflicts are subtle and complex. The blatantly male-dominated, patriarchal family is increasingly an anachronism. Men, however, continue to exercise considerable direct and indirect control in most families and inequality remains a pervasive problem. A full solution to the problem of power in the family will require massive social change. The human costs of family inequality suggest that such change is indeed worth the effort.

THE EMERGENCE OF FEMINIST CRITIQUES OF FAMILY INEQUALITY

Concerns about the family and women's role in the family date back many years. Over a century ago, Frederick Engels wrote *The Origin of the Family, Private Property and the State*, which in many respects formed the foundation for modern critiques of the family. He presented three fundamental propositions: first, the family is a social construct; second, the traditional family is structured to serve men's interests and to restrict women's activities; and third, the solution to the problem of family life is to abolish the family and bring women back into the world of paid work by having society take over women's labours in the home.

Citing the work of historians and anthropologists, Engels maintained that the form of family life varied considerably over time and place. In primitive societies, for example, family life was based on group marriage. Sexual freedom for both sexes was the norm, and descent was determined through the maternal line. Only in modern times, as the economic basis of society changed, did the monogamous, patriarchal family appear. It was clear, to Engels, that the family was neither a biological given nor was it decreed by God. Rather, it was simply a social structure developed by human beings in response to social and, particularly, economic circumstances.

According to Engels, once society became based on private property, men became concerned about assuring the parentage of their sons. Men did not want to work hard all their lives accumulating personal property only to pass that property along to children who might have been sired by some other man. The solution was a form of marriage and family life which restricted and controlled women's activities, particularly their sexual activities. In this new family, women were required to be virgins when they married, and once married they were to be sequestered in the home. While men were free to roam before and after marriage, the strictest sexual fidelity was required from women. Women who transgressed were harshly punished, or condemned to a marginal social role as courtesans or prostitutes.

Men were able to impose this self-serving social structure because they owned the tools, cattle and slaves along with accumulated wealth and property. Women controlled only certain household goods. As men possessed more and more of the social wealth in society, they became more important in the family, and women lost whatever power they once wielded. Through this process, Engels argued, men had long ago taken command of the family and reduced women to servants and instruments for the production of his children. Over time, this subordination of women had been glossed over and modified, but it had never been eliminated (1942, 50).

The solution to the implicit enslavement and prostitution of the wife was, for Engels, a radical reordering of personal life. Women must return to the public domain and work side-by-side with men, while the private work in the home must be taken over by society. The traditional family must be eradicated. These changes would be premised on a revolutionary transformation of the social and economic order where most personal property would become social property and capitalism would be replaced by socialism. In this new social order, since inheritance would no longer be an issue and since women would be economically self-sufficient, the economic basis for the patriarchal family and its trappings (such as the double standard, enforced chastity, restrictions on divorce and prostitution) would inevitably wither away.

Not surprisingly, Engels' position caused a furor in late Victorian England and North America. His anthropological evidence was challenged, his economic emphasis debated and his vision of family life reformulated. Regardless of these wranglings, the critical analysis of the family and women's role in the family developed little until the emergence of the contemporary women's movement in the 1960s. Feminists, such as French author, Simone de Beauvoir (1952), American, Betty Friedan (1963), Australian, Germaine Greer (1970), and, by the early 1970s, a growing number of Canadians—including Margaret Benston (1969); Maxine Nunes and Deanna White (1972); Margret Anderson (1972); Peggy Morton (1972), and Bonnie Kreps (1972)—worked toward a critical understanding of women's role in society. Central to the new feminist literature was a critique of family life which explained in dramatic detail the unsatisfactory quality of many women's lives inside families.

Modern feminist analysis of women and the family emphasizes four basic themes. First, the economic and social structure of the family is based upon and reinforces the power and authority of the husband/father. Second, the content of family life—the roles of wife/mother—function to restrict and inhibit women's lives. Third, the prevailing system of ideas concerning marriage and the family deny women real choices about whether or not to marry and whether or not to bear children. Finally, the subordination of women in the family—as wives, mothers and daughters—accounts for the generalized powerlessness of women in society at large.

Echoing Engel's concerns, feminists point out that the basic structure of the modern family assumes the secondary and subordinant status of women. Most women, even those who work outside the home, are to some degree economically dependent on their husbands, particularly if they have young children. This economic dependence is reinforced by social dependence embodied in the customs and traditions surrounding family life. The bride is 'given' in marriage by her parents and 'taken' by her husband; she usually is 'given' his name and is 'accepted' into his social class (de Beauvoir 1952, 479).

The economic basis of this inequality is perpetuated by the roles women are required to play within the family. As wife and mother, the woman is expected to perform most of the domestic and childcare work generated by the family. Since her time and physical and emotional energy are consumed by these tasks, she cannot undertake other more creative and more personal activities. Even if the husband has the best intentions, once the young woman becomes a mother, her household duties overwhelm her, just as they did in past historical periods (de Beauvoir 1952, 537; Morton 1972, 51; Rosenberg 1987, 185). The home with its endless tasks becomes a trap which excludes women from the real world of creative work and serious challenges (Friedan 1963, 56).

Feminists point out that women's subordination in the family is not simply the product of outmoded customs, burdensome household work and economic inequality. They stress that the ideology surrounding femininity and the family locks women into their traditional role in the home. Prevailing ideas about women's lives, including the dogma of romantic love and the cult of maternalism, are so pervasive and powerful that they discourage women from exploring alternative ways of living.

From a very early age, women are socialized into the culture of romance. Fairy tales, television, magazines, films and books tell women that they will achieve not only personal fulfilment but ecstasy and transcendence once they form a romantic relationship with the right man. The implied message is that failure to fall in love is the mark of an unworthy woman. She may love herself only if a man finds her worthy (Firestone 1970, 149; Nunes and White 1972, 37–55; Mackie 1987, 148). As a result, most women devote a considerable part of their life to the pursuit of love. Cosmetics, aerobics, clothes, fashion magazines, even plastic surgery are employed to create an attractive and desirable image. Predictably, a recent survey of Canadian teenagers finds that young women are far more likely than their male counterparts to express concern about their appearance (Bibby and Posterski 1985, 63).

Energy consumed by this preoccupation with appearing desirable and finding romance is lost to other ventures. Maureen Baker's study of the aspirations of Canadian adolescents reveals that many young women continue to envision highly romanticized versions of married life (1985, 150–54). Dreams of romance deflect young women from confronting

the realities of their educational and occupational futures. By late adolescence the typical young woman has tailored her educational and
occupational plans to suit the romantic script, disregarding the likelihood, whether she marries or not, that she will devote most of her life
to some form of paid employment (Mackie 1987, 157–58).

Through the process of dating and courtship, women are further
socialized into both the culture of romance and the subordinant female
role. Today, the male is still expected to formally initiate and then or-
chestrate the dating relationship (McCormick and Jesser 1983, 67–69).
The woman's part is often reactive rather than active. For example,
Edward Herold's (1984) research into the sexual behaviour of Canadian
young people reveals that while young men are expected to be assertively
sexual, young women are to play a gatekeeper role, establishing the limits
of sexual intimacy (56). The limited power women exercise in setting
sexual boundaries may be ineffectual. Recent research indicates that
many young men do not accept women's right to sexual self-determination. Studies of male college students in Winnipeg and Los Angeles
find that an average of 35% of these young men indicate some likelihood
of forcing sexual relations on a woman, provided they can be assured
of not being caught and punished (Malamuth 1981, 140). In a recent
survey of American college students, more than one-quarter of the men
report trying to coerce women into sexual relations and one in seven
state that they have forced a woman to have sexual intercourse at least
once in the past (Rapaport and Burkhart 1984, 220). Though the majority of young women do not encounter such directly oppressive situations, many discover that the courtship game has as much to do with
power as with romance.

Indoctrinated into the culture of romance from their earliest years,
many women cannot imagine personal happiness and happy endings
except in terms of marriage and family. Once inside marriage, women
often learn that romance appears more frequently in romance novels,
soap operas and commercials for diamond rings than in the day-to-day
routine. In her humorous feminist tract, *The Female Eunuch*, Greer details
the unromantic mundanities of married life. Husbands "forget birthdays
and anniversaries and seldom pay compliments". They are often "per-
functory" and do not make their wives feel desirable. The one great
"adventure" open to women is, at best, short-lived (1970, 186). Feminists
strive to expose popular notions of romantic love as an ideology that
functions to groove women into marriage and domesticity and out of
an independent vision of their lives.

Coupled to the ideology of romance is the cult of maternalism. Once
married, women find that motherhood is increasingly emphasized. Gla-
mourized and romanticized by the media, motherhood appears to offer
women a meaningful, life-long enterprise around which to build their

lives. As Friedan suggests, articles in women's magazines insist that women can only know fulfillment having given birth. In "the feminine mystique", there is only one way for a woman to dream of creation; she can only dream about herself as her children's mother and her husband's wife (1963, 55). Even though modern women have ready access to various birth control technologies, they are still not truly free to decide whether or not to become mothers. Amongst Canadian adolescents, more girls than boys expect to have children, and girls are more likely to state that they definitely want children (Baker 1985, 126). The cult of maternalism and the absence of countervailing images of women's lives deny women the opportunity and freedom to create their own destinies.

Women are also not free to construct their own approaches to mothering. The prevailing ideology expects the mother to devote her life to her children, to make them the core of her life enterprise, to willingly sacrifice on their behalf and to involve herself in their lives as completely as possible. Feminists have long pointed out that these expectations restrict both the parent and the child (Firestone 1970, 72–104, Nunes and White 1972, 107). When women are persistently involved in their children's lives, they may find that their interference is resented or, at least, that there is too little gratitude for their hard work and sacrifice. The resulting relationship may be unsatisfactory to both parent and child.

More recently, some feminists have stressed the positive dimensions of mothering, including both the personal rewards and satisfactions of the mother-child relation and the desirability of nurturing and caring in the society at large (Friedan 1981; Greer 1984; Rowland 1987). Despite these modifications, most feminists continue to agree that motherhood, however necessary and satisfying, is not a substitute for creative, independent enterprise (Levine 1983, 33). As long as the cult of maternalism pushes women into motherhood and mothers are expected to shoulder the lion's share of child-care responsibilities, women, as individuals, will lack the time and energy to create their own projects, and women, as a group, will be unable to construct more egalitarian social structures (Millett 1969, 159).

While feminists may disagree on the ultimate source of women's oppression, almost all agree that women's family responsibilities keep women powerless. Women's roles in the home deny them the opportunity to fully develop an independent social and economic existence. Women have little choice but to gloss over the inequities and frustrations experienced in the family because they lack economic alternatives and independence. This inequality is reproduced within families as each generation of young women accepts some measure of dependence and subordination, inside the family and in society at large, because they lack other models of life.

Contemporary feminists insist women need social and economic power to freely determine their role in the family (to marry or not, to mother or not). Women need the power to demand justice and equality in family relations (the division of domestic labour, freedom from abuse, the right to respect). They also need the power to effect alternative roles in the family and in society. Without these powers, the subordination of women will continue to undermine family life.

Popular humour has often called attention to this seamier side of family life by poking fun at the conflict in male-female relations and at the families which fail to live up to the Happy Days ideal. Jokes aimed at nagging wives, interfering mothers, resentful children and overbearing fathers attest to the unhappiness and frustration of unequal family relations.

A frightfully henpecked man was summoned to the bedside of his dying spouse. For 40 years she had made his life a burden.

> "I think I am dying, David," she said, "and before I leave you I want to know if I shall see you in a better land."
> "I think not, Nancy", he replied, "not if I see you first" (*Canadian Magazine*, May 1914. Quoted in Snell 1986, 79).

Woven into this family humour is the message that women ought to be "loving and submissive" if they want to avoid being ridiculed as "nags" and "gold diggers". Conversely, men are "henpecked" and unmanly if they fail to maintain control over the marriage (Snell 1986).

Feminists, in humourous as well as serious ways, have challenged family inequality. Over the last two decades their work has exposed in detail the dimensions and ramifications of power in family life. Prodded by this feminist scholarship, mainstream sociology of the family has increasingly moved away from its complacent paradigm of family roles and adopted a more critical and questioning perspective on family relations.

FROM 'HAPPY DAYS' TO THE 'MAD HOUSEWIFE' SOCIOLOGY OF THE FAMILY

While feminists have tended to be unequivocally critical of traditional family life, their counterparts in sociology were, for many years, enthusiastically optimistic. In the influential collection, *Family, Socialization and Interaction Process*, Talcott Parsons (1955) assured his readers that high divorce rates, an apparent breakdown in sexual morality, and a decline in birth rates did not signal problems in the family or dissatisfaction amongst family members. These were merely symptoms of "the beginning of a *new* type of stable family structure" (8–9).

Parsons also assured his audience that in this "new" family as in the old, power was present only in age-differentiated, not sex-differentiated, relationships. This power relation was necessitated by the biological helplessness of infants and small children. According to the functionalist perspective, the relations between men and women in the family were premised on "role differentiation", not power (21–26). In the family two types of leaders naturally emerged. The instrumental leader looked after the practical efforts of the group to attain its goals and linked the group to the surrounding social system. This instrumental leader was alternatively described as "boss-manager", "leader", "final court of appeals, final judge and executor of punishment, discipline and control over the children". The expressive leader took care of the emotional needs of the group. This individual was "the mediator", "the conciliator" and "the comforter" (Zelditch 1955, 318).

Parsons did not need to explain the implicit inequalities between these two leaders, since he believed this role differentiation was typical of small groups. He did, however, have to consider why this division of labour was based on sex—why men were almost always the instrumental leaders and women the expressive leaders. He discovered the answer in biology (1955, 23). Since woman's role in child-bearing and early nursing linked her inevitably to the children, men had no option other than to accept instrumental activities. Even if women entered the paid labour force and acquired some instrumental responsibilities, their jobs were generally "of a qualitatively different type" and status. Consequently, they did not compete with the husband's role as "primary status-giver or income-earner" (1955, 14–15).

Whatever the future might hold, Parsons could not envision any possibility that the adult feminine role would cease to be rooted primarily in family affairs while the masculine role would remain firmly fixed in the job and only indirectly in the family (1955, 14). In the Parsonian future these male/female lines would not become blurred. Instead, the isolation of the family from the world of (paid) work, the intensification of women's relationships with children and the growing preoccupation with personal relations suggested to him that gender-role differentiation would become sharper and more distinct (1955, 23–26). Parsonian functionalists did not, however, connect this increasing imbalance between men and women's familial roles to a potential for conflict, dissatisfaction or abuse. Since their paradigm emphasized consensus, conformity and order, the differences between men and women were viewed as natural components of a smoothly running, finely tuned family system.

For many years this conservative model typified sociological analysis of the family. In the 1950s and 1960s, mainstream sociologists generally restricted themselves to detailing the ways in which this family structure functioned. They compared this functioning in various cultural settings and focused on all the mechanisms which maintain familial stability (adjustment in marriage, tradition maintenance, solidarity amongst family members and so on). Serious problems in the 'typical' family were routinely ignored. Topics such as family violence and the sexual abuse of family members were all but completely absent from sociological research until the early 1970s. Delinquency, crime and truancy were seen as social problems, the family was the cornerstone of social stability.

In 1960, Robert Blood and Donald Wolfe, however, did break with sociological orthodoxy by discussing power in their study of husbands and wives. The authors asked wives to tell them who usually makes the final decision in 14 family areas (automobile purchases, vacation plans, and so on). They hypothesized that the spouse with more resources—more income, status and/or education—would have more say in family decision-making (the resource theory of power). Although Blood and Wolfe concluded that American couples were basically egalitarian since wives made as many decisions as their husbands, their research had opened a Pandora's box. More and more research raised the basic questions: Who has power in the family? Are women oppressed by family roles and relations? How can questions about family power and inequality be best studied?

More and more, sociological work suggested that power was indeed a crucial issue in marital relations. Further, women's experience of marriage and the family was often revealed as stultifying and oppressive. In *The Future of Marriage*, Jessie Bernard (1973) argued that men and women experienced a very different reality in marriage. For women, marriage was often a frustrating disappointment that took its toll in physical and psychological well-being. While men benefited from marriage and flourished under its regime, women were so constrained and burdened by their life in marriage that married women were, on average, less healthy and more depressed than their single counterparts.

In 1974, Bernard elaborated on this argument in *The Future of Motherhood*, in which she suggested that the expectation of motherhood (like marriage) was socialized into young women; they had little opportunity to decide whether they wanted to be mothers or what kind of mothering best suited them. In phrases reminiscent of emergent feminist analyses, Bernard argued that modern women often experienced marriage and motherhood as traps which restricted their potential as human beings.

While Bernard and others built up the critical analysis of women's role in the family, several sociologists, notably Constantina Safilios-Rothschild (1970) and Dair Gillespie (1971) addressed the specific issue of power and decision-making in the family. Power in family relations, they argued, cannot be evaluated by simply calculating which spouse makes more decisions. Reviewing the decade of research which emanated from the original Blood and Wolfe study, Safilios-Rothschild criticized decision-making research which concluded that men and women shared equal powers in the family. She pointed out that all family decisions were not equally significant. The wife's decision about which friends to entertain could not be considered equivalent to the husband's decision about which car to purchase for the family. The wife might make many decisions that were only peripherally important to other family members (what to have for supper). The husband might make fewer decisions, but these might have a greater impact on the family as a whole (which job to take).

Gillespie extended these criticisms by suggesting that Blood and Wolfe's personal resource approach ignored the broader dimensions of the gender caste system in modern society. Men, she proposed, had power in the family because of their power in the larger social structure. Men and women were socialized to expect men to occupy positions of power and authority in the educational, economic, legal, religious, political and military institutions. For a woman to achieve equality in marriage, she had to obtain status in the larger society: well-paid employment in the labour force, a good education, and participation in important social institutions. When women sought these opportunities they found that women as a caste were blocked from succeeding in these institutions, while men as a caste had their advancement facilitated. Gillespie argued that equality in the family depended, not on the good will of husbands, but rather on the elimination of gender discrimination in the social structure (1971, 86). Women's subordination in the family was a public issue, not a private trouble.

The work of Bernard, Safilios-Rothschild and Gillespie laid the foundation for a rapid proliferation of critical family research. Canadian feminist scholarship concerning the family developed rapidly throughout the 1970s and early 1980s. These works often focused on women's role in the family as an expression of women's social oppression (Henshel 1973; Veevers 1973; Eichler, 1973; Smith 1973; Taylor 1976). For the first time, serious research examined the dimensions and inequities of Canadian women's labour in the home (Armstrong and Armstrong 1978; Fox 1980). Family violence in Canada, previously ignored by most social scientists, became the subject of serious inquiry (Van Stolk 1978; MacLeod 1980). Meg Luxton's (1980) detailed ethnographic study of housewives in Flin Flon, Manitoba, provided the first in-depth examination of women's day-to-day family lives. Margrit Eichler's (1983) *Families in Canada Today*, which provided a wide-ranging feminist critique of sociological orthodoxy, firmly established feminist thought at the centre of contemporary Canadian research on the family. More recent publications (Baker et al. 1984; Burstyn and Smith 1985; Hamilton and Barrett 1986; Luxton and Rosenberg 1986) attest to the continuing significance of feminist perspectives in Canadian sociology of the family.

A pervasive concern with power and inequality is woven throughout the new feminist scholarship on the family. After more than a decade and a half of research in Canada and many other countries, the actual dimensions and impact of power on family relations are not fully clear. From the advances that have been made, however, it is evident that power is a significant and complex aspect of family dynamics.

POWER DYNAMICS IN THE CONTEMPORARY FAMILY

(i) Who Decides?

Today, researchers using a decision-making approach to family power continue to conclude that modern families are basically egalitarian. Combining data collected in Calgary, Detroit, Tokyo, Paris, Louvain, Athens, Los Angeles, and Haifa, Ruth Katz finds that the modern urban family has almost achieved "an equal allocation of power between marital partners" (1983, 98). This whole approach to family power, however, is still the subject of considerable controversy. After reviewing the decision-making research of the 1970s, Gerald McDonald concludes that researchers have failed to adequately address the criticisms and concerns raised in the 1960s. Only a few of the pressing problems pointed out by Safilios-Rothschild (1970) have been even partially resolved. Very little is actually known about decision-making behaviours (McDonald 1980, 850). In particular, the equal decision-making discovered by researchers appears to reflect a change in expectations, not a change in actual behaviour.

Alongside this apparent egalitarianism, decision-making researchers also find persistent evidence of male dominance in the family. Although most couples in a recent survey of decision-making patterns state that power is shared equally in their home, in a significant minority (one-quarter to one-third of the couples) power is not described as equally shared, and in most of these families the husband is more powerful (Blumstein and Schwartz 1983, 139). In a national survey of American families examining infrequent and important decisions (who decides what house or apartment to live in, where to go on vacation, whether the wife should have a job, and whether to move if the husband gets a job offer in another city) John Mirowsky finds that the balance of power in the average family tends to favour the husband more than the wife (1985, 588). Finally, research in Calgary suggests that there is some indication that the areas where wives make decisions is seen by both marriage partners as not very important. In the areas deemed important by both partners, the husbands tend to have final say (Brinkerhoff and Lupri 1983, 219).

Surprisingly, wives working in the paid labour force do not have more decision-making power (Brinkerhoff and Lupri 1983, 207). The resource theory of power would predict that when women bring more resources into the household, they can expect to have more say in family matters. While it is true that the more the husband earns, the more justified he feels making major family decisions, the implications for women are more ambiguous (Mirowsky 1985, 587).

That 'working wives' do not, in fact, have significantly more power is reflected in decisions about domestic labour. Husbands of employed wives may 'help out' a bit more around the house, but generally, even when the wife has full-time paid employment, the husband contributes relatively little time to household and childcare responsibilities (Coverman and Sheley 1986). For example, Herbert Northcott (1983) reports that in Edmonton, even when husbands and wives express egalitarian sex-role attitudes, it is the wife who routinely takes time off from her job to stay home with a sick child. Further, whatever improvements are achieved towards a more equitable division of household tasks are often the result of manipulation and persistence rather than greater decision-making power for the wife. One woman, who slowly conditioned her husband to do the laundry, complained that he would have refused if she had simply asked him. She had to resort to fooling him into doing it (Luxton 1983, 40)

This lack of improvement when women take paid employment may result from the nature of women's work. Women are not considered "co-providers" in the family until they make one-third of the family income (Hiller 1984, 1009). Married women are traditionally employed in low-wage, part-time and low-status sectors of the economy. Although in Canada more than half of all married couples have two incomes, working wives continue to earn substantially less than their husbands. Women in Canada earn on average only 28% of the family income (Statistics Canada 1985; 70).

Employment differences are only part of the power dynamic. Powerful normative pressures (a good wife, employed or not, lets her husband lead) encourage women and men to accept without discussion or decision women's responsibility for housework. Research on American dual-career families reveals that even when the wife also has a career, she does 79% of all household work. Dual-career husbands do not contribute more time to household duties than professional men married to housewives who have no paid employment (Berardo, Shehan, and Leslie 1987). Within this normative and economic context, the continued movement of women into the paid labour force will not, in itself, resolve family power imbalances.

(ii) Who is Violent?

Almost every Canadian family experiences some violent episode, however minor, each year, and all members of the family seem to engage in some form of violence at some time. However, it is men who continue to be the most frequent perpetrators of severe and repeated violence in the family. As much as the more powerful family members are assumed to have the right to make major decisions and avoid disagreeable tasks, they may also be seen to have the right to inflict physical and psychological abuse. Although family violence is a relatively new area of social inquiry, its overall profile is already apparent.

The recently released report on wife-battering in Canada estimates that 1 million women in Canada are battered each year. In 1985, 15,730 women were admitted to shelters because they had been physically, psychologically or sexually abused by their husbands or partners. Almost all the shelters for battered women were forced to turn away large numbers of women due to insufficient space and funding (MacLeod 1987). National and state-wide surveys in the United States similarly indicate that 10% to 12% of all married women are physically attacked by their spouse or live-in partner each year, and 11% to 21% are attacked at some point during their marriage (Straus and Gelles 1986). Diane Russell's (1982) survey of women in San Francisco reveals that 1 in 7 have been raped by their husbands or live-in partners.

Male familial violence is not restricted to spousal disputes. Men are identified as important agents of child abuse. Women, who do most of the child care, commit only one-half of the abuse and neglect. The other half is committed by men, who have, in general, little responsibility for and much less exposure to children (Van Stolk 1978, 6; Breines and Gordon 1983, 504). Not infrequently, wife abuse results in the indirect or direct victimization of children (MacLeod 1987, 32–33). Recent research on sexual offences against Canadian children not only reveals that many children (one in two females; one in three males) are victims of unwanted sexual acts but, also, that almost all (98%) of the assailants are men. One-quarter to one-fifth of these men are family members (Badgley 1984, 193, 215).

Men are, of course, also the victims of family violence. Many men who batter their wives come from homes where they were abused as children or their mothers were battered. Of the men whose partners sought shelter in Canadian transition houses in 1985, 61% had been abused children (MacLeod 1987, 39). Men are also sometimes the victims of spousal violence, but they are more often the victimizers, and the violence they inflict is more likely to be repeated and is much more serious, resulting in greater injury.

Many analysts argue that these patterns of family violence simply reflect the power disparity between men and women in the family (Rush 1980; Russell 1984). Men abuse their wives because they have economic and physical power over them, because they have been socialized to be the authority in the family, and because our culture condones violence and encourages male aggressiveness. Women abuse their children because of the frustration and disappointment they experience in such unequal family relations (Cole 1985, 32; Straus and Gelles 1980, 42). Recent research suggests, however, that family power relations may be more ambiguous and shifting. A battered woman may feel that it is not her husband's power in the family, but rather, his powerlessness in society (unemployment, minority group status) which triggers his violence towards her. Some battered women feel "important, needed, even powerful" in their relationship. His jealousy, possessiveness and violence may seem, at least in the beginning, to be expressions of an unusually intense and loving relationship (MacLeod 1987, 41–45). Power, even when expressed as violence, may seem ambiguous and complex to family members.

(iii) What Does Power Look Like?

Power in family relations may be expressed in a subtle and indirect manner. Without arguments or disputes, simply by acting out their prescribed roles, husbands and wives may create and sustain a family reality in which the men are more likely than the women to 'get their way', to have their needs and desires respected, and to be personally benefited. Power inequality between men and women is embedded in the normative structures of family life.

For generations, agents of socialization have urged women to accommodate and comply. Canadian women's magazines have long cautioned their readers to be glad, whenever necessary, "to give more than your share" (Killoran 1984, 419). Conversely, many men have been socialized to expect such compliance and accommodation. Luxton finds in her study of Flin Flon housewives, that being a "good wife" often means "doing things his way" (1980, 50). The wife's part in the marriage is to be cautious and not to upset the balance of the relationship by pushing beyond "what their men will tolerate" (Rubin 1979, 152). Good wives do not need to be controlled by their husbands; they are controlled by a life-time of appropriate gender socialization. Without overt struggle, the wife's subordination is written into the marriage script.

As a result, the power dynamics may be so deeply buried that the participants themselves are unaware of them. Lillian Rubin interviewed one such couple. The wife became unintentionally pregnant and wanted an abortion. The husband informed his wife that it was her decision, adding, however, that if she had an abortion he would never agree to another child. The wife decided to have the baby: "It was a hard choice, but it was mine" (Rubin 1976, 98). Neither partner acknowledged that the husband had defined the situation in such a way that the wife could not make any other decision.

This undercurrent of indirect power in family relations may also be found in patterns of communication. Spousal inequality is acted out, for example, in the conversational styles of men and women. Research indicates that women do most of the conversational work in a marriage—trying to get conversations going by asking questions and expressing interest when their male partners speak. Men, in contrast, do much less conversational work and exercise more control over their conversations—by offering minimal responses ('uh-huh') and more frequently establishing 'successful' topics. Gender-based conversational norms set the stage for inequality. When they are not otherwise needed, women are expected to sit and "be a good listener". When there are silences or when the conversation slows down, women's role is to talk a lot (Fishman 1982, 179).

In short, power colours family life not only in terms of who makes decisions and who uses force, but also in terms of the basic parameters of family interaction. Research into both these direct and indirect expressions of power suggests that, in general, it is men who continue to wield power in the family. Research also indicates, however, that within this general pattern there are many shades and subtleties.

Power relations between husbands and wives vary considerably depending on the cultural context, historical and economic factors, region, social class and life-stage. For example, the normative structure of the family varies significantly from one culture to another. In societies with patriarchal norms (such as India and parts of Africa) the husband is expected to dominate, regardless of the wife's resources in terms of education and income. In modified patriarchal societies (such as Japan, Greece, Turkey and Yugoslavia) husbands, particularly well-educated men who have been more exposed to the new egalitarian norms, accept a more equal division of family power (Rodman 1972). There is recent research which indicates that cross-cultural variations in customs of descent and residence also affect power relations in the family. In matrilineal/matrilocal societies, women tend to have more domestic power. Presumably her kin network and continued residence amongst kin members provides the woman with a valuable support system in the event of family dispute. Women in patrilocal/patrilineal societies have significantly less power (Warner, Lee, and Lee 1986).

Women in patriarchal societies are not, however, always passive and powerless participants in family life (Ramu 1988). Although women's strategies and actions may differ from men's, and men may ultimately dominate social and family life, women do not necessarily simply acquiesce. Anthropologist Sharon Tiffany (1979), for example, cites the case of a woman in Papua, New Guinea, who opposed her husband's decision to take a second wife. Through the use of quarreling, public humiliation and threats, the wife succeeded in forcing her husband to change his mind. At one point she climbed on top of the family hut and through a hole in the thatch roof urinated on her husband, the second wife and assembled guests. Tiffany suggests that women in many cultures successfully mobilize their own expressions of power, "manipulation, bluff, influence, gossip, possession, illness, threats of ritual pollution, witchcraft, sorcery, or, suicide" (434). Family power dynamics in patriarchal as well as egalitarian families may be more complex and subtle than generally assumed.

Power relations also vary depending upon historical and economic factors. Certain historical events, such as war, dramatically alter family life. Men go off to war, wives become titular head of the family and, often, wives and daughters acquire a more prominent role in the labour force (Pierson 1986). Even in the absence of crisis, there are considerable historical variations in family life.

Various accounts suggest that the 'frontier family' that typified early Canadian history was relatively egalitarian. As Eichler (1981) points out, this type of family was characterized by symmetrical dependency. Husband and wife were mutually dependent for survival, status and riches. While a wife would have been hard-pressed to survive without her husband's co-operation and contributions, this was equally true of the husband. In contrast, in the contemporary breadwinner-housewife family, there is asymmetrical dependency. While the wife depends on the husband for food, shelter and clothing, the husband can, if necessary, purchase replacements for his wife's services. Since she needs him more than he needs her, he probably has more power in family relations.

There are, in addition, significant regional differences in the family power dynamics. Farm wives in Saskatchewan, Ontario and Prince Edward Island are likely to be more over-worked and isolated than their urban counterparts (Nett 1979, 69–70; Cebotarev, Blacklock, and McIsaac 1986). Similarly, Anglophones hold more egalitarian views of marriage than Francophones, and Francophones are more egalitarian in their views of the wife's role (right to employment, household responsibilities) than Anglophones (Hobart 1973).

Cutting through these regional and cultural variations, there are important social class differences in family power relations. Some research suggests that husband-dominance tends to be more prevalent in upper-class and lower-class families while middle-class families tend to be somewhat more egalitarian (Brinkerhoff and Lupri 1983, 207; Ostrander 1980, 37; Seeley, Sim, and Loosley 1956, 140). The mechanics of family power may also differ from class-to-class. While the upper-class husband simply transposes his public status and prestige to the family setting, the working-class husband may insist on power in the family because he lacks it in the public domain. For the middle-class professional, a (publicly) egalitarian marriage may be part of the respectable front he is required to maintain in his work and in his community. (Rubin 1976; Smith 1973). Further, the meaning of certain powers may differ depending on the class context. Women tend to manage the money in working-class families while men manage the money in professional middle-class families. However, in the typical working-class family there are few real decisions to be made since the money is already allotted to monthly expenses and there is little left over to manage. In contrast, in the (reportedly) more egalitarian middle-class home, money management is often an important task that generally belongs to the husband (Rubin 1976: 106–112).

Power dynamics in the family also vary over time. Despite the massive movement of women into the paid labor force, the birth of children still signals the withdrawal of many women into the home. Two years after having given birth, on average 40% of previously employed women have not returned to paid employment (Waite, Haggstrom, and Kanouse 1985, 270). This period of increased economic and social dependency results in a relative loss in marital power (Gillespie 1971). Some 60% to 70% of mothers experience emotional problems after birth. According to Harriet Rosenberg's (1987) interviews with mothers in Toronto, Vancouver and New York, this is a particularly stressful time for women because high demands on them are coupled with low levels of control over the family situation. Giving up waged work generally results in economic dependence and social isolation. Staying in the job often means overwork and guilt.

This pattern is often reversed when the husband retires or becomes jobless. The resource on which his public and familial status rested is diminished, and with it his power in the family (Brinkerhoff and Lupri 1983, 208). Similarly, as her husband ages or becomes disabled, the wife may become the more powerful member of the couple (Gee and Kimball 1987, 89).

Lastly, the surrounding economic context directly affects family relations. The Nova Scotia fishing community studied by Pat Connelly and Martha MacDonald (1986) underwent important economic changes—war, depression, prosperity—in the past 100 years. With these shifts came changes in family life. When men were unemployed or employed far away from home (fishing, the military), wives might enjoy greater domestic autonomy along with heavier family responsibilities. When paid work for women became available in the local economy, women could enjoy some measure of economic independence. More generally, changes in the national and world economy—the increased demand for women workers, the availability of consumer goods—help to establish the basic parameters of contemporary family relations.

Power relations in the family are, in short, more complex, varied, subtle and changing than appreciated by either 1960s feminists or Parsonian functionalists. The contemporary family does not fit neatly into either a male-dominated or egalitarian model. In general, it is men who have more 'say' in the family, who perform fewer undesirable or onerous chores, and who set the tone for family interaction. However, this male domination is conditioned by cultural, historical, class, life-cycle and socio-economic factors. These complexities must be examined if power in the family is to be fully understood. In particular, as Engels pointed out long ago, the connection between family power relations and the surrounding social and economic conditions must be fully explored. The private troubles of family life are often rooted in public issues—unemployment, lack of childcare, popularization of violence, and erosion of the community. The costs of family inequality to the individual are, frequently, also costs to the society at large.

THE COSTS OF FAMILY INEQUALITY

The power inequalities existing in modern Canadian families exact a heavy toll in terms of familial happiness and satisfaction. Although each marital partner would like to have a bit more power than his/her partner, they are most happy when marital power is shared (Mirowsky 1985, 587; Blumstein and Schwartz 1983, 89). When partners perceive their spouse as being "dominating and powerful" they generally describe their relationships as unhappy (Brinkerhoff and Lupri 1983, 208). Given the general tendency towards male-dominated families, for many wives the lack of power in the family is a serious source of unhappiness.

Echoing Bernard's work of more than a decade ago, researchers still find that in Canada and the United States marriage may be injurious to women's health. While married men continue to benefit from marriage, married women must cope with often onerous household responsibilities, little outside support, social isolation and economic dependency. The net result is "a strong negative impact on their mental health" (D'Arcy and Siddique 1985, 163). At certain points in the family life-cycle (pre-school children in the home), and in certain kinds of family (low-income), wives' feelings of frustration and marital dissatisfaction may be particularly intense (Schumm and Bugaighis 1986). In general, research suggests that when women find themselves relatively powerless in an unequal relationship, they become unhappy and depressed (Mirowsky 1985, 589).

There is some indication that male-dominated family life also does not meet male needs. Carrying the lion's share of power and authority in the family quickly may become an unpleasant, burdensome task. Working from dramatically different perspectives, various analysts conclude that men are eager to be freed from part or all of the life-long economic and social responsibility for wife and children (Ehrenreich 1983; Goldberg 1979). Men who feel they must always be in control of the family, even to the point of using violence, may be the frightened victims of "very narrowly defined social roles for men" (MacLeod 1987, 34). Many men not only want the obligations eliminated, they want to enjoy the benefits of equality. As evidenced in the ongoing Steelworkers Study in Hamilton, Ontario, many men appear to be rejecting traditional marital roles and accepting greater equality for women (*Hamilton Spectator* 1987). Increasingly there are men who do not want to be father figures to their wives and do not want wives who will mother them. They look, instead, for spouses who will share their lives on an equal footing, as friends and companions (Kimball 1983, 48).

Inequities in the power structure of the family not only may foment unhappiness and dissatisfaction, they may create misunderstanding and alienation. Even in sexual relations, where men and women might hope to achieve intimacy and mutual understanding, power struggles may intrude. Women may realize that sexual access is one of their few power resources—they offer sexuality "as a bribe or payment for good behavior" (Rubin 1976, 140). For example, one of Luxton's Flin Flon housewives explained that whenever she needed something for the house, she would use her sexuality. She would "make love like crazy" and then stop. If her husband wanted "more loving' he would have to purchase the needed item (1980, 64).

Conversely, men may approach sexuality as one more domain in which they have a right and responsibility to exercise control. Lillian Rubin describes one such couple. The wife was non-orgasmic until she started reading sex education literature. As soon as the wife became orgasmic and started to show an interest in sexual relations, the husband withdrew. Only as long as he was in control could he remain sexually active. Once his wife became sexually assertive, he could only retain control by rejecting her overtures: "'My husband just lost interest in sex. Now, I can hardly ever get him to do it anymore, no matter how much I try or beg him. . . . Maybe I scared him off or something'" (1976, 150). The possibility of real intimacy is lost whenever issues of power and control intrude (Valverde 1985, 42).

Inequitable power relations may cost the family not only in terms of dissatisfaction, depression and frustrated hopes, but sometimes in terms of lasting or even irreparable damage to family members. Repetitious patterns of violence are also a cost built into the non-egalitarian family. Kersti Yllo reports that the rate of wife-beating in husband-dominant couples is 50% higher than for wife-dominant couples, and more than 300% greater than in egalitarian couples (1984, 314–15). Inequitably distributed power not only facilitates the use of violence, but also the persistent pattern of violence. Subordinate family members repeatedly endure abuse and return to abusive situations because their social, economic and/or psychological powerlessness is built into the structure of the male-dominated family. From their research with battered women in Vancouver, Susan Painter and Don Dutton (1985) conclude that the abused woman is trapped by feelings of powerlessness. She perceives a power imbalance "with the man having the power to make decisions, command behaviour and inflict injury". Her efforts to equalize power by accepting responsibility for what is wrong in the relationship are ineffective. She is left with "feelings of failure and lowered self-esteem" which produce "greater feelings of powerlessness" (371). The male-dominated family sets the stage for violence and abuse.

Finally, another pervasive cost of familial inequality is the lost opportunity for a more fulfilled and satisfying personal life. Research with Montreal couples reveals that equality in the family and, particularly, shared rights and responsibilities are the most promising basis for marriage. Neither a "patricentric nor a matricentric authority structure" create greater happiness. It is joint power sharing which is "strongly related to marital satisfaction" (Mashal 1985, 44). For example, men's psychological well-being improves when they participate in child-care (Shamir 1986, 205) and, conversely, men are not generally distressed when their wives take paid employment (Fendrich 1984). Having interviewed 150 role-sharing couples in the United States and Canada, Gayle Kimball (1983) emphasizes the benefits to women and, especially, men, of 50–50 marriages. Men are permitted to live "less hazardous lives". Women live "with more freedom of choice". The "war between the sexes", sometimes referred to as holy deadlock, is put to an end and men and women can love and enjoy one another more (208).

Unfortunately such egalitarian families are still decidedly uncommon. Research in the early 1970s revealed that only 13% of Canadian families described family power as shared. More recent research indicates that inequality is still common. From their study of Calgary couples, Merlin Brinkerhoff and Eugen Lupri (1983) conclude that there is still "an overall lack of equalitarianism". Decisions tend to be made autocratically with each spouse taking responsibility for specific areas. There is very little joint decision-making (210). In general, the major decision-making studies reveal that "the traditional division of roles and responsibilities between spouses survives" (Katz 1983, 98–99). Even Kimball's difficulties in locating 50–50 marriages in Canada and the United States attest to the scarcity of this type of family. In order to enjoy the benefits of sharing and equality and to avoid the costs of inequality and domination, the typical family and the society in which it flourishes must be extensively overhauled.

TOWARDS THE EGALITARIAN FAMILY

After more than a quarter century of research and analysis, it is clear that power, whatever its complexities and variations, remains an issue in family life. Inequable power relations continue to exact a heavy toll in terms of unhappiness and dissatisfaction. Change, however, has occurred. The traditional patriarchal family, in which a husband could rape and beat his wife with impunity, and in which the wife and children were essentially the husband's property, is now a relic of the past (Dranoff 1977, 23, 27). Though few couples have managed to achieve equality, there is cause for cautious optimism.

Much is being accomplished towards improving family relations. The proliferation of research on women's lives as wives, mothers and daughters provides a crucial basis for action. The emerging critique of men's roles and the struggle by men's groups to articulate a liberated model of masculinity (Kaufman 1987) encourages new approaches to family life. The recent publication of detailed reports on day-care (Canada 1986) and wife-abuse (MacLeod 1987) in Canada indicate the continuing high profile of women's and family issues in public discourse. Community groups providing shelter to abused women, support for single parents, childcare networks and information on work-life alternatives, all sustain the possibility of social change.

The full solution to familial inequality will require a major upheaval in societal and personal life. Traditional gender socialization needs to be abandoned. Each partner will be socialized for participation in both the domestic and public domains (assertive women and men, nurturant men and women). Secondly, the division of labour between men and women will have to be revamped. In the egalitarian family, both paid work and domestic work will be shared by each spouse; the distinction between 'real' paid work and housework will be abandoned.

These changes cannot be separated from a general reordering of the economic institution. Women will have to have equal opportunities and compensation in public work. Childbirth and childcare must no longer handicap women in their jobs and careers. Similarly, men will have to be freed from the traditional 40 hour plus work week in order to have the time and energy to devote to domestic work and childcare. The entire structure of work will need to be reformulated, with explorations into flexitime, job sharing and part-time work, as well as other alternatives.

These changes would inevitably transform the socio-economic order. The old emphasis on productivity and profitability would give way to a new concern about human satisfaction and fulfilment. The old order that is built around the stereotype of aggressive, competitive masculinity and the model of suppliant femininity would be shattered. Every institution—military, political, educational, religious—would feel the impact of these changes. In place of old notions of an isolated, private, family life, the local community would become an integral part of the family.

Community day-care centres run by parents and other interested adults, community centres, along with children's and parents' groups, would provide adults and children with support and guidance. In a society where work is less competitive and where human values are prioritized, there would be less need to seek refuge and peace inside the family unit. There would also be more time to work with and help other members of the community. The very meaning of family might change. Freed from the old ideas, families might take many new and different forms. Rather than referring to a biological, social and/or statistical construct, the term 'family' might come to signify any small group in which there is a strong sense of belonging, intimacy, trust and caring.

The path to a more egalitarian family is clearly long and arduous. The many children, women and men who have been or are now the victims of family power relations will not enjoy the realization of this change. That possibility can, however, be sustained. By learning about the realities of family power dynamics, particularly the subtler dimensions, along with the personal and societal costs, the individual can better understand and address his or her own situation. By participating in social action groups such as day-care lobbies, work alternative institutes, shelters for abused women and children, men's groups, and rape crisis centres, the individual can contribute to a general erosion of family inequality. Together, these efforts contribute to the possibility of a future in which men, women and children will live in relationships premised on equality, mutual respect and human fulfilment.

Bibliography

Anderson, Margret (ed.).
1972   *Mother Was Not A Person.* Montreal: Black Rose Books.
Armstrong, Pat, and Hugh Armstrong.
1978   *The Double Ghetto: Canadian Women and their Segregated Work.*
            Toronto: McClelland and Stewart.
Badgley, Robin F.
1984   *Sexual Offences Against Children Vol. 1.* Ottawa: Minister of
            Supply and Services.
Baker, Maureen, et al.
1984   *The Family: Changing Trends in Canada.* Toronto: McGraw-
            Hill Ryerson Limited.
1985   *What Will Tomorrow Bring?: A Study of the Aspirations of*

Adolescent Women. Ottawa: Canadian Advisory Council on the Status of Women.

Benston, Margaret.
1969   *The Political Economy of Women's Liberation*. Toronto: Hogtown Press.

Berardo, Donna H., Constance L. Shehan, and Gerald R. Leslie.
1987   "A Residue of Tradition: Jobs, Careers, and Spouses' Time in Housework". *Journal of Marriage and the Family* 49 (May): 381–390.

Bernard, Jessie.
1973   *The Future of Marriage*. New York: Bantam Books.
1974   *The Future of Motherhood*. New York: The Dial Press.

Bibby, Reginald W., and Donald C. Posterski.
1985   *The Emerging Generation: An Inside Look at Canada's Teenagers*. Toronto: Irwin Publishing.

Blood Jr., Robert O., and Donald M. Wolfe.
1960   *Husbands and Wives: The Dynamics of Married Living*. New York: Free Press.

Blumstein, Philip, and Pepper Schwartz.
1983   *American Couples*. New York: William Morrow and Company, Inc.

Breines, Wini, and Linda Gordon.
1983   "The New Scholarship on Family Violence". *Signs* 8 (Spring): 490–531.

Brinkerhoff, Merlin B., and Eugen Lupri.
1983   "Conjugal Power and Family Relationships: Some Theoretical and Methodological Issues." In *The Canadian Family*, edited by K. Ishwaran, 202–219. Toronto: Gage Publishing Ltd.

Burstyn, Varda and Dorothy Smith.
1985   *Women, Class, Family and the State*. Toronto: Garamond Press.

Canada
1986   *Report of the Task Force on Childcare*. Ottawa: Minister of Supply and Services.

Cebotarev, N., W.M. Blacklock, and L. McIsaac.
1986   "Farm Women's Work Patterns". *Atlantis* 11 (Spring): 1–22.

Cole, Susan G.
1985   "Child Battery". In *No Safe Place: Violence Against Women and Children*, edited by Connie Guberman and Margie Wolfe, 21–40. Toronto: Women's Press.

Connelly, Patricia and Martha MacDonald.
1986   "Women's Work: Domestic and Wage Labour in a Nova Scotia Community". In *The Politics of Diversity: Feminism,*

Marxism and Nationalism, edited by Roberta Hamilton and Michele Barrett, 35–80. Montreal: Book Center Inc.

Coverman, Shelley and Joseph F. Sheley.
1986   "Change in Men's Housework and Child-Care Time, 1965–75". *Journal of Marriage and the Family* 48 (May): 413–422.

D'Arcy, Carl and C. M. Siddique.
1985   "Marital Status and Psychological Well-Being: A Cross-National Comparative Analysis". *International Journal Comparative Sociology* 26 (Sept.–Dec.): 149–166.

De Beauvoir, Simone.
1952   *The Second Sex*. New York: Vintage Books.

Dranoff, Linda Silver.
1977   *Women in Canadian Life: Law*. Toronto: Fitzhenry and Whiteside.

Ehrenreich, Barbara.
1983   *The Hearts of Men*. Garden City, New York: Anchor Press.

Eichler, Margrit.
1973   "Women as Personal Dependents". In *Women in Canada*, edited by Marylee Stephenson, 36–55. Toronto: New Press.
1981   "Power, Dependency, Love and the Sexual Division of Labour". *Women's Studies International Quarterly* 4 (No. 2): 201–219.
1983   *Families in Canada Today: Recent Changes and their Policy Consequences*. Toronto: Gage Publishing Limited.

Engels, Frederick.
1942   *The Origin of the Family, Private Property and the State*. New York: International Publishers.

Fendrich, Michael.
1984   "Wives' Employment and Husbands' Distress: A Meta-Analysis and a Replication". *Journal of Marriage and the Family* 46 (Nov.): 871–879.

Firestone, Shulamith.
1970   *The Dialectic of Sex*. New York: William Morrow and Company, Inc.

Fishman, Pamela.
1982   "Interaction: The Work Woman Do". In *Women and Work*, edited by Rachel Kahn-Hut, Arlene Kaplan Daniels and Richard Colvard, 170–180. New York: Oxford University Press.

Fox, Bonnie (ed.).
1980   *Hidden in the Household Women's Domestic Labour Under Capitalism*. Toronto: Women's Press.

Friedan, Betty.
1963   *The Feminine Mystique*. New York: Dell Publishing Co., Inc.

1981   *The Second Stage.* New York: Summit Books.
Gee, Ellen and Meredith M. Kimball.
1987   *Women and Aging.* Toronto: Butterworths.
Gillespie, Dair.
1971   "Who Has the Power? The Marital Struggle". *Journal of Marriage and the Family* 33 (August): 445–588.
Goldberg, Herb.
1979   *The New Male.* New York, New York: New American Library.
Greer, Germaine.
1970   *The Female Eunuch.* London: Paladin.
1984   *Sex and Destiny.* London: Secker and Warburg.
Hamilton, Roberta, and Michele Barrett (eds.).
1986   *The Politics of Diversity: Feminism, Marxism and Nationalism.* Montreal: Book Center Inc.
Hamilton Spectator
1987   Male Steelworker's Role Changing—Study. June 4. D1.
Henshel, Anne-Marie.
1973   *Sex Structure.* Don Mills, Ontario: Longman Canada Limited.
Herold, Edward S.
1984   *Sexual Behaviour of Canadian Young People.* Markham, Ontario: Fitzhenry and Whiteside.
Hiller, Dana V.
1984   "Power Dependence and Division of Family Work". *Sex Roles* 10 (June): 1003–1019.
Hobart, Charles W.
1973   "Egalitarianism after Marriage". In *Women in Canada*, edited by Marylee Stephenson, 138–156. Toronto: New Press.
Kaufman, Michael.
1987   *Beyond Patriarchy: Essays by Men on Pleasure, Power and Change.* Toronto: Oxford University Press.
Katz, Ruth.
1983   "Conjugal Power: A Comparative Analysis". *International Journal of Sociology of the Family* 13 (Spring): 79–101.
Killoran, M. Maureen.
1984   "The Management of Tension: A Case Study of Chatelaine Magazine 1939–80". *Journal of Comparative Family Studies* 15 (Autumn): 407–426.
Kimball, Gayle.
1983   *The 50–50 Marriage.* Boston: Beacon Press.
Kreps, Bonnie.
1972   "Radical Feminism". In *Women Unite! An Anthology of the Canadian Women's Movement*, 71–75. Toronto: Canadian Women's Educational Press.

Levine, Helen.
1983   "The Power Politics of Motherhood". In *Perspectives on Women in the 1980s,* edited by Joan Turner and Lois Emery, 28–40. Winnipeg: The University of Manitoba Press.
Luxton, Meg.
1980   *More than a Labour of Love.* Toronto: Women's Press.
1983   "Two Hands for the Clock". *Studies in Political Economy* 12 (Fall): 27–44.
Luxton, Meg and Harriet Rosenberg.
1986   *Through the Kitchen Window: The Politics of Home and Family.* Toronto: Garamond Press.
Mackie, Marlene.
1987   *Constructing Women and Men: Gender Socialization.* Toronto: Holt, Rinehart and Winston of Canada, Limited.
MacLeod, Linda.
1980   *Wife Battering in Canada: The Vicious Circle.* Ottawa: Canadian Advisory Council on the Status of Women.
1987   *Battered But Not Beaten . . . Preventing Wife Battering in Canada.* Ottawa: Canadian Advisory Council on the Status of Women.
Malamuth, Neil M.
1981   "Rape Proclivity Among Males". *Journal of Social Issues* 37 (Fall): 138–157.
Mashal, Meeda M.S.
1985   "Marital Power, Role Expectations and Marital Satisfaction". *International Journal of Women's Studies* 8 (January/February): 40–46.
McCormick, Naomi B., and Clinton J. Jesser.
1983   "The Courtship Game: Power in the Sexual Encounter". In *Changing Boundaries: Gender Roles and Sexual Behavior,* edited by Elizabeth Rice Allgeier and Naomi B. McCormick, 64–86. Palo Alto, California: Mayfield Publishing Company.
McDonald, Gerald W.
1980   "Family Power: The Assessment of a Decade of Theory and Research, 1970–1979". *Journal of Marriage and the Family* 42 (November): 841–854.
Millet, Kate.
1969   *Sexual Politics.* New York: Avon Books.
Mirowsky, John.
1985   "Depression and Marital Power". *American Journal of Sociology* 91 (November): 557–592.
Morton, Peggy.
1972   "Women's Work is Never Done". In *Women Unite! An*

Anthology of the Canadian Women's Movement, 46–68. Toronto: Canadian Women's Educational Press.

Nett, Emily.
1979   "Marriage and the Family: Organization and Interaction". In *Courtship, Marriage and the Family in Canada*, edited by G.N. Ramu, 59–77. Toronto: Macmillan Company Ltd.

Northcott, Herbert C.
1983   "Who Stays Home? Working Parents and Sick Children". *International Journal of Women's Studies* 6 (November/December): 387–394.

Nunes, Maxine, and Deanna White.
1972   *The Lace Ghetto*. Toronto: New Press.

Ostrander, Susan A.
1980   "Upper Class Women: The Feminine Side of Privilege". *Qualitative Sociology* 3 (Spring): 23–44.

Painter, Susan Lee and Don Dutton.
1985   "Patterns of Emotional Bonding in Battered Women: Traumatic Bonding". *International Journal of Women's Studies* 8 (September/October): 363–375.

Parsons, Talcott.
1955   "The American Family: Its Relations to Personality and to the Social Structure". In *Family, Socialization and Interaction Process*, edited by Talcott Parsons and Robert F. Bales, 3–33. Glencoe, Illinois: The Free Press.

Pierson, Ruth Roach.
1986   "Women's Emancipation and the Recruitment of Women into the War Effort". In *The Politics of Diversity*, edited by Roberta Hamilton and Michele Barrett, 101–135. Montreal: Book Center Inc.

Ramu, G.N.
1988   "Marital Roles and Power: Perceptions and Reality in the Urban Setting". *Journal of Comparative Family Studies* 19 (Summer): 207–227.

Rapaport, Karen, and Barry R. Burkhart.
1984   "Personality and Attitudinal Characteristics of Sexually Coercive College Males". *Journal of Abnormal Psychology* 93 (May): 216–221.

Rodman, Hyman.
1972   "Marital Power and the Theory of Resources in Cultural Context". *Journal of Comparative Family Studies* 3 (Spring): 50–69.

Rosenberg, Harriet.
1987   "Motherwork, Stress, and Depression: The Costs of Priva-

tized Social Reproduction". In *Feminism and Political Economy: Women's Work, Women's Struggles*, edited by Heather Jon Maroney and Meg Luxton, 181–196. Toronto: Methuen.

Rowland, Robyn.
1987   "Technology and Motherhood: Reproductive Choice Reconsidered". *Signs* 12 (Spring): 512–528.

Rubin, Lillian.
1976   *Worlds of Pain: Life in the Working-Class Family*. New York: Basic Books, Inc.
1979   *Women of a Certain Age: The Midlife Search for Self*. New York: Harper Colophon Books.

Rush, Florence.
1980   *The Best Kept Secret: Sexual Abuse of Children*. Englewood Cliffs, New Jersey: Prentice-Hall, Inc.

Russell, Diane.
1982   *Rape in Marriage*. New York: MacMillan Publishing Co., Inc.
1984   *Sexual Exploitation*. Beverly Hills: Sage Publishing.

Safilios-Rothschild, Constantina.
1970   "The Study of Family Power Structure: A Review 1960–69". *Journal of Marriage and the Family* 31 (November): 290–301.

Schumm, Walter R., and Margaret A. Bugaighis.
1986   "Marital Quality over the Marital Career: Alternative Explanations". *Journal of Marriage and the Family* 48 (February): 165–168.

Seeley, John R., R. Alexander Sim, and E.W. Loosley.
1956   *Crestwood Heights: A Study of the Culture of Suburban Life*. Toronto: University of Toronto Press.

Shamir, Boas.
1986   "Unemployment and Household Division of Labor". *Journal of Marriage and the Family* 48 (February): 195–206.

Smith, Dorothy.
1973   "Women, the Family and Corporate Capitalism". In *Women in Canada*, edited by Marylee Stephenson, 2–35. Toronto: New Press.

Snell, James G.
1986   "Marriage Humour and its Social Functions, 1900–1939". *Atlantis* 11 (Spring): 70–85.

Statistics Canada
1985   *Women in Canada: A Statistical Report*. Ottawa: Minister of Supply and Services.

Straus, Murray, and Richard J. Gelles.
1980   *Behind Closed Doors: Violence in American Families*. Garden City, New York: Anchor Press.
1986   "Societal Change and Change in Family Violence Rates from

1975 to 1985 as Revealed by Two National Surveys". *Journal of Marriage and the Family* 48 (August): 465–479.

Taylor, Norma.
1976   "All This for Three and a Half a Day: The Farm Wife". In *Women in the Canadian Mosaic*. Toronto: Peter Martin Associates.

Tiffany, Sharon W.
1979   "Women, Power, and the Anthropology of Politics: A Review". *International Journal of Women's Studies* 2 (No. 5): 430–442.

Valverde, Mariana.
1985   *Sex, Power and Pleasure*. Toronto: Women's Press.

Van Stolk, Mary.
1978   *The Battered Child in Canada*, rev. ed. Toronto: McClelland and Stewart.

Veevers, J.E.
1973   "The Child-Free Alternative: Rejection of the Motherhood Mystique". In *Women in Canada*, edited by Marylee Stephenson, 183–199. Toronto: New Press.

Waite, Linda J., Gus W. Haggstrom, and David E. Kanouse.
1985   "Changes in the Employment Activities of New Parents". *American Sociological Review* 50 (April): 263–272.

Warner, Rebecca L., Gary R. Lee, and Janet Lee.
1986   "Social Organization, Spousal Resources, and Marital Power: A Cross-cultural Study". *Journal of Marriage and the Family* 48 (February): 121–128.

Yllo, Kersti.
1984   "The Status of Women, Marital Equality and Violence Against Wives". *Journal of Family Issues* (September): 307–320.

Zelditch, Morris Jr.
1955   "Role Differentiation in the Nuclear Family: Comparative Study". In *Family, Socialization and Interaction Process*, edited by Talcott Parsons and Robert F. Bales, 307–352. Glencoe, Illinois: The Free Press.

PART III

The Pressures from Outside: External Influences on Family Life

CHAPTER 6

Women, Family and Economy

Pat Armstrong and Hugh Armstrong

In the mid-1980s, *Chatelaine* magazine's award for woman of the year honoured work as wife of the Prime Minister. In the same period, hundreds of women in lone-parent households lost their mother's allowance or welfare benefits because inspectors found a man in the house (Barron 1986). Thousands of other women moved in and out of the labour force as the "exigencies of marriage, pregnancy or childcare had a major impact on the continuity of work for a large majority of women, but almost no impact for men" (Burch 1985, 26). Although the Prime Minister's wife, the lone mothers on welfare, and the women with interrupted paid employment are widely separated in terms of power, resources and opportunities, together they symbolize the continuing and complex interconnections amongst economy, families and women's work.

Understanding families and women's work entails untangling these complex interconnections. For feminists, the project begins with the assumption that the consequences of work and family life not only are different for women and men but also frequently serve to perpetuate the subordination of women. For feminists who are political economists, the project begins as well with the assumption that the constantly changing ways women and men co-operate to provide for the necessities of daily life and for the next generation set the conditions for families and for work.

Although women are divided by differences in social class, race, ethnicity, region, age, and marital status, women's subordination still means that they share a wide range of experiences. "Each successive socio-economic stage in Canada, from seigneurialism to liberal capitalism, has allocated substantial advantages to males within every rank and class," conclude Strong-Boag and Fellman (1986, 2). Women's subordination has not, however, simply meant passivity or resulted from passivity. Individually and collectively women have fought to alter their conditions. The contradictory nature of economic development has itself provided a basis for much of this activity. Similarly, ideas emerging with new economic forces or retained from past experiences and spread by women talking with each other in kitchens, church halls, hospitals, schools and on shop floors have helped them to shape their histories.

Starting with these assumptions and drawing on theoretical lessons learned from our research, we outline in this chapter broad developments in the Canadian political economy and their interrelationships with families and with women's work. The overall patterns are familiar: the emergence and development of a formal economy increasingly dominated by large, international corporations, the concomitant growth of the state, the decline of household production, the transformation of domestic tasks with the introduction of new products, machines and energy sources, and the increasing reliance on wage labour as a means of obtaining the necessities of life. Less familiar are the explanations for these trends, the contradictions in these developments, the regional variations, the different impacts on women and men, the largely invisible informal economy, the continuing interpenetration of household with formal economy, and what we call the adjudication by the state of the relationship between ostensibly public and private spheres.

Bringing together the familiar and the unfamiliar, we argue that the search for profit shapes work and family structures for women and men in particular but often contradictory ways. This search serves to denigrate women's knowledge and skills while ensuring their responsibility for crucial caring work in and out of the household. Women's household responsibilities continue to lock them into domestic labour at the same time as the decline in household production has made wage labour more and more necessary. Combined with and reinforced by the segregation of women's work, these responsibilities have made women more dependent on families and on the state. By contrast, men's rising labour force participation and decreasing domestic workload have helped them become more independent of households (Ehrenreich 1984).

However, the growing labour force involvement of women has also contributed to the expansion of their choices, the strengthening of their power, and the alteration of their ideas about women's place. At the same time, the economic crisis has made many men more dependent economically and emotionally on their families. Meanwhile, the state has contributed to both the shoring up and the breaking down of family structures, through legislation, support payments and employment programs. Although capitalist development and state intervention have shaped women's alternatives, they in turn have been shaped by women's actions, as women defend their families, engage in an informal economy, change their purchasing and fertility patterns, and organize around demands directed at employers or the state.

BASIC TRENDS IN CANADIAN ECONOMIC DEVELOPMENT

As the Conservative government of Brian Mulroney and the Macdonald Royal Commission on Canada's economic future make clear, Canada remains a private enterprise system in spite of, and perhaps because of, extensive state intervention. The driving force of such a system is accumulation or, in more popular language, profit growth and reinvestment. The then Conservative minister of state for finance, Barbara McDougall, explained this clearly to the Native Business Summit: "There's one underlying motivation in business shared by all. It's called greed. It's what keeps the world of commerce going: the desire to make a profit" (quoted in Laurie 1986).

This motivation creates certain tendencies within the economy. To increase profits, owners seek to increase sales and reduce costs. These twin objectives are primarily achieved on the one hand by introducing new goods and services to the market, by eliminating competitors and by stimulating demand, and on the other hand by developing ways of making workers cheaper, more productive and more compliant. The process of making more goods and services available for sale in the market—of making more of them commodities—is called *commodification*. With increasing commodification, new needs emerge. Many of these needs cannot be satisfied outside the market because fewer and fewer people have the means or skills to provide directly for themselves, because these goods and services are often produced more cheaply in the market, and because many are difficult, if not impossible, to produce in an individual household. For example, few people have either the space or the legal right to raise chickens, many do not have the skills required to make a coat, bread is cheaper to buy than to make from scratch, and toilets or vacuum cleaners cannot be made at home. As old means of household production have been eliminated and new needs created, more and more people have been pushed into the market to seek wages.

With increasing *intensification* of labour comes new technology and methods of organizing work. Much of this wage work is broken up into small fragments, the skill involved is often reduced, and the control exercised by owners over the work process is frequently enhanced as each employer seeks to make employees more easily trained, more readily replaced, more structured into a rapid pace, and thus not only more productive but also more obedient. For example, a secretary's job is divided into typing, reception, filing and processing tasks which can be performed by different workers, each of whom needs to learn only one job. Each task can be more simply measured, the time required to switch from one area to another is eliminated, and each worker can be more closely supervised.

Meanwhile, competition pushes owners to expand or disappear. This competition, along with the uneven availability of credit, encourages the growth of larger and larger but fewer and fewer companies, a trend known as the *concentration* and *centralization* of capital. "Mom and Pop" corner stores are replaced by giant supermarket chains, which in turn own many of the companies supplying the goods for their shelves as well as many of the shopping centers in which they are located. With these processes, wage work in all areas is constantly being restructured and reconstituted. At the same time, new divisions amongst people, new social classes, are emerging.

Although these tendencies are created by the search for profit, their development is not smooth, linear or predetermined. Contradictions are built into the system and place limits on these tendencies. There is a constant tension between owners' efforts to decrease wage costs and workers' efforts to increase them. Even if employers are successful in reducing wages and the number of workers, they are then left with the challenge of finding buyers, since workers are also consumers. Pushing workers to produce more under more tightly controlled conditions may not only encourage rebellion but may also endanger the availability of future labour supplies. Workers get sick from poor conditions and women may have fewer babies. Increasing production and eliminating competition may lead to economic crisis. Drawing women into the labour force may mean that men can be paid less but it may also mean that more jobs need to be created in order to avoid dangerous levels of unemployment. Women working both at home and in the labour force may refuse to supply the next generation of workers in sufficient numbers. They may also develop new ideas about their needs, worth and potentialities. Their rising labour force participation and worsening working conditions may destroy that "haven in a heartless world" (Lasch 1977, xiii), that warm home that male workers have long counted on to renew their energies and that employers have long counted on to dampen opposition (see Armstrong and Armstrong 1984, 64–106; Cowan 1983; Hayden 1981; Luxton 1980; and Strasser 1982).

One way of handling these contradictions is the expansion of the state. As James O'Connor (1973) explains in *The Fiscal Crisis of the State*, the state often functions to promote profits by providing various kinds of support to owners and by regulating competition. At the same time, it encourages popular support for the private enterprise system by compensating for its worst consequences and by reproducing existing social relations. To these accumulation and legitimation functions—and to the coercive function of the state, invoked when legitimation fails (Panitch 1977, 8)—we would add the role of adjudicating the relationship between the seemingly public and private spheres, a function which overlaps the others. Through legislation in areas such as the minimum wage, birth control and property rights, through social programs in fields such as unemployment insurance, family allowance, health and education, and through employment strategies which serve to expand or contract state sector employment (Armstrong 1984, chapter 6), the state plays a crucial role in the distribution of work, control and financial responsibilities between families and private enterprise, as well as between women and men. Of course the state is not always successful in carrying out these functions, given the contradictory nature of the tasks themselves. Nor is the state neutral, serving as it does more often the interests of owners and men than those of workers and women.

Canadian society has been fundamentally shaped by these tendencies towards commodification and intensification, towards concentration and centralization, and towards state and labour force expansion. None of these tendencies is sex-neutral, however. They have been structured by sex divisions and themselves have structured sex divisions. The consequences of these basic tendencies have been different for women and men, both in and out of families. Women and men have reacted to and resisted these tendencies in different ways. In order to understand the sex segregation of contemporary Canadian society and the 'his' and 'hers' realities of family life (Bernard 1973), we must examine the course of these key historical trends and consider their differing implications for women and men.

THE EARLY EUROPEAN PERIOD

It was the search for profit that brought many Europeans to Canadian soil. Canada's first waged workers were men employed either in extracting raw resources from widely separated areas of the country or in defending first French, then British, sovereignty. Both kinds of work required lengthy and difficult travel—a problem for women in their reproductive years—and traditionally had been performed by men. The nature of fur trading society, however, meant that many Indian women played "an integral socio-economic role because there was little division between public' and private' spheres" (Van Kirk 1980, 4). In addition to performing crucial liaison work, Indian women were able to provide their trader husbands with many of the goods and services necessary for survival, possessing as they did "a range of skills and wilderness know-how that would have been quite foreign to a white wife" (Van Kirk 1986, 61).

In the east, part of the defence and extraction strategy involved settlements. Land grants were given by the state to "the militia, soldiers, and sailors", to French seigneurs, English merchants and land developers; in other words, to men (Teeple 1972, 46). Women were transported to labour as unwaged workers for the church or as direct producers of goods, services and children in the household. Legal authority and property rights were given by the state to men, and for the most part these were denied to married women (Plamondon 1986, 47). But because women's household labour was as obviously essential as men's in a time when families produced most of what they consumed, because women bore the very necessary children, because there was a shortage of women in most areas, and because women often had to handle the family enterprise during their husband's long absences on trading or other business trips, marriages were often relatively egalitarian relationships (Langton 1950, 49; Mitchell 1981, 47–48). Some women enjoyed "an unusually privileged position", engaged as they were "not just in the usual tending of families and farms but in arranging financing, immigration and defences that played a major role in the colony's survival" (Noel 1986, 24).

These state-supported rights of men were to prove significant, however, as capitalism developed unevenly across the country. It was possible for many male owners, as direct producers, to accumulate capital "in the form of cleared land, buildings, tools and livestock" (Johnson 1974, 17–18). Moreover, male production on the land was often oriented not only towards providing for household requirements but also for the market. Women's work was directed much more towards immediate household demands, frequently through the provision of personal services. The products and services, such as eggs and clothes-washing, that women did sell yielded low returns and were difficult to produce in large quantities in a private household, especially when women had so much other caring work to do. In the agricultural United States and Canada, "as the husband struggled to succeed in production for the market, building up capital goods and saving up cash income for future investment, his wife worked to reduce family expenditures by providing for most of the family's basic subsistence needs" (Matthaei 1982, 31).

Journals and diaries from central Canada in the early years and from western and eastern regions well into this century testify to the highly skilled nature of women's and men's work (Conrad 1986; Langton 1950; Rasmussen et al. 1976; and Traill 1969). Men tilled, planted and harvested the fields, tended larger animals, felled trees and chopped wood, made furniture, implements and leather goods. In addition to frequently assisting men with these tasks, women looked after smaller animals and vegetable gardens, collected, preserved, cooked and served food, made cloth, wool and clothes, soap, candles and quilts, bore children and cared for them as well as for the sick and the elderly. Mutually dependent, both women and men created their own visible products in collective work situations which involved their children and often un-related live-in help who were paid little, if any, wages (Harrison 1979).

Workloads were heavy for all household members, whether or not they were relatives. Male owners and their wives usually performed the more complicated tasks and directed the labour of others. However, work distinctions between employer and hired help, between parent and child, were not large in these agricultural households. Similar conditions existed in households based on craft or service production for exchange, although distinctions between employer and employee increased, es-pecially in urban areas, along with the development of wealth from private enterprise (Mitchell 1981, 8 and 155).

The work of women and men was distinguished, then, not primarily in terms of effort, location, necessity, strength or even skill but mainly in terms of ownership, access to the market, and the large personal service component of women's work. It was, of course, also distinguished by the fact that only women have babies. Much of their personal service work was related to this unique capacity. This relationship between bear-ing and caring for children was socially rather than biologically struc-tured. With the development of capitalism, it was to have an increasingly important impact on the maintenance of women's subordination (Arm-strong and Armstrong 1983a and 1984).

In most households, then, mother, father, children and hired help worked together within those households to produce most of what was required for survival.

But as some men accumulated capital on the basis of their land holdings, craft production, fur or other trading, and as the state, re-sponding to demands from entrepreneurs for the maintenance of a more stable labour supply, restricted the amount of land available (Teeple 1972), fewer and fewer men were able to acquire the means to provide directly for their own needs. Interest in producing a surplus for the market encouraged the early development of technology to reduce la-bour in household areas where men worked. Interest in producing goods for sale also tended to have a greater impact on male household labour. For example, new farm field equipment reduced the number of male hands required in sowing and harvesting while railways reduced the male labour necessary to take farm products to market. Similarly, stoves "were labour saving devices, but the labour they saved was male" (Cowan 1983, 61) because their main impact was to reduce the need for massive supplies of wood, not to diminish the work involved in cooking. Men had been producing more goods than services in the household and these were becoming cheaper to acquire through the market. At the same time as the demand for labour on the land was declining, demand in the market was growing. Increasingly, men entered the market search-ing for wage work. With this developing commodification, the formal economy grew in size and strength, creating and often dominating the private household. More and more, there was a distinction between 'public' and 'private' spheres, home and 'work'. Increasingly, 'work' was restricted to those activities undertaken directly for pay or profit.

Women's household labour changed not only at a different pace but in a different way. Women's domestic workload remained heavy well into this century for a number of reasons. First, many of women's tasks were difficult to mechanize. An article appearing in an 1876 edition of the *Christian Guardian* (Cook and Mitchinson 1976, 170) predicted that "artificial substitutes for cooks and housemaids will not probably be perfected before the close of the next century". Second, entrepreneurs initially "ignored most of the patents for household labour-saving devices" that could mechanize some work "because they could not produce them profitably" (Strasser 1982, 8), because they had little interest in making domestic workers more productive, given that their labour did not directly create profit or surplus, and because there was still room for expansion in profits making other goods. Third, the nature of women's personal service work in particular made it difficult to provide these services cheaply in the market through the application of factory methods and new technology. Assembly lines could not be used to care for children, the sick or the aged. Besides, married women were already doing much of this work for no wages at home, limiting the demand for cash service alternatives in the market.

The slow development of devices and services to save women's labour kept most married women and many single women in the household. Single women who did not work in their parents' households had fewer choices than men, given that they had less access to land or to other means of accumulating capital. Consequently, especially those arriving alone as immigrants, had little alternative to seeking paid employment. Although many did factory, waitressing or sales work, and some taught school, the largest proportion were employed in private households as general servants, nurses, cooks, laundresses, seamstresses and kitchen maids until well after the turn of the century (Ramkhalawansingh 1974). As late as 1941, domestic service was far and away the largest single occupation for women in the Canadian labour force (Armstrong and Armstrong 1984, 34). When the women working in factories or other labour market jobs married, almost all of them left their paid jobs to undertake the heavy domestic tasks in their private households.

Most married women remained out of the labour market not only because there was so much domestic work to be done but also because, unlike an increasing number of men, many still had the means of providing directly for family needs or of gaining income without leaving the household. Even in the twentieth century, many women did market gardening or at least grew and preserved food for their families' own needs. Many took in sewing, ironing, washing or boarders while others did "tailoring for the wholesale trade in their homes" (Thomas 1976, 181). Of course, the goods and income produced in these ways were seldom adequate to provide for all the needs of the household. Consequently, when husbands deserted, died or were unemployed, married women often sought paid work. Married women regularly did short-term seasonal work in factories or in laundries (Thomas 1976, 181) to boost family income. This was often the case in areas such as the Maritimes where men were able to avoid wage labour by fishing or other forms of direct production, but did not provide enough cash income to meet changing family requirements. Until the Second World War, however, most married women were fully occupied with household labour, even though some intermittently entered the formal and informal economies.

Children also kept married women in the household. In 1889, Jean Scott Thomas (1976, 181) explained that "Women whose husbands are dead or who are not able to support them, will not go out as long as they have children at home to care for, but prefer, if they can, to engage in some work which will keep them at home." Twenty-five years later, Elizabeth Mitchell (1981, 48–49, emphasis in original) concluded that "the man *has* to go out to his work, and the wife *has* to look after the babies and cook the food and bake the bread and do the washing and keep the house decent, though she may leave any egg-collecting or milking to the man at bad times". As long as household and economy were united, the fact that women bore the children interfered little with their full participation in work. But as capitalist development increasingly separated the formal economy from the household, women's childbearing capacities restricted, if only for a very short period, their continuous participation in market work, outside the household. And there was little material or social support in the market for women who were having or had had children. Children remained in the home and the mothers and female servants who were there looked after them, a relationship that was strongly supported by the dominant ideas of the time.

From the earliest years of capitalist development, then, men constituted the overwhelming majority of those owning enterprises and of those working for wages outside the household, even though many single and some married women worked for pay. Both female and male wage earners faced dismal working conditions, low pay and had few alternatives to paid employment. Women, however, received "from one-third to one-half less wages" (Phelps 1976, 182) than their male counterparts. These low wages meant that they, unlike men, "often worked after hours at home, mending, washing, preparing meals or helping out" (McCallum 1986, 43). Bad working conditions, often seasonal employment, low pay and marriage meant that women seldom stayed long in their jobs. "This continual turnover not only enabled the employers to keep the wages of women low but also permitted them to dub women unreliable, uninterested in learning a trade or in applying themselves to it seriously" (Trofimenkoff 1986, 89). That there was an enormous variety in the particular jobs classified as women's work and that these classifications changed significantly over time and regions while the segregation and subordination remained suggests, however, that ideas about women's place were not the primary factor in women's subordination. The mostly male employers hired women and ghettoized them in particular jobs in order, as a nineteenth century observer explained, mainly to "cheapen the cost of labour" (Thomas 1976, 180). Stiff competition amongst women who laboured "too much in a few occupations" (Phelps 1976, 184), the location of many in small shops or private households, little male support or perhaps male opposition, high turnover rates, and women's double shift contributed to keeping wages low, work segregated, and organized opposition limited.

Men were generally easier to organize. Concentrated in large numbers, more continuously in the labour market, more justified by the ideology and less burdened by household tasks, men were more likely to band together to resist unfair working conditions. Men more than women tended to be employed in industries where technology allowed each worker to produce more, where profits were higher and where employers could better afford concessions to workers' demands. But both in spite of and because of their conditions, some women did organize, did strike and did win a few victories (Fager 1983; Klein and Roberts 1974).

It was not only employed, single women who organized for and won concessions, however. Women married to men who owned the expanding factories, shops and farms paid domestics to perform an increasing number of the household tasks. This practice tended to strengthen "the social barrier which exists between mistress and maid" (Thomas 1976, 183), and frequently left the mistresses with little useful work to do. It was such well-to-do women who formed the core of the early women's movement. They came together to demand from the state the right to vote, to enter universities and professions. they also sought protective legislation for female workers and public health measures for everyone. They often glorified women's superior morality and motherwork (Kealey 1979), using such arguments to support their demands. For them, the purpose was often to shore up women's traditional work.

Victories for women frequently had contradictory effects. Typically, state reforms prevented any single employer from bearing alone the consequences of improving conditions and forestalled the development of demands that might prove more difficult to accommodate (McCallum 1986; Ursel 1986). Access to university for some women, for example, served to reinforce class differences amongst women. Protective legislation, such as a minimum wage for women only, set at a rate so low it would just provide for the subsistence of a "working girl" (quoted in McCallum 1986, 43), served to reinforce differences between women and men in the market, women's economic dependence on men in marriage and their responsibility for children. Such legislation was "imposed to protect women not as wage earners, but as reproducers and nurturers of the labour force of tomorrow" (McCallum 1986, 41) and "to restrict the role of women in the workplace" (Ursel 1986, 163).

INTO THE TWENTIETH CENTURY

By the beginning of this century, capitalism was firmly established as the dominant mode of production. More than 80% of the men were counted as part of the labour force. Although half of them still worked in primary sectors such as farming and mining, a third did manual work in factories, on construction sites or in transportation industries (Connelly 1978, Table 7:2b). By contrast, more than 80% of the women were not counted as part of the formal economy. Almost all married women worked full-time in the household. Meanwhile, more than one in three of the single women (Connelly 1978, Table 7.2a) who were counted as members of the labour force were employed in households as well.

Women's domestic work was, however, changing. Growing commodification and the accompanying development of mass production techniques did mean that more and more goods previously produced by women in the household were available more cheaply in the market. Services such as electricity and running water provided by either entrepreneurs or the state eventually eliminated many of women's domestic tasks. As the twentieth century developed, clothes, candles, bread and jam no longer had to be made at home, water no longer had to be lugged nor chamber pots emptied.

But many personal services—the caring for children, the sick and the aged, the making of beds and the serving of food—were relatively untouched until the welfare state expanded enormously in mid-twentieth century. Moreover, the impact of many of these new commodities was to lock women's work more firmly into a household that was increasingly isolated from the paid work of men. Searching still for the most profitable commodities (those which could be produced in a centralized, capital-intensive, cost-efficient manner which would encourage demand), entrepreneurs invested in producing individual washing machines rather than public laundry services; in private refrigerators rather than collective food delivery. Often they sought state support in the form of legislation or services for their projects (Cowan 1983). But, while washing machines lightened women's load, they also kept laundry in the home.

As Strasser (1982, 8) points out in her study of domestic technology "Capitalism had socialized only those aspects of domestic work that could be replaced by profitable commodities or services, and left the cooking, cleaning and nurturing to the housewife."

But commodification, state services and the growth of wage labour in the formal economy did more than introduce some store bought goods, some modern conveniences and some machines into the household, while leaving the labour-intensive personal service work to wives and mothers. It also fundamentally altered the nature and relations of women's domestic work. Much of the work became less visible, more isolated, less obviously skilled, less rewarding and more dependent on those paid a wage, namely men. Analyzing conditions just before the First World War, Elizabeth Mitchell (1981, 52) concluded that half of women's work "no longer deals with the primary necessities". Social duties and cleaning accounted for larger and larger amounts of work and "thus housekeeping is still burdensome, but it is no longer so vitally necessary or so personally interesting—it has lost the splendor and reality of the fight for life." With clean floors, dusted furniture and defrosted fridges rather than bread, clothes and candles as products of their labour, that labour was more difficult to see and appreciate.

New products and services not only made it increasingly possible, but also increasingly necessary, for one woman to do the work alone. At the same time, more and more single women escaped from domestic service to respond to the growing demand for workers in the formal economy. Meanwhile, the introduction of legislation which made formal education compulsory meant that more and more older children who had done most of the least skilled tasks were away at school. Left alone with the children's and servants' work to do and with only very young children as witnesses, women's work became increasingly invisible, lonely and boring.

The new managerial, social and child-rearing skills required by the altered nature of domestic work, and promoted by experts and women's groups alike, were less visible than older skills such as bread-making. The growth of expert advice in all areas of domestic work tended to denigrate women's knowledge, leaving them with the responsibility but not the authority in most areas of work (Strong-Boag 1982; Reiger 1985).

Market-produced underwear and socks, stoves and toilets, bottles and blankets, electricity and water supplies cost money. With little access to paid jobs, with even less to decent wages, and with the possibilities for producing goods or earning income at home gradually shrinking, women became more and more dependent on men who earned wages. And more and more distant from them. As one prairie woman explained, "On the farm, I was a *real* partner with my husband, sharing with him in almost every detail of daily work. Now his work is carried on in a downtown office, with professional help. There is little I can do to assist him" (quoted in Sundberg 1986, 103). Consequently, Barbara Ehrenreich argues in *The Hearts of Men* (1984, 2–3), "women need men more than the other way around", creating "an inherent instability that predates the sexual revolution". The dominance of wage labour often made men feel that they were bearing alone the work of the household. Women and men, by working in different locations, receiving different kinds and amounts of reward, and making different sorts of social contact at work, shared less and less in their marriages. In addition, more and more of women's household labour was directed towards providing personal services to husbands, children and elderly relatives (Heller 1986). In other words, an increasing amount of women's time was devoted to responding to the needs of others, to serving others. Such work often not only involved deference and subservience, it was also less visible and quickly disappeared. These developments tended to make all married women's work more similar—in spite of differences related to husbands' income—as an increasing number of women did this domestic work themselves.

With a growing proportion of household work-time devoted to the production of services rather than goods, women's domestic duties in some ways became more flexible. Bread and candles had to be regularly produced in pioneer households or families would starve in the dark, but there were a few dire consequences resulting from unmade beds. While service work is still necessary, much of it can be delayed, done less often, done more quickly by working harder with more machines, or, increasingly for those with money, purchased in the market. The least flexible part of the work is the care of children, the sick and the elderly. Such work is difficult to delay or intensify, and very expensive to purchase in the market. This flexibility was to have important consequences for women's labour force participation as the household's need for income and the demand for female employees grew at the same time as the state provided more and more care outside the home.

Commodification and state intervention then had contradictory and different consequences for women and men. Men's access to land and other means of providing directly for their own needs within the household was rapidly declining. Meanwhile, access to the ownership of growing private enterprises or, more commonly, to wage labour, was rapidly increasing, giving them advantages over women in the market. Money income made men less financially dependent on the household, but more responsible for household economic needs. So did state legislation. Women, on the other hand, were slower to lose their ability to contribute directly to meeting the household needs, but this served to isolate them from the increasingly dominant market and to put them at a disadvantage in that market. Market goods and services made women's household work less strenuous but it also made it less skilled, visible, collective and satisfying. It made women's work more flexible but more dependent and more oriented towards personal service. It freed women from many onerous tasks but locked them into what was emerging as the private household, separated in distance and in relationships from the experiences of men. State protective legislation, fought for by women, eased conditions but reinforced the segregation of work in and out of the home.

As the household was moving gradually from the production of goods to the provision of services, employment in the market shifted first towards goods production, then increasingly to services. The twentieth century began with 44% of the labour force engaged in extracting and processing primary resources. This dropped, mainly as a result of the intensification of labour with mechanization, to 13% as Canada entered the Second World War. Because almost all workers in these occupations were male, the job loss here was borne by men. During the same period, the percentage of those working in manufacturing, construction and labouring occupations remained relatively steady because, although some mechanization was taking place and new methods such as the assembly line were introduced to make workers more productive and more easily replaced, demand was growing steadily. Except for the very labour-intensive textile and garment industries, the overwhelming majority of workers in these jobs were male. Although union numbers and gains were limited during these years, rising profits and greater investments in machinery helped male workers, in particular, to win some improvements in wages and hours.

Meanwhile, the proportion of workers employed in service jobs—in professional, clerical, commercial, transportation and communications occupations—increased from one-in-five to almost one-in-three (Meltz 1969, Table A1). As enterprises grew in size, more managers and more paperwork were required to keep track of workers, clients and other enterprises (Braverman 1974). Banks and insurance companies expanded with the introduction of credit approved by the state and with the increasing size of financial transactions between larger and larger companies. Employment in transportation grew with the mass production of cars, with state investment in railways and roads, and with the movement of more and more goods. At the same time, the development of the telephone, telegraph and radio increased jobs in the communication field. There was more work for teachers as a result of state legislation on compulsory education, and more for doctors and nurses as hospitals and health services expanded. These developments, in turn, were related not only to demands from women's groups and unions, but also to discoveries in medicine which indicated the need for public health measures and which increased the effectiveness of medical care in general. Jobs in these service-producing industries were difficult to mechanize. Although new methods of job organization and supervision were introduced, and although employers got more work for the money by making employees work harder and longer (Lowe 1980; Sangster 1986), more work to be done usually meant more workers had to be hired.

Men were able to capture the majority of especially the most attractive jobs in these service-producing areas. However, employers increasingly were drawing on the reserve of single females to lower their costs and fill demand where male labour was scarce. In teaching, for instance, few males were available to fill the rapidly expanding work at the turn of the century, and school trustees were searching for ways to reduce expenses as numbers grew. Low salaries for women teaching the early grades meant relatively higher salaries could be used to attract men to fill the "super-intendents, inspectors, principal teachers and headmasters" jobs (Prentice 1977, 51; see also Prentice 1985, 104–107). With a dramatically increasing number of clerical jobs, employers sought to get more work for the money and more control over the work process by fragmenting the jobs into hierarchically organized simple tasks, each requiring little training. Women were hired to do the least skilled, lowest-paid jobs "which male clerks were unsuited or unwilling for a variety of social and economic reasons, to perform" (Lowe 1980, 378). The growth in size of retail stores also meant that employers could use similar techniques there (Roberts 1976, 27).

The gradual rise of female labour force participation reflected the expansion of demand for female workers in the service-producing industries, the subsequent feminization of teaching, clerical and sales work, and the declining demand for the labour of single daughters in the home. Even though these jobs were more attractive than work as servants in private households, they did not mean significant gains for women. Women's high turnover continued to reflect their dominant pattern of leaving their paid work when they married, a practice ensured in many areas by state regulations or by employers' policies designed to prevent women from keeping their jobs after marriage. Poor conditions in these paid jobs, and employers' propensity to fire employees who complained, also contributed to their continuing subordination and high turnover rates.

The First World War consolidated the industrialization process, more firmly establishing the perceived separation of the private household from the public political economy. The shortage of male workers in some areas facilitated the entry of more single women into the labour market, as did the postwar boom. "Women used their war-time achievements and contributions to demand to vote" (Ramkhalawansingh 1974, 262), and to win pensions for war widows, and to win mothers' allowances as well (Finkel 1979, 347). Such legislation provided women with financial assistance but it also reinforced their place as wives and mothers. Men, too, were able to win some improvements in their conditions of paid work, in the process solidifying their positions as household wage earners.

The Great Depression halted, and even reversed, many of these trends. While unemployment was, "primarily at least, a male problem" (Marsh 1939, 55), for the many single women without paid work, unemployment was "an even more serious problem of dependency than to a man" (Marsh 1939, 255). Moreover, it was women who had to make the rapidly diminishing dollar feed and clothe the family. It was women who usually had to bear the brunt of the growing tensions in households where the male breadwinners were no longer winning bread, or when husbands left to search for work elsewhere. Many women went back to canning and growing food, or to earning money at home (Milkman 1976). Families doubled up to save heating and housing costs; many married women searched for paid employment. The number employed, especially as domestics, rose. The economic crisis and the rebellion it spawned led to wide-ranging proposals for state intervention not only to restore the economy and to prevent starvation, but also to maintain the family. The fragility of the economy was exposed, the very system brought into question, and the interpenetration of household with formal economy demonstrated.

The Second World War marked the end of the Depression. It also drew, for the first time, a large number of married women into the labour force. With men off to war or employed in industries that had gone back to full production, the state worked actively to attract first, single women, then, married women without children, and finally, mothers, into the market. Hours were adjusted, day-care centres were organized, taxation incentives were introduced, counselling services were offered, and efforts were made to accommodate women with jobs near their homes. Campaigns were developed to increase and extend women's volunteer and domestic work.

Female volunteers moved into new areas such as salvage work, and housewives remade clothes, planted gardens and cut back on purchases (Pierson 1986, chapter 1). Better conditions and pay encouraged single women to leave domestic service in private households, and encouraged married women to leave their homes. Women had the opportunity to demonstrate their capacity to perform a wide range of men's jobs in the market and to handle the household alone. They also demonstrated that they were quite willing to take on paid work if support services were available. Most took on this paid work, not primarily because of ideas, such as those of patriotism, but because they were "in need of money to help their families" (quoted in Pierson 1986, 47).

THE POSTWAR PERIOD

With the end of the Second World War in sight, the state became concerned about jobs for returning soldiers. A commission set up to investigate the "problems of women" was convinced that "women's normal urge towards marriage home and family life" would reduce dramatically the numbers who stayed in paid jobs, "provided there is sufficient well-paid employment for men" (Canada, Advisory Committee on Reconstruction 1944, 16). Neither the commission nor the state was prepared, however, to rely on this normal urge. Supportive services and legislation were withdrawn. Women were forbidden to keep jobs in the public service that could be filled by men. Family allowances were introduced to help relieve the pressure on wages and to help maintain demand for commodities. Paid directly to women, many of whom had become accustomed during the war to having a pay cheque, these 'allowances' also were intended to encourage women's departure from the labour force.

Although some married women remained in paid jobs after the war, these strategies, combined with high rates of male employment and pay, high fertility rates, and media messages extolling the virtues of full-time mothering, led to a dramatic decline in women's labour force participation. It was during these immediate postwar years that the idea of mom at home, kids at school, dad in the labour force and a station wagon in the suburban garage best fit the reality for a large proportion of the population. Even during these boom years, however, women who were unattached to men with decent jobs faced a different reality. Low welfare benefits meant that those relying on the state lived in poverty, while job segregation and low wages legitimated by the state meant that few of those women with paid employment fared better.

Indeed, the postwar prosperity, which contributed to the growth of the welfare state and the winning of better working conditions in the labour force, had contradictory effects on women and different consequences for women and men. The expansion of employment-related programs such as pensions, workers' compensation for injury, and unemployment insurance for the still primarily male employees served to provide some income security, to sustain demand and to limit revolt. At the same time, they reinforced men's attachment to the labour force. The extension of education and pensions, and the gradual, if uneven, introduction by the state of a 40-hour work week, reduced male participation in the labour force slightly and made full employment for men easier to approximate. State education, medical care and labour regulations improved living as well as working conditions while ensuring a continuing supply of trained, healthy and disciplined workers without creating an undue disadvantage for any individual employer.

Seeking to increase sales, entrepreneurs developed new household appliances and other goods and services for domestic consumption. Washers and dryers, cake mixes and frozen foods, apartment houses and no-wax floors became increasingly available. The rising cost of such goods and services made households more dependent on rising male incomes. At the same time, goods and services such as these, along with, for example, TV dinners, laundromats, relatively secure wages, hospital care and unemployment insurance all helped to make many men less dependent on their families.

Women's benefits from improved market conditions were mainly indirect, through their attachment to employed men. Relatively full male employment limited pressure on women to seek paid work, and limited competition from men for women's paid jobs. But it also made many women even more dependent on men.

Because women constituted the majority of those qualifying for welfare and family allowances and of those requiring medical care and supplements to old age pensions, women's benefits from the welfare state's extension of universal programs was mainly direct. These programs, too, helped sustain purchases and prevent opposition. Simultaneously they supported women's dependency on the state or men and discouraged their full participation in the labour force. To some extent, both the new 'consumer goods' and the new state services reduced women's knowledge and fragmented their domestic work without eliminating it entirely. Serious illness was handled by professionals employed in the market; home care was directed by doctors but still done by mothers. Machine loading and unloading, purchasing, chauffeuring and scheduling replaced more visible and connected household tasks (Armstrong and Armstrong 1984, chapter 3; Kome 1982; Luxton, 1980). Children took up even more of mother's time as professionals stressed the complex nature of child development and the mother's share of the responsibility for its success.

Although the expansion in the market service sector was transforming and reducing women's domestic work, by the late 1950s it was also increasing the demand for female workers in the market. The male-dominated agriculture sector continued to decline, growth in manufacturing, construction and transportation slowed, while service, finance and trade industries—where women were more likely to find work—expanded rapidly. Work in the state sector increased dramatically, especially with new health care support and the extension of education. Although men captured almost all the senior administrative jobs created in the state sector between 1941 and 1961, and although they dominated such departments as defence, two-thirds of the additional workers in education, health and welfare were drawn from the large reserve of women not in the labour force (Armstrong and Armstrong 1986). Women were hired because they were cheap, because they were considered to have the appropriate attitudes as well as skills, because they were available, and because most men already had jobs.

But these women did not remain cheap and compliant for long. Brought together in large, impersonal structures, formally educated but not adequately compensated, many fought for and won significant improvements in their conditions. They were strengthened by the shortage of certified workers, by full government coffers and by the public support for these services. By the end of the 1960s, more than half of all unionized women worked for the state (White 1980, 27). It was here that women found their best jobs in terms of conditions, fringe benefits, pay, seniority and possibilities for promotion (Armstrong 1984; Denton and Hunter 1982, 40).

Women responding to the growing demand in other state sector jobs and in clerical or service work in the private sector were less successful. Women in the private sector faced employers who could and did move their enterprises when protest threatened. Many of these employers operated on a seasonal basis or hired primarily short-term and part-time workers. Few of the jobs required recognized skills, further limiting women's strength. Moreover, women were often forced to choose among the few jobs within commuting distance of their husbands' higher paying work. The nature of the paid employment often encouraged women to leave as soon as possible, helping to keep turnover rates high and opportunities for unionization, promotions and decent wages low. Women's strength in these jobs was also limited by the large supply of married women who did not have paid jobs and who had little choice about seeking employment, replacing other women in these easily learned, fragmented jobs.

While the demand for female workers was growing, so too was the economic need of many married women. As it became more and more expensive in relative terms to produce alternatives to the new, commodified goods and services at home, the requirements of households for cash income tended to increase faster than did the real wages of the men in them. Lengthening education, expanding services and changing ideologies made children more expensive. Taxes, mortgages, heating and transportation costs grew much more rapidly than those related to goods women could still produce in the home, placing further stress on household budgets (Armstrong 1984, 104; Vickery 1979).

This growing economic need was hidden by simple measures of real wages or consumer prices. Even during the boom years, there were widening income disparities, increases in unemployment, rising prices and falling profits. These trends heralded future economic decline and pushed more married women into the market searching for pay. From the late 1960s on, slight declines in real male wages and increases in male unemployment prompted many more married women to seek paid employment. Rising divorce and separation rates also meant there were more women without access to male incomes.

Obviously, a variety of factors influenced married women's rising labour force participation. Those in areas where demand was high or wages decent, those with many years invested in formal education, those who had recently immigrated, those who were young, and those who were convinced that women should have paid employment were more likely to seek jobs in the market. But the two most important factors were household income and the presence of young children (Armstrong and Armstrong 1984, chapter 6). Children often kept women out of the labour force. The high cost and scarcity of day-care combined with women's low wages in the market and an ideology that stressed the benefits of full-time mothering put pressure on women to stay at home. On the other hand, low male incomes pushed women into the market. And as the 1960s progressed, more and more households found that men's incomes were no longer adequate for household economic needs. At first, the addition of mother's wages often allowed for some improvement in living standards. Between 1971 and 1981, however, the income of Canadian wives "was the significant factor in preventing family income from declining in real dollars". Family economic resources have continued to deteriorate, and by 1979–81, "increases in wives' income were no longer able to offset the decline in husbands' average income" (Pryor 1984, 102).

During the last decade or so, this growing economic need has also encouraged increasing numbers of women with small children to stay in the labour market, even though childcare services, the range of jobs open to women, and their wages have not improved significantly. Primarily as the result of women's demands, legislation has been adopted which requires employers to grant some maternity leave and which pays maternity benefits under employment insurance. Benefits remain low, however, and job security tenuous. With only limited maternity leave, few possibilities for future employment if they drop out for longer periods, and with growing economic needs, more and more women "make do" by leaving their preschool children with husbands, with other relatives, or with women caring for children in their private homes (Statistics Canada 1982; Status of Women in Canada 1986). This pattern, in turn, has meant that many other women with small children can still earn money at home by caring for the children of employed women.

THE CURRENT SITUATION

By the 1980s, then, major changes had taken place in the economy, in women's work and in families. Few men or women were able to provide directly for their own needs. The majority of both sexes were in the labour force and the proportion who worked for wages, rather than for themselves, increased from two-thirds to 90% between 1946 and 1981 (Riddell 1986, 9). At the end of the war, 60% of the labour force was employed in primary industries, construction and manufacturing; more than three-quarters of the employed were male. By 1981, 60% worked in trade, finance, insurance and real estate and other services. And two-fifths of them were women (Riddell 1986, Table 1–3). In 1941, less than 5% of married women were counted as part of the labour force; in 1981, more than 50% were (Armstrong and Armstrong 1984, Table 20). In the boom years of the early 60s, 65% of families were couples relying on one income and only 6% of families were headed by single parents. Just 20 years later, a mere 16% of families consisted of couples with one income earner, and the proportion of single-parent households had doubled (Status of Women Canada 1986, Figure 1.1). The transformation of domestic work made it both possible and necessary for married women to take on two jobs. Now, for the largest proportion of families, both mom and dad are in the labour force, young children often are looked after outside the home, more of the food comes from McDonald's and more of the dishes are washed by machine.

The massive and relatively permanent movement of married women into the formal economy has increased women's strength and choices in and out of the market. As economic need has encouraged women to stay in the labour force, they have become a less flexible and less docile labour supply, organizing for better working conditions, better access to jobs and more equal property rights. The number of female doctors, lawyers, dentists and managers has grown significantly. Some women have gained power within their households, and more women have been able to leave unbearable marriages. The burden of providing economic support is more obviously shared, as is the experience of working for a wage. Along with these changes have come new ideas about women's work in and out of the house, about women's place in families and in the labour force.

These dramatic changes have not, however, all served to improve women's conditions. Although many more are in the labour force, most are still segregated into women's jobs at women's wages. "In 1983, 77% of all female employees worked in just five occupational groups—clerical, service, sales, medicine and health, and teaching. This was only a three percentage point drop from what the proportion had been in 1975" (Statistics Canada 1985a, 43). This slight decline in concentration has not been matched by the movement of women into new and better jobs or into traditional male areas of work. Over the last 40 years, there has been an increase of only 1.4 percentage points in the proportion of women employed in professional and technical jobs, and most of these have gone into technical rather than professional work (Armstrong and Armstrong 1984, 41). Indeed, more men have moved into traditionally female teaching than women into traditionally male medicine, law, architecture and engineering combined. The small number of women who have entered traditionally male, blue-collar work now find their jobs in jeopardy as these sectors decline.

It is this segregation which accounts in large measure for women's continuing low wages (Ornstein 1983). "In 1982, the average earnings of women who were employed full-time were just 64% of those full-time male employees" (Statistics Canada 1985a, 46). The gap between male and female earnings was even greater in those occupations, such as sales and services, where jobs are growing for women (Statistics Canada 1985a, 62). In addition, such comparisons fail to take fringe benefits—which have been growing faster than wages—into account. Women's low rate of unionization (24.5% in 1982), their limited length of service, the small average size of their employers' enterprises, and exemptions in labour legislation all serve to deny many women fringe benefits. With benefits based on salaries, even those women who are eligible receive less than men. If fringe benefits are included, the wage difference between full-time employed women and men has been increasing (Dulude 1985, 5).

The gap is still greater if part-time employment is taken into account. Although more than half of all women were counted as part of the labour force in 1984, only 35% of them had a full-time job and full-time pay, while 63% of the men had full-time work. More than a quarter of employed women had part-time jobs, and they accounted for more than 70% of those working part-time. Such figures underestimate the numbers who work part of the year, who work under part-time conditions, or who have irregular employment. For most of this century, employers have used female workers as a means of intensifying labour, employing them to fill sudden rises in demand or to do labour which was so burdensome it could be done for only short periods of time. As many full-time female workers have become a less flexible reserve, employers increasingly have turned to part-time female workers to perform a similar function (Armstrong and Armstrong 1986).

Employers have been hiring increasing numbers of part-time workers primarily because they are cheaper—and getting even cheaper as new microelectronic technology makes payment, scheduling, supervision and training easier (Armstrong and Armstrong 1986). In the main, they are not following this strategy as a favour to women. And women increasingly are taking these part-time jobs because they have few alternatives. Between 1975 and 1983, "women who work part-time because they cannot find other work accounted for 51% of the growth in part-time work" (Statistics Canada 1985a, 45). Although many others indicate they accept part-time work because of family responsibilities, part-time work may take women away from their families on weekends and at night. Part-time employment also may be detrimental to future employment possibilities, locking women into particular areas of work rather than maintaining their skills and "keeping their hands in". It also may offer little challenge, reward or even contact with other workers. In addition, it may serve to discipline workers "on call" when they are not at their paid jobs, disrupting their family life.

Women's segregation, their part-time work and their low wages both reflect and reinforce their continuing responsibility for domestic work and childcare. The wages for the minority of women employed full-time constitute only 40% of household income in husband-and-wife families. The one-in-four married women who are employed part-time contribute less than a quarter of household budgets (Status of Women Canada 1986, Figures 1.3 and 13; Statistics Canada 1985a, Tables 10 and 11). These lower wages make women's jobs secondary in terms of family priorities. If anyone has to stay at home with the children, the elderly or the sick, or to give up a job to move, it will be the woman. Women's childbearing capacities also mean that their employment is interrupted for a short period of time in a society where household and formal economy are split. In the absence of good, inexpensive alternatives, it makes financial sense for women to stay home full- or part-time with young children or others needing care. Only a third of women with preschool children remained employed full-time and we have no figures on those who give up full-time work in order to look after granny or a sick husband. Moreover, the poor working conditions women face in the labour force encourage many of them to leave when they can (Armstrong and Armstrong 1983b).

These withdrawals then serve as a justification for limiting the employment opportunities of all women. The longer hours women work in the home, combined with their smaller direct contribution to family income, also serve as a justification for their domestic responsibilities. And this sexual division of labour is further reinforced by an ideology that defines these tasks as requiring skills unique to women.

Women's responsibility for caring and domestic tasks as well as their segregation into low-wage market jobs means that most women must continue to rely on men for support. Those unattached to employed males—whose numbers are growing with increasing divorces and separations, with women's greater longevity, and with high male unemployment rates—frequently face poverty. More than one in ten single women is unemployed, and many are ineligible for unemployment insurance. Those who do collect benefits often receive less than the minimum wage, not enough to live on decently. Low-wage earners also frequently live below the poverty line, and women constitute the majority of those paid minimum or part-time wages and of those without benefits or pensions. Without husbands, women with children are often poor. "One in 10 Canadian families is headed by a lone parent woman and 50% of these women are supporting their families on incomes that are below low-income cut-off lines." Without husbands, old women are also poor. "One in three Canadian women over 65 years of age lives alone, and 60% of those who live alone are supporting themselves on an income that is below the low-income cut-off lines" (Statistics Canada 1985b, 2). High male unemployment rates mean that even women with husbands—and especially those with young husbands—increasingly are experiencing periods of poverty. Moreover, the separation of household from formal economy has left most of the caring work to women at home. "For children, and for men, economic dependency is the cost of being cared for: for women, economic dependency is the cost of caring" (Graham 1983, 24–25).

The separation of home and work also masks the interpenetration of household and formal economy, the crucial links between what happens in the home and in the market. Working conditions structure not only choices and the division of labour but also relationships within the home. "What happens during the day on the job colors—if it doesn't actually dictate—what happens during the evening in the living room, perhaps later in the bedroom" (Rubin 1976, 164). When tensions or exhaustion build at work for women or men, they are often taken out in the home (Luxton 1980). And as one woman we interviewed for our as yet unpublished hospital study explained, "there is no sex when your husband's unemployed". As more and more women take and lose part-time jobs, two sets of frustrations are brought home, and women are often too tired to handle the tensions.

While more women face poverty, segregation and dependency, some women have acquired careers, independence and paid substitutes for household labour. The differences amongst women have increased, especially between those career women married to men with good jobs and those women without paid work or employed husbands. Our research also suggests that differences are increasing between younger and older women. Young women now have little choice about staying in or returning to labour market jobs. Their husbands' jobs are frequently insecure, while their combined and often interrupted incomes are in many cases too low to purchase housing that is now very expensive.

And the future offers little promise of relief. Continuing high rates of unemployment, short-term jobs and increasing long-term unemployment places pressures on women to take any job available in the formal or informal economy. These trends also create more labour in the household as women work to reduce family expenditures and family tensions. Increasingly, the state and employers are explicitly recognizing the dual-earner family and using this as a justification for limiting programs designed to maintain full male employment or to provide support during periods of unemployment. In the process, men are becoming more dependent on families (Armstrong and Armstrong 1986).

Continuing attempts to reduce the deficit by cutting state services also have multiple consequences for women. Employment in the state sector, where women have found some of their best jobs and opportunities for advancement, are being reduced. At the same time, large supplies of qualified workers are limiting women's strength. Many services which are no longer offered by the state must be performed by women at home, or by female volunteers located between market and home. The movement of large numbers of married women into the labour force means, however, that many women are unable or unwilling to assume these additional tasks. Furthermore, many state services have never been provided in the home and thus cannot be "sent back" there. Complicated medical procedures and advanced education, for instance, cannot be offered at home. Not only is the state trying to shift the burden from paid to unpaid female workers, it is also proposing to reduce expenditures in ways which will tie women more closely to the home or push them to take any labour force jobs. Because women are the majority of those who receive family allowances, use medical services, benefit from childcare and after-school programs, and receive welfare or pension cheques, cutbacks in these areas will particularly restrict women's situations.

At the same time, employers' efforts to further intensify labour through the introduction of microelectronic technology and more part-time or short-term work threaten to reduce the paid jobs available to women, and to transform those which remain by making many of them more fragmented and deskilled. In addition, this new technology also makes it possible to have many paid jobs performed by women working alone in their households. This strategy not only reduces cost but also reduces the possibilities for organized resistance as it further isolates women in the home (Armstrong 1984, chapter 7).

CONCLUSION: SHAPING THE FUTURE

Work and family life are socially constructed, shaped by the search for profit, by the contradictory effects of that search and by the active participation of women and men. Commodification has at one and the same time released women from many of their onerous domestic tasks and locked their caring and personal service work into the household. It has made it both possible and necessary for women to enter the labour force, but has also made it difficult for them to equally participate there. Their labour force participation has opened up new opportunities for many women, often creating a basis for more power and independence, while segregation and low wages reinforce their responsibility for household tasks and their dependency on men. While some women gain positions of power, more live in poverty. Similarly, the expansion of the state has relieved women of some work and provided many with support, protection or good jobs, although it has also served to denigrate women's knowledge and encourage their dependency on men and their responsibility for children. Intensification has often provided the basis for women's employment, because women frequently have constituted a cheap and flexible reserve of labour, but it has also transformed women's work, making it more fragmented and less skilled. It has provided the basis for the rapid expansion of part-time work for women. This part-time employment ensures women's responsibility for domestic work and their secondary position in the market. The search for profit has led both to the separation of household from formal economy and to their continuing interpenetration, albeit in altered form.

Women's work and family life have been and are being transformed. Women have made some significant gains and men have undergone some losses. As women remain longer in the labour force, their exhaustion and changing ideas have increasingly led to demands for more services from the market, for more control over fertility, and for more help at home. Their lives are becoming more similar. While women, like men, now face a lifetime in the labour force and can survive without a family, unlike men, women take on two jobs, have babies and more frequently experience poverty if they end up parenting alone. Historical analysis clearly demonstrates that if women and men are to share equally in family life, they must also share equally in work in and out of the labour force.

Bibliography

Armstrong, Pat.
1984   *Labour Pains. Women's Work in Crisis.* Toronto: The Women's
              Press.
Armstrong, Pat, and Hugh Armstrong.
1983a   "Beyond Sexless Class and Classless Sex: Towards Feminist
              Marxism". *Studies in Political Economy* 10 (Winter): 7–43.
1983b   *A Working Majority. What Women Must Do For Pay.* Ottawa:
              Supply and Services Canada for the Canadian Advisory
              Council on the Status of Women.

1984   *The Double Ghetto: Canadian Women and Their Segregated Work.* Toronto: McClelland and Stewart.

1986   "More for the Money: Redefining and Intensifying Work in Canada". (Paper presented to Conference on Work and Politics: The Feminization of the Labour Force). Center for European Studies. Harvard University.

Barron, Shari.

1984   "Is There a Man in the House?" *Perception* 9, no. 4 (March–April): 12–14.

Bernard, Jessie.

1973   *The Future of Marriage.* New York: Bantam.

Braverman, Harry.

1974   *Labor and Monopoly Capital: The Degradation of Work in the Twentieth Century.* New York: Monthly Review Press.

Burch, Thomas K.

1985   *Family History Survey: Preliminary Findings.* Ottawa: Supply and Services Canada (Cat. no. 99–955).

Canada, Advisory Committee on Reconstruction.

1944   *Post-War Problems of Women: Final Report of the Sub Committee.* Ottawa: King's Printer.

Connelly, Patricia M.

1978   *Last Hired, First Fired.* Toronto: Women's Press.

Conrad, Margaret.

1986   " 'Sundays Always Make Me Think of Home': Time and Place in Canadian Women's History". In Veronica Strong-Boag and Anita Clair Fellman, *Rethinking Canada: The Promise of Women's History,* 67–81. Toronto: Copp Clark Pitman.

Cook, Ramsay, and Wendy Mitchinson (eds.).

1976   "Employment for Women, 1876". In *The Proper Sphere,* 169–172. Toronto: Oxford University Press.

Cowan, Ruth Swartz.

1983   *More Work for Mother: The Ironies of Household Technology from the Open Hearth to the Microwave.* New York: Basic Books.

Denton, Margaret A., and Alfred Hunter.

1982   "Economic Sectors and Gender Discrimination in Canada: A Critique and Test of Bloch and Walker . . . and Some New Evidence". Women's Bureau Series A (Equality in the Workplace) No. 6. Ottawa: Labour Canada.

Dulude, Louise.

1985   "Fringe Benefits and the Female Workforce". In *Towards Equity. Proceedings of a Colloquium on the Economic Status of Women in the Labour Market,* edited by the Economic Council of Canada (November 1984) 71–78. Ottawa: Supply and Services Canada.

Ehrenreich, Barbara.
1984   *The Hearts of Men: American Dreams and the Flight From Commitment*. Garden City, New York: Anchor.

Fager, Ruth.
1983   "Women Workers and the Canadian Labour Movement, 1870–1940". In *Union Sisters: Women in the Labour Movement*, edited by Linda Briskin and Lynda Yanz, 44–64. Toronto: The Women's Press.

Finkel, Alvin.
1979   *Business and Social Reform in the Thirties*. Toronto: James Lorimer and Company.

Graham, Hilary.
1983   "Caring: A Labour of Love". In *A Labour of Love. Women, Work and Caring*, edited by Janet Finch and Dulcie Groves, 13–20. London: Routledge and Kegan Paul.

Harrison, Phyllis (ed.).
1979   *The Home Children*. Winnipeg: Watson & Dwyer.

Hayden, Dolores.
1981   *The Grand Domestic Revolution*. Cambridge, Mass.: MIT Press.

Heller, Anita Fochs.
1986   *Health and Home: Women as Health Guardians*. Ottawa: Advisory Council on Status of Women.

Johnson, Leo.
1974   "The Political Economy of Ontario Women in the Nineteenth Century". In *Women at Work Ontario 1850–1930*, edited by Janice Acton, Penny Goldsmith and Bonnie Shepard, 13–31. Toronto: The Women's Press.

Kealey, Linda (ed.).
1979   *A Not Unreasonable Claim: Women and Reform in Canada*. Toronto: The Women's Press.

Klein, Alice, and Wayne Roberts.
1974   "Besieged Innocence: The 'Problem' and Problems of Working Women—Toronto, 1896–1914". In *Women at Work. Ontario 1850–1930*, edited by Janice Acton, Penny Goldsmith and Bonnie Shepard, 211–259. Toronto: The Women's Press.

Kome, Penney.
1982   *Somebody Has To Do It*. Toronto: McClelland and Stewart.

Langton, H. H. (ed.).
1950   *A Gentlewoman in Upper Canada*. Toronto: Clarke, Irwin & Company.

Lasch, Christopher.
1977   *Haven in a Heartless World. The Family Besieged*. New York: Basic Books.

Laurie, Nate.
1986   "Tories have idealized 'greed' but it won't solve our problems". *The Toronto Star*, June 6.
Lowe, Graham.
1980   "Women, Work and the Office; The Feminization of Clerical Occupations in Canada, 1901–1931". *The Canadian Journal of Sociology* 5, no. 4 (Fall): 361–381.
Luxton, Meg.
1980   *More Than a Labour of Love: Three Generations of Women's Work in the Home*. Toronto: The Women's Press.
Marsh, Leonard.
1939   "The Mobility of Labour in Relation to Unemployment". Offprint of Papers and Proceedings of the Canadian Political Science Association.
1975   *Report on Social Security For Canada 1943*. Toronto: University of Toronto Press.
Matthaei, Julie A.
1982   *An Economic History of Women in America*. New York: Schocken.
McCallum, Margaret E.
1986   "Keeping Women in Their Place. The Minimum Wage in Canada, 1910–25". *Labour/Le Travail* 17 (Spring): 29–56.
Meltz, Noah M.
1969   *Manpower in Canada 1931 to 1961*. Ottawa: Queen's Printer (Cat. no. MP 34–368).
Milkman, Ruth.
1976   "Women's Work and Economic Crisis: Some Lessons of the Great Depression". *The Review of Radical Political Economics*. 8, no. 1 (Spring): 73–97.
Mitchell, Elizabeth B.
1981   *In Western Canada Before the War. Impressions of Early Twentieth Century Prairie Communities*. Saskatoon: Western Producer Prairie Books.
Noel, Jan.
1986   "New France: Les Femmes Favorisees". In *Rethinking Canada: The Promise of Women's History*, edited by Veronica Strong-Boag and Anita Clair Fellman, 23–44. Toronto: Copp Clark Pitman.
O'Connor, James.
1973   "Equality in the Workplace. Accounting For Gender Differentials in Job Income in Canada: Results of a 1981 Survey". Ottawa: Supply and Services Canada for the Women's Bureau, Labour Canada.
Ornstein, Michael D.
1983   Accounting for Gender Differentials in Job/Income in Can-

ada: Results from a 1981 Survey. Women's Bureau Series A (Equality in the Workplace), No. 2. Ottawa: Labour Canada.

Panitch, Leo.
1977   "The Role and Nature of the Canadian State". In *The Canadian State: Political Economy and Political Power*, edited by Leo Panitch, 3–27. Toronto: University of Toronto Press.

Phelps, Minnie.
1976   "Women as Wage Earners". In *The Proper Sphere*, edited by Ramsay Cook and Wendy Mitchinson, 182–186. Toronto: Oxford.

Pierson, Ruth Roach.
1986   *"They're Still Women After All". The Second World War and Canadian Womanhood*. Toronto: McClelland and Stewart.

Plamondon, Lilianne.
1986   "A Businesswoman in New France: Marie-Anne Barbel, The Widow Fornel". In *Rethinking Canada: The Promise of Women's History*, edited by Veronica Strong-Boag and Anita Clair Fellman 45–58. Toronto: Copp Clark Pitman.

Prentice, Alison.
1977   "The Feminization of Teaching". In *The Neglected Majority*, edited by Susan Mann Trofimenkoff and Alison Prentice, 49–65. Toronto: McClelland and Stewart.
1985   "Themes in the Early History of the Women Teachers' Association of Toronto". In *Women's Paid and Unpaid Work: Historical and Contemporary Perspectives*, edited by Paula Bourne, 97–121. Toronto: New Hogtown Press.

Pryor, Edward T.
1984   "Canadian Husband-Wife Families: Labour Force Participation and Income Trends 1971–1981". In *The Labour Force* (May 1984). Ottawa: Supply and Services Canada.

Ramkhalawansingh, Ceta.
1974   "Women During the Great War". In *Women at Work. Ontario 1850–1930*, edited by Janice Acton, Penny Goldsmith and Bonnie Shepard, 261–307. Toronto: The Women's Press.

Rasmussen, Linda, Lorna Rasmussen, Candace Savage, and Ann Wheeler.
         A Harvest Yet to Reap: A History of Prairie Women. Toronto: The Women's Press.

Reiger, Kerreen.
1985   *The Disenchantment of the Home. Modernizing the Australian Family 1850–1940*. Melbourne: Oxford University Press.

Riddell, Craig W.
1986   "Work and Pay: The Canadian Labour Market: An Overview". In *Work and Pay: The Canadian Labour Market*, edited by Craig Riddell, 1–75. Toronto: University of Toronto Press

in cooperation with the Royal Commission on the Economic Union and Development Prospects for Canada and the Canadian Government Publishing Centre.

Roberts, Wayne.
1976   *Honest Womanhood.* Toronto: New Hogtown Press.
Rubin, Lillian.
1976   *Worlds of Pain: Life in the Working-Class Family.* New York: Basic books.
Sangster, Joan
1986   "The 1907 Bell Telephone Strike: Organizing Women Workers". In *Rethinking Canada: The Promise of Women's History,* edited by Veronica Strong-Boag and Anita Clair Fellman, 137–156. Toronto: Copp Clark Pitman.
Statistics Canada.
1982   Results From the 1981 Survey of Child Care Arrangements. Labour Force Survey Research Paper No. 31. Ottawa: Supply and Services Canada.
1985a   *Women in Canada. A Statistical Report.* Ottawa: Supply and Services Canada.
1985b   *Infomat* (March 2).
Status of Women Canada.
1986   *Report of the Task Force on Child Care.* Ottawa: Supply and Services Canada.
Strasser, Susan.
1982   *Never Done.* New York: Pantheon.
Strong-Boag, Veronica.
1982   "Intruders in the Nursery: Childcare Professionals Reshape the Years One to Five, 1920–1940". In *Childhood and Family in Canadian History,* edited by Joy Parr, 160–178. Toronto: McClelland and Stewart.
Strong-Boag, Veronica, and Anita Clair Fellman (eds.).
1986   *Rethinking Canada: The Promise of Women's History.* Toronto: Copp Clark Pitman.
Sundberg, Sara Brooks.
1986   "Farm Women on the Canadian Prairie Frontier: The Helpmate Image". In Veronica Strong-Boag and Anita Clair Fellman, *Rethinking Canada: The Promise of Women's History,* 95–106. Toronto: Copp Clark Pitman.
Teeple, Gary
1972   "Land, Labour, and Capital in the Pre-Confederation Canada". In *Capitalism and the National Question in Canada,* edited by Gary Teeple, 43–66. Toronto: University of Toronto Press.
Thomas, Jean Scott.
[1889] 1976 "The Conditions of Female Labour in Ontario". In *The Proper*

Sphere, edited by Ramsay Cook and Wendy Mitchinson, 172–182. Toronto: Oxford University Press.

Traill, Catherine Paar.
1969   *The Canadian Settler's Guide*. Toronto: McClelland and Stewart.
Trofimenkoff, Susan Mann.
1986   "One Hundred and Two Muffled Voices: Canada's Industrial Women in the 1880s". In Veronica Strong-Boag and Anita Clair Fellman, *Rethinking Canada: The Promise of Women's History*, 82–94. Toronto: Copp Clark Pitman.

Ursel, Jane,
1986   "The State and the Maintenance of Patriarchy: A Case Study of Family, Labour and Welfare Legislation in Canada". In *Family, Economy and State*, edited by James Dickenson and Bob Russell, 150–191. Toronto: Garamond Press.

Van Kirk, Sylvia.
1980   "Many Tender Ties". *Women in Fur Trade Society, 1670–1870*. Winnipeg: Watson & Dwyer.

1986   "The Role of Native Women in the Fur Trade Society of Western Canada, 1670–1830". In *Rethinking Canada: The Promise of Women's History*, edited by Veronica Strong-Boag and Anita Clair Fellman, 59–66. Toronto: Copp Clark Pitman.

Vickery, Claire.
1979   "Women's Economic Contribution to the Family". In *The Subtle Revolution*, edited by Ralph E. Smith, 159–220. Washington: The Urban Institute.

White, Julie.
1980   *Women and Unions*. Ottawa: Supply and Services Canada for the Canadian Advisory Council on the Status of Women.

CHAPTER 7

Women's Roles, Reproduction and the New Reproductive Technologies: A New Stork Rising

Susan A. McDaniel

Reproduction and childbearing are hot topics for discussion among people in Canada in the late 1980s. The Canadian birth rate is at its lowest level in history. Politicians are expressing concern about women's changing roles and about possibly providing incentives to raise the birth rate. Women are faced with difficult choices about whether and when to become mothers. Abortion is a contentious issue across Canada. New reproductive technologies are available to deal with various types of infertility. In short, the increasingly complex issues of reproduction, reproductive control and reproductive rights have emerged from the privacy of bedrooms to be openly debated and discussed by Canadians at many levels in society.

Childbearing is at the same time very private and uniquely feminine and highly political and male-controlled. It is this tension between private and public, between female and male control that both blinds us to the social and political aspects of reproduction and can make women highly sensitive to the socio-political context of reproduction. These tensions, their consequences for Canadians and for women, as well as contemporary challenges to reproduction, are explored in this chapter.

"The rate of fertility has fallen so low in Canada that the replacement of present generations is no longer assured" (Statistics Canada 1984a, 7). There seems to be rather strong, although inconsistent, indications that this low rate of childbearing among Canadians is here to stay (Statistics Canada 1984a, 83; Grindstaff 1985). In a few decades, Canada has moved from baby boom to baby bust. Several factors explain the present low birth rate in Canada. These include the overriding desire for smaller families, a reduction in unwanted and unplanned births (although they still occur), a changed perception that children comprise only part of a satisfying and full life, increased labour force participation of married women, and the increased costs (both economic and social) of children. Perhaps most significant, however is that Canadians, like citizens of most other Western countries, have been experiencing a long-term decline in fertility begun in the mid-nineteenth century (McLaren and McLaren 1986, 11; Statistics Canada 1984a). Seen this way, the high birth rates of the post-war baby boom might be an aberration rather than the norm.

REPRODUCTION AS A SOCIO-POLITICAL PROCESS

Despite the fact that pregnancy and childbirth are biological events, reproduction is more of a social than a biological process. Reproduction involves the mating of two individuals (although this may become an archaic notion as a result of the new reproductive technologies) in a social context that includes families, social structure, political systems, and cultural beliefs. Although babies are biologically born of women, at least for the moment, everything else surrounding reproduction is social. The process of mate selection, whether based on choice or not, is highly social, as is the timing of childbearing, child spacing, family size and the meanings given to having children. Nowhere in the world do people reproduce to biological maximum. In every culture, society intervenes in one way or another, to control the biological potential to reproduce.

It is not at all difficult to understand and accept that reproduction is a largely social process, yet a prevalent cultural belief in our society is that reproduction is primarily biological. Many excellent articles and books have been written, including some by biologists, which reveal how and why this has come to be (a summary of some of this research is provided in Hubbard, Henifin and Fried 1982). Maintenance of the myth of women as biological suggests that it is not easily possible to change women's situations because they are after all, rooted in the flesh. The belief that reproduction and women are biologically determined enables us to see motherhood as women's natural role. Women, therefore, who are not mothers, or wives for that matter, are seen to be not fulfilling their biological destinies. The work associated with child-raising, often termed motherwork, tends to be redefined, not as unpaid labour, whether joyfully done or not, but as an extension of the natural biological process of reproduction. The cultural belief that reproduction is biological obscures the role of social and political structure in defining and controlling reproduction and women's roles.

The widespread belief that biology takes priority over social factors in reproduction has received considerable reinforcement from social science, particularly from functionalist sociology (Eichler 1984), but also from psychology, economics and political science. A natural, biologically based functional differentiation of roles within families has been assumed by many sociologists and psychologists. The explanation for women's and men's different opportunities and talents is then found in our biologically specialized roles. This assumption is particularly powerful, as well as insidious, because it is widely accepted by both men and women. It further has the potential of being self-fulfilling—if, for example, a woman believes herself to be limited by her reproductive capacity, then she will act within those limits, thereby curtailing her opportunities. Alternatively, if society expects less of us as women because of the belief that our biology limits us, society will provide less to us.

The generally accepted reason for the secondary social status held by women in Canadian society is our reproductive roles (McDaniel 1986b). The childbearing role of women, of course, is usually extended to include primary responsibility for child-raising and childcare. Reproduction often is seen as women's essential social role, compared to which all else we do comes second. This assumption is the rationale provided for why women earn less than men in Canada, why we are promoted less often, why we work in different occupations than men and why we see things differently. In short, the belief that biology is women's destiny is still very much alive and well in Canada in the late 1980s. The belief that motherhood should be at the core of women's lives has in fact robbed many women of full independent adult lives (Levine 1983, 29). Making motherhood the central job for women in society has elevated reproduction to a life's work for women. Women are so defined as natural mothers whose motherhood role transcends everything else we are or might become, that women who do not 'choose' to be mothers are often perceived as poorly adjusted misfits (Veevers 1980; Levine 1983).

The irony of all this, of course, is that the complex process of socially constructing the myth that reproduction is biological reveals, without question, that it is social. If reproduction were as biological as our cultural beliefs would have us believe, there would be less need for an elaborate social explanatory scheme, which has become an ideology, for justifying the biology of reproduction. We would simply act in accordance with our biological natures and search for questions to tease our intellects elsewhere.

Reproduction is also a political process, which may seem startling at first because we are so carefully taught to see reproduction as private and personal, an individual choice made by us (Lange 1976). From the above discussions of the policy and social issues involved in reproduction, it is clear that reproduction is emerging as a public social issue of growing importance. In Canada today, the reproductive issue of abortion is one of the hottest items on the public agenda. Reproductive issues being publicly debated in Canada now include policies to increase the birth rate, contraceptive availability, ads in the media for condoms to prevent AIDS, whether organizations that provide abortion referrals or contraceptives to minors should be given public funds, surrogate motherhood, the rights of the unborn compared to the rights of women, and who should be given priority of access to the new reproductive technologies. It could be argued that issues related to reproduction and reproductive control, far from being private, are among the most politically contentious of our times.

Women's reproduction serves social purposes, thus can be, and has been, harnessed to political agendas (McDaniel 1985a). Hitler, for example, recognized the centrality of reproduction as a cornerstone of his bizarre and misguided quest for a "super-race" (Corea 1985b, 272–274). Women of the sort deemed right by Hitler became reproductive prostitutes or breeders in his scheme of planned reproduction. "Himmler established the Lebensborn Registered Society on December 12, 1935 . . . where 'racially valuable' pregnant women could bear children and where those children could be cared for until they were adopted by German families" (Corea 1985b, 272). This program apparently involved kidnapping "racially valuable" female children in the occupied countries of Czechoslovakia, Hungary, Poland and Rumania for eventual use as breeders. Once they had been mated with equally "racially valuable" men, often Hitler's own SS troops, and borne several children, they were exterminated. Hitler defined reproduction as women's patriotic duty, "It must be considered reprehensible conduct to refrain from giving healthy children to the nation" (Hitler in *Mein Kampf*, cited by Steinem 1983, 311).

Black women under slavery were seen as the means by which slave-owners could capitalize on their investments (Burnham 1983; Corea 1985b, 272). Slave-owners determined the worth and value of their slave women not only by their work in the fields and the slave owner's home, but also by their reproductive capacity. Some early documents of slave buyers cited by Burnham (1983, 31), suggest that slaves were bred in ways similar to cattle, "with good husbandry". Unborn progeny of slaves were passed on in slave owners' wills to their children as part of their inherited wealth. Maternity prizes were offered to slave women who produced lots of children. One planter offered his slave woman freedom if she produced one slave child for each of his heirs (Burnham 1983, 32). Courts in the southern U.S. ruled that slave mothers had no legal rights to the children they bore because the children were on the same footing "as other farm animals" (Corea 1985b, 272). The bodies of slave women were traded for profit in a socio-political system that sold their reproductive work for profit. Subversion for the black women in this dehumanizing system consisted of abortion and contraception (Jones 1985).

Reproduction, in the conservative climate of the 1980s in Canada and in the United States, has emerged as a central political issue. The new right, in the guise of being pro-family (Eichler 1985; McDaniel 1985a), has developed a political agenda with reproduction at its core. There is even a new political party in western Canada, the Christian Heritage Party, which defines itself, and the sole reason for its existence, as defending the traditional family against invasions by those who wish to change it ("Party Opposes Gays, Abortion", *Globe and Mail* 1986). The essential political program of the new right is family strength tied to free enterprise, patriotism and tough treatment for anyone who is different or deviates. On the family front, the new right sees contemporary changes in the family as dangerous and threatening to the family as they understand it, to the social order and to patriarchy. Reproduction and the family are clearly stated by advocates of the new right as politically crucial to maintenance of social order.

Specifically, the new right expresses concern about the declining birth rate, what they see as the high rate of abortion, women's escalating demands for equality and fair treatment, public day-care and sex education in the schools. The new right also expresses disquietude about deviant lifestyles (which they see as including everyone outside the traditional family), high divorce rates and women generally undermining the male-dominated patriarchal family with complaints about child abuse, incest and wife battering (Eichler 1985). The solution is seen by the new right in what Eichler (1985, 27) aptly terms "the movement for the restoration of the patriarchal family". Families, according to the new right, should exist on only one model, that of the two-parent nuclear family with father as breadwinner and mother as homemaker, in which the father has complete authority over women and children. Women's function is to bear and raise children, without question or complaint about the circumstances under which this is to be done. Hence, women's renewed attention to their primary social roles as reproducers is expected, by the new right, to solve most of the social problems facing society today.

This political agenda of the new right is anti-women, in that it attributes women's lack of attention to their perceived responsibilities to men, hence to society and the social order, as the root cause of society's troubles. The strength of their anti-woman bias (or misogyny) becomes fully clear in their stand on abortion which will be discussed in the next section. Many analysts see the new right as, in part, a backlash against the gains made by feminism for women in society and in the family. The new right sets feminism up as a kind of "straw man", to use the colloquial phrase, as being comprised of man-hating and children-hating women who have no interest in motherhood or family, but who are in a quest to dominate men and fulfill their selfish ambitions. In truth, feminists value family and motherhood, but seek to change the patriarchal family into a more egalitarian family. Reproduction, argue feminists, should be a choice made by women or by couples, not forced on women as a duty. In this way, of course, reproduction and women's roles are political among feminists too. Reproduction and the issues surrounding it are highly political in the late 1980s in Canada and could perhaps become even more politically heated in future.

REPRODUCTIVE CONTROL IN SOCIO-POLITICAL CONTEXT

The quest for reproductive control for women, by women, has a long history in Canada (McLaren and McLaren 1986). It is, in fact, inseparable from any analysis of the social and political aspects of reproduction. McLaren and McLaren (1986), in their study of the history of contraception and abortion in Canada, reveal that issues of reproductive control always have been more closely linked to the broader issues of sexual, moral, social and political power than to family size *per se*. If reproduction is to be anything other than service to society or to patriarchy, then women must have some control over when and whether they wish to become pregnant. As in discussion of any social aspect of reproduction, the issues involved in reproductive control take many unexpected twists and turns as women and men vie for domination. In this instance, the battle for determination is over the issue of control— who manages reproduction for what purpose, under what circumstances. The answers are interesting and portend the issues involved in the new reproductive technologies, to be discussed next. Only a brief summary of some of the issues involved in reproductive control in a socio-political context can be provided here.

Given what has been said so far about the perception of women as reproducers, it is not surprising that the quest for reproductive control has been, in large measure, a quest for control over women's reproduction rather than over men's. Although it has long been recognized that men and women are both important in conceiving a child, it is around women's bodies that reproductive control has centered. Contraceptive devices go back to ancient history, although many people seem to have the impression that they came into being only with the vulcanization of rubber for condoms, or the development of hormone-based contraception in the past few decades. The notion that reproduction is a feminine process is equally ancient and no doubt accounts for the focus on women in reproductive control.

Many of the efforts made by male-dominated society to control women's reproduction, or as they might argue to enable women to control our own reproduction, have had bad consequences for women. Many people are now familiar with the risks to some women of long-term use of the birth-control pill, which was developed by male-oriented pharmaceutical companies and researchers for use by women. Similarly, intra-uterine devices (I.U.D.s) have been used for a long time to prevent pregnancy, although medical research still has not shown how exactly the devices work. It is suspected that the coils made of plastic or various metals irritate the lining of the uterus in such a way as to prevent implantation of a fertilized egg. I.U.D.s have been linked with infertility, scarring of the fallopian tubes, pelvic infection and even, in the case of the Dalkon shield, various cancers and death. I.U.D.s are no longer commonly prescribed in Canada, but still are used in many other parts of the world.

Although not related to fertility control, it is the same medical pharmaceutical industry that brings us birth control that brought us the thalidomide tragedy of the 1950s and early 1960s, and the diethylstilbestrol (DES) and Benedictin problems of today. All three drugs were given to pregnant women to prevent morning sickness or miscarriage. Thalidomide produced severely deformed babies, often born without arms or legs. DES has been discovered to be a cause of cancer among teenage and adult daughters, and possibly sons too, of women who took it while pregnant, ostensibly to prevent miscarriage. Interestingly, most controlled laboratory tests of DES done prior to its widespread prescription for pregnant women, showed it to be ineffective in preventing miscarriages ("DES", National Film Board film). Nonetheless, it was prescribed for this purpose for over a decade. Benedictin is alleged to cause mental retardation and physical co-ordination problems in babies whose mothers took the drug to prevent morning sickness while pregnant. Cases are still before the courts in Canada and in the U.S. Although pharmaceutical companies have never conceded that there are problems with Benedictin, it has been withdrawn from the market.

It is on the abortion debate, however, that the socio-political context of reproductive control emerges most clearly (Luker 1984). Abortion has become a central political issue of our time, with candidates in the 1984 federal election in Canada being asked to state their views (McDaniel 1985b). During this election as well, a national Catholic newspaper in Canada encouraged Catholics not to vote rather than to cast their vote for a pro-choice candidate. Similar escalations in political activity surrounding the abortion issue have occurred in the United States. There, a new political party, The Right to Life Party, was formed; it ran a slate of candidates in the 1980 and 1984 elections. Recently, several amendments have been proposed to the American constitution which, in varying ways and to varying degrees, would prevent abortion and give greater rights to an unborn fetus than to the woman carrying it (Pogrebin 1983, 185–186). One can imagine a situation in which, if these amendments passed, a pregnant woman could be tried for murder if she sought an abortion. Alternatively, a woman who smoked or drank or failed to eat properly during pregnancy might be tried on criminal charges of child abuse (McDaniel 1985a; Pogrebin 1983, 183). A pregnant woman with cancer might be denied treatment or be afraid of seeking treatment because she could be charged if her unborn fetus were harmed (Pogrebin 1983, 183). These images are alarming and may seem far-fetched until it is pointed out that one of these proposed amendments, the Hatch amendment, which would have given the American Congress and the States the power to restrict abortion, lost on a vote of 50–49 in the United States Senate on June 28, 1983 (Pogrebin 1983, 185).

The activities of anti-abortion groups effectively reduced women's access to abortion in Canada in the years prior to the landmark Supreme Court decision in early 1988, which struck down Canada's abortion law. Pressure was brought to bear on abortion committees and on local gynecologists to stop approving or doing abortions (McDaniel 1985b, 85–86). This resulted in a severe reduction in the number of Canadian hospitals with therapeutic abortion committees or with committees that actually meet (McDaniel 1985b, 86). Under the circumstances of the 1969 abortion law, fewer and fewer gynecologists were willing to risk what they see as public censure by performing abortions. Closures of free-standing abortion clinics, most notably in Toronto and Winnipeg, had been common. Since the abortion law was struck down, free-standing clinics have become legal and abortion decisions are made by a woman with her doctor. Both anti-abortion and pro-choice forces continue to be active in lobbying for a new abortion law.

The political campaign of the new right sees the anti-abortion issue as central. Curtailing women's access to abortion is defined by the new right in terms of protecting the rights of the unborn and the privacy and sanctity of the family (McDaniel 1985b). What this means, of course, is that women's rights are seen as coming second to the rights of fetuses and male-controlled families. Women's reproductive rights are not an issue of importance to the political agenda of the new right. Political control over women's reproduction means control by a society in which women's interests and rights are overlooked. It is the return to raw patriarchal control of women by men that is advocated by the new right.

HIGH TECH REPRODUCTION

In Margaret Atwood's *The Handmaid's Tale*, women have become reproductive robots in the repressive theocracy of Gilead as part of the attempt to quell social unrest, women's growing demands for equality, and to raise the declining birth rate. This vision is frightening in the spectre it calls forth—not because it is so far-fetched, but precisely because it may *not* be. In many ways, Gilead is a rather small extension of tendencies and realities well entrenched in Canadian society in the late 1980s, although little known and even less well understood by most Canadians.

Average Canadians, when they think of the new reproductive technologies such as surrogate motherhood, artificial insemination or *in vitro* (or test-tube) fertilization, tend to think of the happiness brought to childless couples who are able to have their own child. This happiness is real for some couples and offers the end of a long quest. The feelings of crisis and isolation experienced by the infertile can be addressed (Rowland 1987, 56). It seems like a miracle, a gift from science and technology, what earlier might have been called a gift from heaven. Few Canadians think beyond these happy images brought to us by the news media, about what the implications of the new reproductive technologies might be for society, for social relations between women and men, for our fundamental relations to ourselves as women and for our future (Rowland 1987).

Already in the late 1980s we can produce test-tube babies, babies conceived through artificial insemination or carried by surrogate mothers. These techniques are now being franchised in the United States under the venture capital scheme called "Baby U". We can buy Nobel laureate sperm or Mensa-ranked sperm from sperm banks, or bank that someone special's sperm for possible later use. We can transfer or freeze embryos and use sex selection techniques in either laboratory conception or selective abortion to guarantee that preferred sons are born. The stork, the cabbage patch and the woman are being left behind by these technological advances.

It was only in 1971 that Shulamith Firestone argued in a landmark book that women might be set free by reproductive technology. The thinking at that time was that women's reproductive roles, socially defined, tended to limit our opportunities in other realms, as discussed earlier. Firestone speculated that if reproduction could take place without women's direct involvement, then possibly equality could be attained. Now feminists have begun to revaluate reproduction and to attempt to recreate the experience of motherhood as non-exploitative (Rowland 1987, 512–513). The reproductive technologies have become real and available, but it is far from clear that these techniques will indeed be freeing for women. A growing number of feminists are expressing grave concerns about what they might mean for women's roles and rights in the future.

Exploring the complex implications of the new reproductive technologies is not an easy task. One could discuss each in the light of its associated intricate problems, whether these be social, political, medical or legal. One could discuss the emergence of these technologies in historical context, revealing that some of what is perceived as new may in fact be a high tech version of an old practice. Books, however, could be, have been, and will be written on these topics (Arditti *et al.* 1984; Corea 1985a; Corea 1985b). The task here is to summarize, highlight and synthesize some of the issues raised by the new reproductive technologies for women that affect women's roles in the family and society. To ease this daunting task, issues will be grouped into five categories, each posing a question: What are the new reproductive technologies and how new are they? Who benefits from and who controls these technologies? What are the political (or class) dimensions involved? Will motherhood change as a result? And, what does the future hold?

HOW NEW ARE THE "NEW" REPRODUCTIVE TECHNOLOGIES?

This question is a variation on the title of an often quoted article by Klein (in Corea *et al.* 1985, 64–73). It is a question that recurs in the growing feminist literature on the subject. The answer is important in that it reveals the construction of reproduction as a social, political and legal process. The answer also permits us to see the continuity between what has occurred in the past and what is likely to occur in the future. Seen this way, the new reproductive technologies are removed from their futuristic 'star galaxy' imagery and become comprehendible.

What is generally included in the 'new' reproductive technologies are sex selection techniques (both pre- and post-conception), various types of artificial insemination (by donor, known as AID, by husband, known as AIH, and combined semen from donors and husband, known as AIC), and the whole range of 'test-tube' techniques including *in vitro* fertilization, embryo replacement, transfer and 'flushing', and embryo freezing. Sometimes surrogate motherhood involving artificial insemination by the man who intends to become the legal father is included as well. All of these technologies are available and in use now, with varying degrees of accessibility and success. None are governed by law in any clear way in Canada. Looming on the horizon of the future are cloning, artificial placentas (or 'glass wombs'), genetic engineering and the somewhat silly, but perhaps symbolic, prospect of implanting and, presumably, gestating, a fertilized egg in the abdomen of a man.

These techniques have in common that they are medical practices which, to varying degrees, are invasive of the female body. All centre the control of reproduction somewhere other than with women. All involve the increasing involvement of doctors in reproduction; all subsequently redefine women who cannot reproduce as medically deficient in some way, even if the 'problem' is their husbands' and not their own. All, particularly taken together, tend to centre women's roles on reproduction, which we are now expected to go to great lengths and expense to fulfill. Perhaps most importantly, all tend to lead in the direction of removing childbearing from women. Technology has opened the possibility for women as child-bearers to become obsolete.

It is now *parts* of women's bodies that are used and controlled rather than the *whole* of women's bodies. Klein suggests that, women now are to be seen as uteruses, ovaries, eggs and embryos which can all be separated and reassembled so the parts work in unison (Klein in Corea *et al.* 1985a, 66). The medical profession's involvement in reproduction is also not new. Childbirth, for example, was taken out of the hands of the traditional experts, midwives and women themselves, and placed firmly under the control of obstetricians, usually male (Oakley 1980). Contraception, under the control of women for millenia, has now become a largely medical procedure, with distinctly mixed consequences, as most of us well know. The 'new' reproductive technologies clearly have much in common with some long established trends and practices. They are the latest on a continuum of change which separates women further and further from reproduction on their own terms.

Many of the seemingly new reproductive approaches date back rather a long way in history. For example, surrogate motherhood is found in the Book of Genesis of 4000 years ago when Rachel, Jacob's infertile wife, had her maid Hagar bear two children for them. Similarly, the long-standing system of adoption, both public and private, has served as a kind of surrogate motherhood by which poor and young women bear children for those who are better off and older (Brodribb 1984, 2; Ferguson 1984). The first recorded artificial insemination occurred in 1884 at Jefferson Medical College in Philadelphia, but this technique has been practised since the eighteenth century by humans (Brodribb 1984, 3). A patient of a Dr. Pancoast was discovered to be infertile because of her husband's lack of sperm. Without the woman's knowledge, the doctor injected sperm provided by one of his medical students into her uterus under anesthesia, while a group of male medical students watched. She gave birth to a son nine months later. Her husband was apparently informed and was happy about it. The woman herself was never told (Corea 1985b, 12; Achilles 1986, 6).

What is new about the new reproductive technologies is that they open up possibilities for fuller and more complete exploitation of women. Reproduction as high technology divorces women from that experience in terms of both power and joy: medical scientists then assume control of fundamental decisions about who should reproduce and who should not (Achilles 1988; Currie 1986). While the media has responded positively to the novelty and allure of the new reproductive technologies wherever these are introduced, it has overlooked some of the dark concerns and issues raised, not only for women, but for us all as a society.

WHO CONTROLS AND BENEFITS FROM THE NEW REPRODUCTIVE TECHNOLOGIES?

The new reproductive technologies are brought to us by the same medical researchers who brought us the old reproductive technologies such as the birth control pill, DES and the Dalkon shield (McDaniel 1985a). This alone is cause for concern, since our experience shows that the best interests of women are not always part of the motivation to develop reproductive control technologies. Unfortunately, the complex issues of who has control and who benefits from the new reproductive technologies extend far beyond the conflicts between the interests of scientists and those of women. These issues include scientific ethics, male control and dominance, the pre-eminence of women's biological roles over their social roles, and fathers' rights.

As seen earlier in this chapter, reproduction is a process deeply embedded in the socio-political structure. Any attempts to change it or control it must be discussed with reference to the wider context in which reproduction takes place. Science, too, takes place in a socio-political context, despite its image as objective and unbiased. Scientists, indeed, the place given to scientific pursuit itself, are products of society, social beliefs and political priorities, as well as biases and vested interests. Numerous critiques have been produced of science and the ways in which it tends to validate existing myths about women, minorities, and theories that are popular with the dominant group at any given time (Messing 1983; Johnson 1984; Keller 1982, among many others).

Examples of the ways in which women have been overlooked and victimized by science are numerous. One striking example is the publication of an article in *Psychology Today* by David Barash in which he argues that the double standard of sexual behaviour among humans is biological, based on his observations of birds (Messing 1983, 84). This theme was picked up by *Playboy* magazine under the title, "Do Men Need to Cheat on Their Women? A New Science Says Yes". Another example from a different science is the lack of decent representative studies of wife battering and incest in Canada, compared to the large amount of research focused on delinquent boys and crimes involving property (Eichler 1984, 37). Clearly, the practice of science is not above the distortion of reality to fit existing beliefs.

Scientists also are part of society. The process of recruiting scientists, including the expense involved, tends to exclude people without money, without fairly traditional families, and those who do not think in ways similar to practising scientists. In this way, the scientific community tends toward homogeneity: white, male, and middle class. To people who resemble each other in these ways and reinforce each other's views on what is important to study, such issues as wife battering, incest, the social causes of the double standard, or how to provide safe abortion or contraception to women, may not be important. Funding agencies, often under indirect pressure from the very lucrative pharmaceutical industry, tend to reinforce scientists' definitions of what is important to study. Sometimes biases show up explicitly in science, as in the example cited earlier about the sexual double standard. Other times, the influence of prevailing beliefs is more subtle but no less clearly present.

Given the context in which science is done and in which scientists practise, it must be acknowledged that the new reproductive technologies did not emerge in a vacuum. Their development reflects the interests and needs of science and scientists as part of the wider society. That wider society as well as science itself, is patriarchal. Our experience as women with the old reproductive technologies of birth control and access to safe abortion alerts us clearly to some of the problems involved in social control over women's reproduction. The new reproductive technologies enable an extension of that control of women's reproduction into unprecedented arenas, despite the media hype about the opportunities it may provide infertile women to have babies of their own (Rowland 1984).

Who, in fact, does benefit from the new reproductive technologies? Given their high tech medical orientation, researchers who develop the techniques and those who perform them benefit in terms of their careers. Doctors Steptoe and Edwards of England, who developed the technique of *in vitro* fertilization which in 1978 produced Louise Brown, the first "test tube" baby, became known in almost every household. They are still frequently sought for interviews by the media about the implications of the new reproductive technologies. Their names, along with those of Doctors Bernard and Jarvik, have gone down in the annals of medical history, no mean accomplishment in the fiercely competitive world of medical research.

Doctors who do *in vitro* fertilization at hospital clinics also tend to have the high status that accompanies those on the frontiers of new medical techniques. The fairly esoteric knowledge required by these techniques distances the medical expert from the patient. This gives these doctors power over their patients, who of course are women. Determining which circumstances present acceptable risks, what is appropriate drug usage, and who are appropriate subjects for these techniques, are crucial decisions made by doctors for women.

More significant and perhaps more terrifying for women than the vested interests of doctors in the new reproductive technologies are the interests of society generally. The new reproductive technologies have not been tested with primates (Williams 1986b), thus, it could be argued that women who use them, often at *their* own expense, are being reduced to "living laboratories, to 'test-tube women'" (Klein 1985, 65). In the case of *in vitro* fertilization, the process is often painful, extremely expensive, and time consuming. The failure rate of *in vitro* fertilization is about 80% (Achilles 1988, 13), a figure not publicized sufficiently. This experimentation on women, often upper class or middle-class women because of the prohibitive expense involved, is reminiscent of the experiences of poor women in Puerto Rico during the early human trials of the birth control pill. Images of happy couples leaving hospitals with healthy babies fades quickly when one is reminded of the potential physical and psychological damage to countless women that results from fertility drugs and the repeated use of highly invasive surgical techniques.

A particular concern among feminist critics of the new reproductive technologies is the degree to which they are male controlled and enable an increase in male dominance (Rowland 1987, 517–518). Feminist research has shown the many ways in which medical control of women's bodies, and particularly of reproduction and sexuality, has occurred and has been an important factor in women's oppression (Ehrenreich and English 1978 provide a good summary of this research). Male dominance, of course, is closely related to medical control since medicine remains a largely male profession, with women even rarer in medical research and the high prestige specialities such as reproductive technology. Frye has suggested that "the progress of patriarchy *is* the progress toward male control of reproduction, starting with possession of wives and continuing through the invention of obstetrics and the technology of extrauterine gestation. Giving up that control would be giving up patriarchy" (1983, 102).

Male control over childbirth is now almost complete, the overwhelming majority of babies being born in hospital with a male obstetrician in attendance, or, if that obstetrician is female, she was taught her skills in accordance with the male model of obstetrical practice (Oakley 1986). The new reproductive technologies now enable control by medicine and by males of the beginning of reproduction, conception. This concerns feminists a great deal when they consider the implications for women of the widespread use of the new reproductive technologies (Brodribb 1984; Overall 1986; Williams 1986a). Female-centered technologies are controlled almost entirely by males. The issue of male dominance over female reproduction becomes particularly important when it is considered that discussions of the legal aspects of the new reproductive technologies are premised on the same tenets of male dominance which have always governed reproduction (Brodribb 1984; Ontario Law Reform Commission 1985; Williams 1986a).

Male control of the development of the new reproductive technologies has created a new language and approach to child-bearing and conception. What used to be called begetting, siring, procreation, or even genesis of new life has now taken on the terminology of the factory—reproduction as similar to production (Achilles 1985, 10). The profoundly mysterious and wonderous process of conception, which many philosophers have argued to be women's greatest source of creativity and the source of envy on the part of men in many parts of the world, has now been turned into a medical technological riddle solvable by male-dominated science, or what Rowland (1987, 527) refers to as "technopatriarchs".

That women's reproductive consciousness is altered as a result of male determination of reproduction is rarely taken into account by male medical researchers. For example, a woman submitting to artificial insemination by donor in a medical clinic must relinquish her right to choose, or even know, who the biological father of her child is. This certainly marks a profound shift in reproductive relations between women and men. Similarly, a woman using *in vitro* fertilization admits that infertility is a medical problem which she hopes the medical profession can resolve. New reproduction techniques are seen as 'cures' for infertility, thus rendering infertility a new status as a medical disorder. All infertile women can be stigmatized by this new label, perhaps as much if not more than with the old label of the barren woman. Royal barren women were sometimes beheaded for their incapacities. One can easily imagine a situation, not far removed from Atwood's Gilead, in which modern infertile women cannot easily choose to remain childless when technology exists to help them 'cure' their deviance.

Access to the new reproductive technologies is controlled by men as well—male doctors, hospital and clinic committees and, perhaps most important in the long run, legislators. Williams' (1986a, 1986b, 1986c) research on the admittance criteria of the Ontario *in vitro* fertilization clinics reveals this clearly. For example, doctors, in deciding what medical conditions must exist for women patients to be deemed appropriate for their technologies, allow into the treatment program only patients who have been referred by other doctors. In addition, only patients with certain prespecified medical conditions (women with any fertility problems but malfunctioning fallopian tubes were barred initially from the *in vitro* programs, and women whose husbands have no sperm count are still excluded), and importantly, only women under the age of 37 to 40, depending on the hospital (Williams 1986b) are allowed to enter treatment. Significantly, social criteria are also included in the admittance criteria. For example, only married or stable cohabiting couples are eligible, requiring assessments to be made by doctors or other professionals of how stable any relationship is. In some clinics, couples are screened to find out how many children they have, priority being given to couples with no naturally born children. Adopted children, apparently, do not count, which suggests the primacy given to biological parenthood over social parenthood by the clinics, a point to be discussed in more detail in a moment.

Recommendations of the 1985 Ontario Law Reform Commission on the control of the new reproductive technologies reinforces male and medical dominance. The OLRC, for example, emphasizes the importance of regarding all forms of artificial insemination as medical procedures to be controlled and administered by doctors (OLRC 1985, 175). No means of grievance or appeal should be open to women who are denied 'treatment' by the new reproductive technology clinics, according to the OLRC recommendations (OLRC 1985, 275). Artificial insemination and other technological 'treatments' are to be confined to married women or to heterosexual women *with* partners. This bars access to single women, both heterosexual and lesbian, who are deemed by the Commission as less suitable for parenthood.

Behind the new reproductive technologies lurks the belief that biological parenthood takes precedence over social parenthood. Basic to the talk of gamete banks in the OLRC report and to the processes by which technology lets us have *our own* children, is an emphasis on the importance of genetic links between parents and children. Women become the means by which male genes are given life, as evidenced by both the medical practices surrounding the new reproductive technologies and the emerging legal recommendations. Emphasis is not placed on the joy of childcare which could be done by childless couples and childless women and men through adoption, fostering, informal care of relatives' and friend's children, or even shared parenthood, but rather on *biological* reproduction. Infertility, which many experts suggest is on the rise due to environmental pollution, workplace hazards, diet and lifestyle (Achilles 1985, 11), now is seen as a medically curable biological deficiency. This means that infertile women come to see their infertility as a source of anguish, a life crisis or even an illness. Previously, this might have occurred too, but the solution was found in social contact with children rather than in a quest for a biological role, compared to which all else paled.

The opening of possibilities for genetic engineering, for 'harvesting' only perfect babies out of the many that could be conceived in petri dishes, the selection of only 'correct' sperm or ova, or women as breeders, looms large on the immediate horizon. Clearly, priority is being given now and likely will be given even more in the future, to biology and genetics, while people in unacceptable categories such as the handicapped, the single, the poor, the gay or lesbian, or even ethnic minorities, may be denied the opportunity to reproduce by these expensive and inaccessible 'brave new world' techniques. The prospects are nightmarish indeed.

The issue of fathers' rights in the new reproductive technologies appears again and again. For example, in Williams' study (1986b) of the admittance criteria for the Ontario *in vitro* clinics, she discovered women are seen as eligible for 'treatment' by IVF even if they are healthy *and* fertile! Women are treated with an invasive, painful, traumatic and possibly dangerous procedure, *and* it is seen as medically good practice, when the infertility problem is not theirs but their husbands' (Williams 1986b, 9). Corea (1985b, 121) suggests that "the biggest population (for external fertilization) are going to be men with low sperm counts". Williams further found that women whose partners had no sperm count are declared ineligible for IVF in Ontario, despite the presence of any medical conditions the patients themselves might have.

Questions of male consent underlie the discussion of both artificial insemination and surrogate motherhood. For example, the OLRC recommends that husbands'/partners' consent be obtained for artificial insemination procedures for fear that these could be seen as adultery. Fears run high that women might be able to use the new reproductive technology to procreate without males or to engage in sexual relationships not under male control. For example, the Dean of the University of Manitoba Law school has remarked,

> if artificial insemination becomes common, it may cause wives to deceive their husbands. A childless wife, after obtaining her husband's consent to resort to artificial insemination, would be able to carry on with impunity sexual intercourse with her lover, secure in the knowledge that she could attribute any pregnancy which might result to artificial insemination (quoted in Brodribb 1984, 19).

With surrogate motherhood, it is generally husbands who contract with the surrogate, not wives. One way to interpret this is that the husband has two wives, similar to Jacob in Genesis or to the system of concubines, where one 'wife' reproduces, the other is for social purposes. Fathers' rights take precedence over the rights of mothers. The term surrogate, like the term 'artificial' when used in relation to reproduction, is in fact a father-oriented image, based on male consciousness of reproduction and birth. Any woman who gives birth to a baby is its mother, no matter how it is conceived. The male bias in the new reproductive technologies becomes eminently clear.

Women's roles as reproducers also are affected by the patriarchially controlled reproductive technologies. Some of the class and political issues involved will be discussed in the next section. Here, the issues involve a redefinition of woman as breeder, first and foremost. Some of the new reproductive technologies have been derived from stock breeding. With emphasis on patriarchal control of women's reproduction by means of technology, women become breeders too, the receptacles by which men reproduce themselves and their power. This, of course, is not new, as we have seen earlier in this chapter, but the degree of control over women's reproduction by male science and power for men's purposes has increased. It may be, as Mary O'Brien argues, that men are "alienated from their seed" and therefore seek other means by which to repossess it (O'Brien 1981).

Another important aspect of women's roles as reproducers which is affected by male domination of the new reproductive technologies is the increased commodification of women as reproducers, and the commodification of children. Women's reproduction has always had market value in some way. In some societies in Africa, women's reproductive potential must be tried before her marriage market value can be assessed. We have noted the value placed on slave children. In our own society, rich men often buy fertility by marrying young fertile women. In addition, the new reproductive technologies mean that fertile women can sell their reproductive capacity. The typical fee for surrogate mothers in Canada is around $10,000. Similarly, women might be able to sell ova, or even uteruses, fallopian tubes or ovaries for transplants in the future. Frozen embryos may come to have a market value, as light-skinned babies in Latin America have come to have for those willing to pay high prices to adopt them in the U.S., Canada and Israel.

POLITICAL AND CLASS DIMENSIONS OF REPRODUCTIVE TECHNOLOGY

The political and class implications of the new reproductive technologies are truly frightening in their scope. Although the potential exists for women to become united in their concerns about the new reproductive technologies, the likelihood is that existing divisions among women will be exacerbated. These divisions are worth exploring in some detail, as their implications for society and for the future of feminism may be profound.

The first and most obvious division among women is between those women with children and the childless, a distinction made more vivid by the advent of the new reproductive technologies. Childlessness of the involuntary sort may become seen as a failing or an imperfection about which one should do something, as in a weight-loss diet, smoking cessation program or plastic surgery for baggy cheeks. Childlessness which is voluntary might become as unimaginable in the new world of reproductive technology as it is in Atwood's Gilead. Among childless women or infertile women who have children, adopted or natural but not as many as they want, there are further divisions possible. One can easily imagine a schism between women who are acceptable for the interventions of the new reproductive technologies and those who are not. Women who are eager to have children of their own, whatever the reasons, but are denied access to the technology because of their marital status, age, sexual preference, or the fact that their mates lack sperm, might resent women who easily gain access. A black market in the more portable reproductive technologies could easily develop. The interests of women who use the reproductive technologies, whether successfully or not, may be at variance with the interests of women who choose not to use them. Women who stand to benefit from the technologies may be less willing to criticize the way they are controlled than women who are not involved with them or are denied access. Already, the demand for access to the new technologies is so high among women that the media and legislators tend to see only the benefits, and perhaps view the criticisms offered with some skepticism.

The prohibitive costs involved in obtaining access to the new technologies, in combination with the screening process through which candidates must go, tends to create further divisions among women. Poor women who cannot afford access to the new reproductive technologies, the expense involved in foreign adoptions, or who may be deemed unworthy of an adopted child by the Canadian adoption system, may become reconciled to life without children, no matter how strong or real their desires for children. Meanwhile, poor women might observe other poor women facing sanctions, either formal or informal, against childbearing. As we have seen, motherhood is very much a class issue, with sympathies going to rich childless couples and negative sanctions going to the poor with many children (Pogrebin 1983, 175–191). A boost might be given to a two-tiered system of child-bearing where the rich get every encouragement in their quest for children, while the poor are not only denied access to reproductive technologies, but are discouraged from having children generally by welfare systems and social attitudes.

The advent of surrogate motherhood and the sympathetic views of it being expressed by Canadian politicians as well as philosophers (see Brodribb 1984, 10–15), suggests that it could soon be institutionalized and governed by law, rather than simply by precedent as it is now. This could mean the emergence of a class of breeders among poor women who are paid to bear children for the rich, or what Corea calls a "caste of childbearers" (Corea 1985b, 272). The issues of moral concern that have been raised about surrogate motherhood focus less on the class dimension than on the morality of accepting money for childbirth. For example, Dr. Roy of the Centre for Bioethics at the Clinical Research Institute of Montreal finds that "the profit-making aspect of surrogate motherhood can render it immoral, and he calls for regulatory legislation with sanctions against women who accept anything more than expenses associated with the pregnancy" (quoted in Brodribb 1984, 15). Not only will we have two distinct classes of women, but the richer class could have legislated sanction to exploit the lower class, without any compensation going to the poor!

Seen in another way, the case could be made that surrogate motherhood is an extension of prostitution, in the sense that a woman's body is rented for a specific purpose with no ties beyond that purpose. Reproduction, like sexuality, becomes a commodity women can offer on the open market. While the issues involved in both prostitution and surrogate motherhood are far from simple, it is clear that poorer women are more vulnerable to exploitation once a service, sexual or reproductive, becomes commodified. In both cases, rich men hold the power to bargain and to control the contractual arrangements made. In the case of surrogate motherhood, unlike prostitution generally, the wives of richer men might also be involved in the exploitation of poor women for their benefit. The political issues raised by this is reminiscent of those issues discussed earlier as part of the political dimensions of reproduction.

In yet another view, surrogate motherhood could be seen as an institutionalization of the long-standing practice that has been the poor and young bearing children for the rich. Essentially, this is the system of adoption we have had in Canada for a hundred years. Poor women more often face unwanted pregnancy due to lack of access to contraception and abortion and lack of opportunity in other realms to find meaning in their lives. These children were, until rather recently, often given up for adoption, and generally adopted by 'proper' middle-class or upper-middle-class families whose lifestyle fit the definition of 'good for children' set out by the Children's Aid Societies. Interestingly, the CAS criteria for suitable candidates for adoption are very similar to the admittance criteria for IVF clinics (Ferguson 1984). Social pressures are immensely strong for only those in the right categories to become parents. It may not be without significance that the new reproductive technologies emerged at just the time when fewer babies are available for adoption, not because of the abortion rate as many people argue, but because fewer women are willing to relinquish their children for adoption at birth. Surrogate motherhood could be seen as an extension of the adoption system which commodifies children as Cabbage Patch dolls and compels poor women to use their reproduction as part of a system of commodity production.

With the emphasis being placed on quality of babies, on screening of potential clients for artificial insemination and for IVF, it may not be too far-fetched to imagine a situation where 'higher quality' sperm, or ova, can be bought by those able to afford 'the best'. Given the cultural view, androcentric and patriarchal as it is, that intelligence comes largely from sperm rather than ova, one can imagine a sperm bank of the future in which vials are marked with IQs, and the costs increase as the IQs increase. If this seems like science fiction, it should be noted that in California in 1982 the first baby was born from a sperm bank set up for Nobel Prize winners in 1980. The bank was called "The Repository for Germinal Choice" ("Sperm Bank Has First Birth", *Kitchener-Waterloo Record*, May 25, 1982, p. 29). This story took an unexpected turn when it was discovered that the mother of the first Nobel Sperm Bank baby, previously reported to be of high intelligence, was in fact an ex-convict who had lost custody of two children after her husband was accused of child abuse ("Sperm Bank Mom Ex-Con, Spouse Cited in Child Abuse", *Kitchener-Waterloo Record*, July 18, 1982, p. 47).

A variation of the theme of quality sperm banks might be a ranking system for aspiring surrogate mothers in which those with higher intelligence, better family backgrounds, better looks and very likely white skin, are given higher priority as surrogates than other women. Issues of surrogate motherhood as economic opportunity aside, this tendency could result in an increase in the birth rate among certain types of people, and a decrease among others. It could resemble Hitler's plan for a master race, discussed earlier (Corea 1985b, 272–273). It is not much of a jump in projecting the future to envision a situation where poor women with the socially defined 'right' attributes might be coerced economically into becoming virtual reproduction machines for another class.

A very contentious political and social issue emanating from the new reproductive technologies is the issue of who are the parents of the new infants born as a result of technology. It is possible to have genetic mothers, birth mothers and social mothers, all separate. For example, one woman would supply the ova which when fertilized would be implanted in the uterus of a second woman for gestation. A third woman who contracted for the baby then would become the mother. Similar complexities, of course, exist for fathers. Given the serious social and legal issues being raised now about adopted children's right to know about their birth parents, one can imagine the social and legal wrangles possible on this one. On the negative side, women could become splintered into speciality groups—gene givers, breeders, and mothers—each representing a particular class and political position. There is, however, a positive side here, albeit paradoxical. An aspect of the new reproductive technology involves the quest for biological parenthood, a child of one's own. Yet, the real world possibilities inherent in the new reproductive technologies may force the realization, as in adoption, that social parenting is much more important than biological parenting both to the child and the parents.

A final political issue involved with the use of the new reproductive technologies which deserves attention here relates to the use of sex selection techniques. Many ways are being explored and perfected for selecting or detecting the sex of a fetus. Among these are separation of X chromosome from Y chromosome prior to conception, diet control, and timing (the latter two, once thought to be 'old wives' tales', are now written about in the prestigious *New England Journal of Medicine*), selective abortion after amniocentesis, and implanting only one sex fetuses after IVF, to name only a few of the many possibilities (Holmes and Hoskins in Corea *et al.* 1985a, 15–20). The motivation is strong to possess the power to predetermine the sex of one's child. It seems to be a growing part of the process of birth planning, but there is a more insidious aspect. Several prominent people, among them the newspaper editor Clare Booth Luce, have argued that preferential births of boys will lower the birth rate ultimately, since it is females who give birth (cited by Holmes and Hoskins, in Corea 1985a, 21).

Most people, all across the world, prefer sons to daughters as first-borns. After that, daughters may be welcomed as helpers, caretakers or as potential wives for the better off. Sometimes the preference for first-born sons is so strong that females are subject to infanticide. We also know from many studies that first borns of whatever sex have distinct advantages. In Third World countries, they may have access to more and better food. In countries like Canada, they may be given more parental attention. Further, and this is important for women's future achievements, girls from single-child families or all-girl families tend to be higher achievers than girls from other family types. Sex selection techniques and the strong preference for sons may mean that girls will be born far less often than boys, and when born will be born second to the preferred first-born male. Cultural views about women can literally become manifest at birth. Sex selection techniques enable women never to be born at all except as needed to continue reproducing the species. These prospects are all the more frightening because they are so real and so close to the present.

HOW WILL MOTHERHOOD CHANGE?

As we have seen, the new reproductive technologies have broad implications for women, for families and for society. Motherhood, that seemingly unassailable image often enshrined with apple pie, is changing in many ways. Only some of these changes, not so far discussed, can be considered here.

The new reproductive technologies, particularly when considered in addition to the problems associated with the old reproductive technologies, tend to make reproduction and motherhood increasingly public. Standards of motherhood increasingly tend to be agreed upon as new reproductive technologies become accepted. These social standards increasingly define and constrain definitions of proper parenting to the traditional, middle-class norm of parenting.

Associated with the establishment of clear standards of good parenthood is a homogenization of motherhood images. All mothers may be expected to have a decent income before they consider motherhood, or to have no genetic problems, or to be married legally, or not to be lesbians. Whatever the standards become, they are shoving aside women whose lives do not fit the rules but who, in fact, might be wonderful mothers. This is similar to Barrett and McIntosh's (1982) comment that over-emphasis on the nuclear family, as the only place where loving intimacy can occur, diminishes the possibilities of strong loving relationships occurring elsewhere, because energy devoted to the nuclear family sucks the life out of all other possibilities. In the case of motherhood, seeing only some non-deviant women as legitimate candidates for motherhood may have the same consequences. The diversity of mothers and mother-child relationships so important in our society today could dwindle.

Motherhood, with the new reproductive technologies, takes on a mandate. It becomes *the* reason for women's existence, as women submit to years-long quests for a baby of their own. Doctors, legislators and society generally may interpret this quest (and have already) as a reproductive urge built into women's biologies. Women without it in the future may appear, by contrast, to be even stranger than they appear today. As well, women's quest for motherhood may usurp their quest for opportunity in the work place, thereby feeding nicely into the agenda of the new right which sees women's place at home first and foremost. Somewhat paradoxically, the renewed positive attitude toward motherhood, fostered by feminism in the 1980s, may inadvertently give a boost to the technopatriarchs' experimentation (Rowland 1987, 527).

Mothers may be drawn more completely into the service of patriarchy by the new reproductive technologies, although some of course will be able to have their wishes for maternity answered. We have seen, to some extent, how this works in the earlier discussion of class and political dimensions of the new reproductive technologies. As women seek motherhood on terms decided by men for the benefit of men, motherhood becomes more specifically serving rather than liberating or freeing. When the implications of sex selection are considered, it becomes ever more clear that women may become vessels for patriarchal maintenance and regeneration. Motherhood as an expression of womanhood or as a feminist act is no longer easily possible, and when possible, takes on a distinct air of subversiveness.

The new reproductive technologies are being marketed to women as a means to increase our choices about childbearing. The irony here is that our choices may actually decrease as more women are pressured into seeing themselves primarily as mothers. The choice of voluntary childlessness, for rich women, is already difficult to make, given the strength of social pressure on women to reproduce (Veevers 1980). With the new reproductive technologies, families, mates, the media and society may encourage women even more to fulfill themselves as mothers by 'choosing' reproductive technology.

BABY M: A CASE STUDY

The Baby M case which was tried in a New Jersey courtroom in the spring of 1987 and widely publicized, raises a number of points relevant to the present discussion. A surrogate mother, Mary Beth Whitehead, and the biological father, William Stern, were locked into what was called a custody case over their child, called Sarah by Mrs. Whitehead, and Melissa by Mr. Stern. The outcome of the case may have been preordained when the court decided to call the child Baby M, rather than Baby S, or even the neutral Baby X. The decision to view this as a custody case between the biological father and biological mother rather than a dispute over an adoption or parentage, or a contract breach, is telling. Primacy is given by the courts to biological, rather than social or legal, parenthood.

It was assumed throughout the trial and in media reports that Mr. Stern had rights with respect not only to Baby M, but to Mrs. Whitehead. For example, Stern demanded that Whitehead undergo amniocentesis over her doctor's objections. He maintained the right to demand an abortion if the fetus was imperfect. If the baby turned out to be unacceptable to him at birth, he was not required to pay the agreed fee of $10,000 or to assume custody (Landsberg 1987, A2). All the risks rested with Whitehead, yet Whitehead was the child's undisputed biological mother. The father's rights took precedence, even in the initial definition of the situation.

In other ways, too, the rights of Mr. Stern took on considerable weight in comparison to those of Mrs. Whitehead and even of Mrs. Stern, who faded into the background of the trial. Stern's right to enter into a contract, under the conditions outlined above, was never questioned. Indeed, neither his adequacy as a father nor the competence of either of the Sterns to raise a child was ever questioned. It was simply assumed that they would be good parents, possibly because of their high socio-economic status. The competency of Mrs. Whitehead to mother was questioned throughout the trial, however. Even her mental stability was questioned as she struggled to keep her child, while Mr. Stern cooly recorded her emotional reactions to his threats to take her child that he made by telephone. Her choice to dye her prematurely white hair black was seen by the court as pathological narcissism (Landsberg 1987, A2). Throughout the trial the man's right to procreate was emphasized to the neglect of the rights of either of the two women involved in the case. In several instances, Mary Beth Whitehead was referred to as a surrogate uterus. Her attempts at underlining the importance of the mother-child bond were dismissed by the court as irrelevant. In any ordinary custody case, this could not be done so readily, nor would a mother be so completely and permanently denied access, even visiting rights, to her child.

The gap in socio-economic status between the Whiteheads and the Sterns provided a backdrop to the entire proceedings. The Sterns are solid, high-earning professionals, while the Whiteheads had financial and social problems. Given that Mrs. Whitehead had contracted to be a surrogate mother for the money she could earn, this is not entirely unexpected. To those who believe that surrogate mothers should not be given any compensation for their efforts, one might respond that perhaps upper-class women would be more appropriate surrogates on behalf of the poor. They would be in a far better situation to donate their services. In the case of Baby M, there can be little doubt that William Stern bought a baby of his own because he could afford it. Mrs. Stern was fertile but had not tried to conceive out of concern for her health. The Sterns had never approached an adoption agency despite the surplus of abandoned babies in New Jersey. Clearly, a man's right to reproduce himself genetically took priority over all else.

WHAT MIGHT THE FUTURE HOLD?

It is always difficult to predict the future of society or social phenomena. Demographers, those who specialize in population trends, have a notoriously bad reputation for predicting what will happen to the birth rate (Statistics Canada 1984a). Predicting future developments related to the new reproductive technologies is even more difficult because of the involvement of medical, legal, ethical, social, economic and political factors. Nonetheless, some tendencies present today provide hints of what the future might hold.

Given the infatuation in North American society with technology and the desire to push back the frontiers of nature so that it can be controlled (both distinctively masculine orientations), it can be predicted with some certainty that fooling with reproductive technology and ever greater interventions in women's bodies is not likely to stop, barring a social revolution or a massive change in orientation. The potential profits to be reaped through development and marketing of these new technologies contributes further to the incentive to pursue them. With cloning, development of glass wombs, possibly reproductive brothels or baby factories, men's control over and usurping of women's reproduction will likely become more complete.

Women's control over their bodies may become an even larger political issue than it is today. As feminists' attention shifts from reproductive control to reproductive rights, one can imagine the rallying cry of women shifting from women's rights to access to abortion or contraception, to women's right to bear children on their own terms. Women's reproductive consciousness may become as discontinuous as O'Brien (1981) describes men's as being historically.

On the bright side, the new reproductive technologies, if controlled by women for the benefit of women, do have the potential of making women's range of reproductive choices wider. One could imagine an underworld of women who pre-select female babies and encourage feminist, lesbian and deviant women to have children and to raise them with love and caring. Ultimately, this would make a wonderful natural experiment to see whether social environment or genes prevail in children's adult lives, achievements and happiness. When the evidence is in, it will likely show that a wanted child, growing up in a loving environment, does better than all the gene-spliced and Nobel sperm-banked babies produced by technological 'advances'. At that juncture, all this technological reproduction may be canned as we return to old fashioned coupling, motherhood and non-scientific childrearing.

Bibliography

Achilles, Rona.
1985   "New Age Procreation". *Healthsharing* 6(4): 10–14.
1986   "The Social Meanings of Biological Ties: A Study of Participants in Artificial Insemination by Donor". Unpublished Ph.D. thesis, University of Toronto.
1988   "Artificial Reproduction: Hope Chest or Pandora's Box?" In *Changing Patterns: Women in Canada*, edited by S. Burt, L. Dorney, and L. Code. Toronto: McClelland & Stewart. *Forthcoming.*
Arditti, Rita, Renate Duelli Klein, and Shelley Minden (Eds.).
1984   *Test-Tube Women: What Future Motherhood?* London: Pandora Press.
Atwood, Margaret.
1985   *The Handmaid's Tale.* Toronto: McClelland and Stewart.
Barrett, Michele, and Mary McIntosh.
1982   *The Anti-Social Family.* London: Verso Editions/NLB.

Beaujot, Roderic.
1986   "Dwindling Families: Making the Case for Policies to Sustain the Birth Rate in Canada". *Policy Options* September: 7(7) 3–7.
Brodribb, Somer.
1984   "Reproductive Technologies, Masculine Dominance and the Canadian State". *Occasional Papers in Social Policy Analysis* No. 4. Toronto: OISE.
Burnham, Dorothy.
1983   "Black Women as Producers and Reproducers for Profit". In *Woman's Nature: Rationalizations of Inequality*, edited by Marian Lowe and Ruth Hubbard, 29–38. New York: Pergamon.
Canadian Journal of Women and the Law.
1986   Special issue on Women and Reproduction: 1(2).

Cassidy research done at Wilfrid Laurier University. Cited by John Asling, "Childless Couples Back the Wrong Riches". *Kitchener-Waterloo Record* July 5, 1986, p. B2.
Collins, Larry D.
1982   "The Politics of Abortion: Trends in Canadian Fertility Policy". *Atlantis: A Women's Studies Journal* 7(2): 1–20.
Corea, Gena (Ed.).
1985a   *Man-Made Women: How New Reproductive Technologies Affect Women*. London: Hutchinson.
1985b   *The Mother Machine: Reproductive Technologies from Artificial Insemination to Artificial Wombs*. Toronto: Fitzhenry and Whiteside.
Currie, Dawn.
1986   "Thinking About Motherhood: How much 'Choice' Have Technologies Given Women?" Paper presented at Canadian Research Institute for the Advancement of Women Conference, Moncton, N.B., Nov.
Denton, Frank T., Christine M. Feaver, and Byron G. Spencer.
1980   *The Future Population and Labour Force of Canada: Projections to the Year 2051*. (A study prepared for the Economic Council of Canada. Ottawa: Minister of Supply and Services.
DeSeve, Micheline.
1985   "Prospects for Feminist Research: Towards a New Paradigm?" *Feminist Perspectives* No. 3.
Dickinson, James, and Bob Russell (Eds.).
1986   *Family, Economy and State: The Social Reproduction Process Under Capitalism*. Toronto: Garamond.

Ehrenreich, Barbara, and Deirdre English.
1978   *For Her Own Good.* Garden City, New York: Anchor.

Eichler, Margrit.
1984   "Sexism in Research and its Policy Implications". In *Taking Sex into Account: The Policy Consequences of Sexist Research,* edited by Jill Vickers, 17–39. Ottawa: Carleton University Press.
1985   "The Pro-Family Movement: Are They For or Against Families?" *Feminist Perspectives* No. 4a.

Ferguson, Evelyn E.
1984   "The Real Cabbage Patch Kids: An Examination of the Canadian Private Adoption System". *Occasional Papers in Social Policy Analysis* No. 2. Toronto: OISE.

Firestone, Shulamith.
1971   *The Dialectic of Sex: The Case for Feminist Revolution.* London: Jonathan Cape.

Frye, Marilyn.
1983   *The Politics of Reality: Essays in Feminist Theory.* Trumansberg, New York: Crossing Press.

Glenn, N.D., and S. McLanahan.
1982   "Children and Marital Happiness: A Further Specification of the Relationship". *Journal of Marriage and the Family* 44: 63–72.

The Globe and Mail, Toronto. Sept. 23, 1986, p. A14.

Grindstaff, Carl.
1984   "The Consequences for Women of Early Childbearing—an Analysis of Statistics Canada Data". Colloquium given at the University of Waterloo, October 11.
1985   "The Baby Bust Revisited: Canada's Continuing Pattern of Low Fertility". *Canadian Studies in Population* 12(1): 103–10.

Johnson, Judith.
1984   "Feminism and Science: Dissecting the Bias". *Broadside* 6(1): 8–9, 14.

Hanmer, Jalna.
1983   "Reproductive Technology: The Future for Women?" In *Machine Ex Dea: Feminist Perspectives on Technology,* edited by Joan Rothschild, 183–197. New York: Pergamon Press.

Harris-Adler, Rosa.
1987   "Who Pays for Pregnancy?" *The Globe and Mail Report on Business Magazine* (March): 60–63. Toronto.

Healthsharing: A Canadian Women's Health Quarterly
        (Fall 1985): 6(4).

Holmes, Helen B., and Betty B. Hoskins.
1985 "Prenatal and Preconception Sex Choice Technologies: a Path to Femicide?" In *Man-Made Women: How New Reproductive Technologies Affect Women*, Gena Corea *et al.* (Eds.), 15–29. London: Hutchinson.

Hubbard, Ruth, Mary Sue Henifin, and Barbara Fried (Eds.).
1982 *Biological Woman—The Convenient Myth*. Cambridge, Mass.: Schenkman.

Johnson, Judith.
"Feminism and Science: Dissecting the Bias". *Broadside* 6(1): 8–9, 14.

Jones, Jacqueline.
1985 *Labor of Love, Labor of Sorrow: Black Women, Work and the Family from Slavery to the Present*. New York: Basic Books.

Keller, Evelyn Fox.
1982 "Feminism and Science". *Signs* 7(3): 589–602.

Kitchener-Waterloo Record.
May 18, 1982, p. 47; May 25, 1982, p. 29.

Klein, Renate Duelli.
1985 "What's 'New' about the 'New' Reproductive Technologies?". In *Man-Made Women: How New Reproductive Technologies Affect Women*, Gena Corea *et al.* (Eds.), 64–73. London: Hutchinson.

Knoppers, Bartha Maria.
1985 "Women and the Reproductive Technologies". In *Family Law in Canada: New Directions*, edited by Elizabeth Sloss, 211–225. Ottawa: Canadian Advisory Council on the Status of Women.

Lahey, Kathleen A.
1985–86 "The Criminal 'Justice' System and Reproductive Technology". *Resources for Feminist Research* 13(4): 27–30 (Dec./Jan.).

Landsberg, Michelle.
"Baby M Judge was Needlessly Harsh with Mother". Toronto: *The Globe and Mail*, April 9, 1987, p. A7.

Lange, Linda.
1976 "Reproduction in Democratic Theory". In *Contemporary Issues in Political Philosophy*, edited by William Shea and John King-Farlow, 131–146. New York: Science History Publications.

Levine, Helen.
1983 "The Power Politics of Motherhood". In *Perspectives on Women in the 80's*, edited by Joan Turner and Lois Emery, 28–40. Winnipeg: University of Manitoba.

Luker, Kristen.
1984 *Abortion and the Politics of Motherhood*. Berkeley, Calif.: University of California Press.

Maroney, Heather Jon.
1985   "Embracing Motherhood: New Feminist Theory". *Canadian Journal of Political and Social Theory* 9(2): 40–64.
McDaniel, Susan.
1984a   "Explaining Canadian Fertility: Some Remaining Challenges". *Canadian Studies in Population* 11(1): 1–16.
1984b   "Family Size Expectations among Selected Edmonton, Alberta Women: A Comparison of Three Explanatory Frameworks". *Canadian Review of Sociology and Anthropology* 21(1): 75–91.
1985a   "Abortion, Reproductive Technology and Women's Roles as the Barter of the New Right". Paper presented at the Ontario Association of Sociology and Anthropology, Waterloo, Ontario.
1985b   "Abortion Policy Implementation in Canada as a Women's Issue". *Atlantis: A Women's Studies Journal* 10(2): 74–91.
1986a   *Canada's Aging Population.* Toronto: Butterworths.
1986b   "Women's Roles and Reproduction: The Changing Picture in Canada in the 1980's". *Atlantis* (forthcoming).
1986c   "An Alternative to the Canadian Family in Crisis Model". Paper presented at the Family in Crisis Conference, Symposium of the Federation of Canadian Demographers and the Royal Society, University of Ottawa, November.
McLaren, Angus, and Arlene Tigar McLaren.
1986   *The Bedroom and the State: The Changing Practices and Politics of Contraception and Abortion in Canada, 1880–1980.* Toronto: McClelland and Stewart.
Messing, Karen.
1983   "The Scientific Mystique: Can a White Lab Coat Guarantee Purity in the Search for Knowledge about Women?" In *Woman's Nature: Rationalizations of Inequality,* edited by Marion Lowe and Ruth Hubbard, 75–88. New York: Pergamon.
Oakley, Ann.
1980   *Women Confined: Towards a Sociology of Childbirth.* London: Martin-Robertson.
O'Brien, Mary.
1979   "The Politics of Reproduction". *Resources for Feminist Research* special No. 5: 27–37.
1981   *The Politics of Reproduction.* Boston: Routledge and Kegan Paul.
Ontario Law Reform Commission.
1985   *Report on Artificial Reproduction and Related Matters.* Toronto: Ministry of the Attorney General.

Overall, Christine.
1986   "Sexuality, Parenting and Reproductive Choices". Paper presented at the Canadian Association of Sociology and Anthropology meetings, Winnipeg, June.

Pogrebin, Letty Cottin.
1983   *Family Politics: Love and Power on an Intimate Frontier.* New York: McGraw-Hill.

Rowland, R.
1984   "Social Implications of Reproductive Technology". *International Review of Natural Family Planning* 8(3): 189–205.

————   "Technology and Motherhood: Reproductive Choice Reconsidered". *Signs: Journal of Women in Culture and Society* 12(3): 512–528.

Singer, Peter, and Diane Wells (Eds.).
1984   *The Reproductive Revolution: New Ways of Making Babies.* Melbourne: Oxford University Press.

Singh, B.K., and J.S. Williams.
1981   "Childlessness and Family Satisfaction". *Research on Aging* 3: 218–227.

Smart, Carol.
1984   *The Ties that Bind: Law, Marriage and the Reproduction of Patriarchal Relations.* London: Routledge & Kegan Paul.

Smith, Dorothy E.
1973   "Women, the Family and Corporate Capitalism". In *Women in Canada*, edited by Marylee Stephenson, 2–35. Don Mills: General Publishing.

Statistics Canada.
1984a   *Current Demographic Analysis, Fertility in Canada: From Baby Boom to Baby Bust.* Written by A. Romaniuc. Catalogue No. 91524E Occasional. Ottawa: Minister of Supply and Services.

1984b   *Current Demographic Analysis, Report on the Demographic Situation in Canada in 1983.* Prepared by Jean Dumas. Catalogue No. 91–209E Annual. Ottawa: Minister of Supply and Services.

Steinem, Gloria
1983   *Outrageous Acts and Everyday Rebellions.* New York: Holt, Winston and Rinehart.

Tait, Janice.
1985   "Ethical Issues in Reproductive Technology: A Feminist Perspective". *Canadian Woman Studies* 6(2): 40–45.

Veevers, Jean E.
1980   *Childless by Choice.* Toronto: Butterworths.

Westoff, Charles.
1983   "Fertility Decline in the West: Causes and Prospects".
          Population and Development Review 9(1): 99–104.
Williams, Linda S.
1986a   "But What Will They Mean for Women? Feminist Concerns
          about the New Reproductive Technologies". *Feminist
          Perspectives* No. 6. Canadian Research Institute for the
          Advancement of Women.
1986b   "Who Qualifies for In-Vitro Fertilization? A Sociological
          Examination of the Stated Admittance Criteria of Three
          Ontario IVF Programs". Paper presented at the Canadian
          Sociology and Anthropology Association meetings, Winni-
          peg, June.
1986c   "Wanting Children Badly: The Social Construction of Par-
          enthood Motivation in Women Seeking In Vitro Fertiliza-
          tion". Paper presented at the Second International Congress
          on Women's Health Issues, Halifax, Nova Scotia, Nov.

CHAPTER 8

Preserving Patriarchy: Women, The Family and The State

Norene Pupo

It is possible not to be interested in what the state does; but it is not possible to be unaffected by it (Miliband 1973, 3).

In recent years federal and provincial legislators have been forced to declare their views on a number of issues raised by women's groups. Diverse issues, such as employment equity, homemakers' pensions, daycare, sexual harassment, domestic violence, and family law reform have been raised at every political level. All political parties have been publicly questioned on their platforms and individual local election campaigns have pivoted around family life questions. While matters of family, women, and social welfare historically have been presented as secondary to free trade talks, economic summits, banking and high finance issues, even labour disputes, it is through the politics surrounding home and family life that Canadians may glimpse the contradictions that plague state politics within a liberal democracy.

Despite the sometimes trivialized treatment of family issues in news coverage, state decisions regarding private life are profound. Policy changes in marital property arrangements, for example, not only potentially alter the family's lifestyle, but more fundamentally, may affect underlying power arrangements between men and women. The state operates on both public and private levels, but the boundaries between these levels are indistinct. Underlying family policy questions is the relationship between family, home, and the economy. Whatever their political opinions, women should examine the impact of that relationship on their lives. The state should be seen as a 'feminist issue'.

It is often difficult to accept the family as a political issue. Traditionally, public and private worlds have been viewed separately. Home and family usually conjure images of free emotional expression, privacy, and protection from the impersonal world of politics and bureaucratic rule. Such images are, however, ideological constructs. In reality, the private home stands in a complex, entangled, and historical relationship to the public sphere. This relationship between the state and family life is a dynamic one that evolved as the family form adapted to meet the changing needs of capitalism, and as the state grew to accommodate advanced capitalism and its inherent contradictions. Rather than viewing the home as a private sphere and discussing the state's meddling in that sphere, it is essential to examine the family in the context of the state's development and functions. Perhaps then, the often quoted notion that "the personal is political" may be more sharply focused.

This chapter examines the state's role in family policy. Over the past few years, Canadian women have experienced limited victories, such as the enactment of pay equity legislation, along with setbacks, such as the decision to prosecute doctors procuring abortion, and inaction on, for example, the pension issue. Given this inconsistency in addressing women's issues, the state is often perceived as a 'neutral' body which does not cater to the needs of any particular group. By focusing on historical and current actions of the welfare state, the question of whether the state plays an implicit or explicit role in maintaining the traditional patriarchal family structure will be explored. In particular, recent policy initiatives in childcare and family law will be examined.

THE FAMILY AND THE STATE: THEORETICAL CONCERNS

There is considerable disagreement among scholars with respect to the role of the state. The question of the state's role is complicated by a number of perceived inconsistencies—the state's responsiveness on some issues, inaction on others, and women's struggles for more or less state involvement. Among the most popular interpretations of the state's role are the liberal democratic and Marxist positions.

A prominent and popular view—the position of liberal democrats—sees the state as an arbitrator. This view regards the state as a neutral force in which consequences of action (or inaction) are carefully evaluated, and decisions are based on research, logic, precedent, and historical example. This position assumes that state actions are directed toward the achievement of social progress and the attainment of the 'social good'. Liberal democrats suggest that decision-making may be influenced by pressure groups, organized lobbies, and charismatic leaders. The ability to influence policy seems to be contingent upon a group's political resources, level of organization, persistence, quality of information, and its allegiance to broad social goals. In casting the state as an arbitrator, liberal ideology promotes the view that the state is independent and fair.

According to this position, any group may garner its political resources and acumen, present a persuasive case, and thereby tip the balance of social change.

Implicit in the liberal democratic position are the notions that all interest groups may potentially affect state policy, that all have equal opportunity to represent their interests before state authorities, and that in this task all are confronted with obstacles but may rely on a number of political resources (such as organizing skills, effective group leadership, access to power, and finances) to gain recognition. The fact that one group may represent dominant class interests is not necessarily regarded as significant. Rather, the state is seen to operate for the 'social good'—an undefined and somewhat vague purpose.

Viewed from this perspective, state actions are scored as victories for some, losses for others. Movement on the employment equity issue may be seen as a victory for an organization such as the National Action Committee on the Status of Women, whereas indecision with regard to homemakers' pensions would be considered that group's loss. This apparent inconsistency is regarded as a confirmation of the state's impartiality. This position, however, assumes that politicians and state authorities act voluntarily and that their decisions are based on their own assessments of lobbyists' presentations, election promises and party platforms, personal commitments to issues, and a sense of social justice.

In contrast to this liberal democratic position, Marxist scholars first analyze the state in terms of its nature and role under capitalism, and then discuss specific state policies and decisions with regard to its general functions. Writers within this tradition generally emphasize the state's function as representative of capitalist class interests; that is, the state functions to preserve the privileges and power of the dominant class. There is disagreement, however, over the course of state actions in that task. A key point of discussion centres around the relationship between the state and the capitalist class. One interpretation, the 'instrumentalist' view, maintains that the state serves the capitalist "ruling" class or its most powerful component by acting directly or indirectly on its instructions (Cuneo 1979, 148). The instrumentalists focus their attention on the institutional positions, examine the personnel residing in the "command posts" of the political and economic orders, and trace the close interpersonal connections between economic and political spheres (Miliband 1973). This approach, which may have been derived from a cursory reading of Marx, views the state as operating under the direction of the capitalist class, rather than as acting for the benefit of that class (Panitch 1977, 3–4).

Departing from this 'instrumentalist' approach and recognizing the existence of competing groups within the capitalist class, the 'structuralists' are not as interested as the instrumentalists in the personnel within the dominant class. They begin their analysis by examining the way in which the state operates within the constraints of capitalism (Panitch 1977; O'Connor 1973; Poulantzas 1973; Piven and Cloward 1971; Cuneo 1979; Walters 1982). These writers have identified two basic functions of the state: (1) accumulation and, (2) legitimation/social control.

The most important structural constraint acting upon the state is the fact of the private ownership of the means of production. The state aids the process of profitable capital accumulation, and thereby benefits the capitalist class, because the state is dependent upon the prosperity of this class for its own survival—its own revenues are derived through taxation from the economy's surplus production capacity. The state promotes profit-making by maintaining an opportune economic climate, by underwriting risks and assuming costs of production, and by providing education, health, and welfare services to maintain the labour force. Simply put, the state cannot risk drying up the sources of its own revenue so it draws from the "public purse" to provide support services and to maintain an economic environment attractive to private profit-makers (O'Connor 1973).

The picture, however, is further complicated. In order to facilitate capital accumulation, the state must maintain harmonious social conditions. It must be seen by the average citizen to be neutral in order to adopt and administer policies, such as social welfare, which foster or restore social harmony, and it may legitimately employ force to impose or maintain social order (Panitch 1977). In contrast to the instrumentalists, the structuralists do not regard the state simply as an agent for the capitalist class. Structuralists recognize that the capitalist class as well as the working class is internally differentiated, and that capitalist and working-class interests are fundamentally conflictual. Structuralists maintain that the state enjoys "relative autonomy" from the capitalist class. This allows them to explain how the state may sometimes meet working-class demands and disagree with members of the capitalist class (Cuneo 1979, 148). Without a degree of autonomy the state would be unable to serve the long-term interests of the whole capitalist class. Rather, it would likely serve only those particular interests with greatest influence over state authorities. With relative autonomy state policies may deny fractional or short-term interests in order to ensure capital's long-term interests.

The state, of necessity, seeks to promote capital accumulation; through its agencies and the enactment of social welfare legislation, it preserves the notion of the system's neutrality and legitimation. These roles, however, are often in contradiction. For example, the history of the Canadian state's actions in the development of social welfare and health policy reveals a complex and often contradictory process (Moscovitch and Albert 1987; Dickinson and Russell 1986; Struthers 1983; Walters 1982;

Swartz 1977; Finkel 1977). In the short run, state policies may appeal to act for disenfranchised groups, but in the long run, legislation is designed to maintain existing class relations and aid profit-making (Walters 1982, 429). Concessions to working-class demands depend on the socio-economic climate. The contradictions and constraints under which the state operates may become evident by asking why particular policies are introduced, and by examining the historical and economic conditions in which legislation is introduced, defeated, or reformulated.

The role of the Canadian state in preserving the traditional family structure may be seen by examining the growth of social welfare legislation.[1] Historically, women have had fewer financial and political resources than men. The impoverishment and powerlessness of women has facilitated a paternal connection to the state. Social welfare and family protection legislation was designed to support women and children and to preserve the concept of the household as a distinctive unit within the broader community structure. Such legislation, however, resulted in persistent inequalities of power and resources.

Women's relationship to the state may be characterized in a variety of ways. During the social reform phase of the nineteenth century, social welfare legislation was enacted primarily to preserve the family tie and the moral structure. By 'saving' children and protecting women, patriarchal authority and a puritanical spirit were maintained. With the emergence of modern social welfare, family allowances, survivors' pensions, and other 'income' legislation, the administration of the legislation became a central issue and women were treated as traditional clients or recipients of the services of a 'benevolent' state.

Women have played a major role in shaping state relations as recipients, clients, protagonists, and lobbyists. Women have struggled against the state's function of social regulation by voicing the need for less state interference and more independence of action. Women have objected, for example, to the intrusiveness and implications of welfare workers' interview questions regarding cohabitation and sexual relations.[2] Yet, in other instances women have encouraged state involvement as mediator in their fight for protection, service and justice within family relations. Women rely on the state, for example, to intervene in violent home situations and to sponsor childcare and nursing care in order to avoid privatized, profit-making ventures. Recently, the Ontario government established a Support and Custody Enforcement Programme. This computerized system of collecting and paying court ordered or separation agreement support payments is expected to improve the dismal 15% rate of compliance with support orders (*The Globe and Mail* July 2, 1987, A1–2).

While it is necessary to document the state's resistance to feminist demands and its actions in maintaining the traditional patriarchal structure, it is also essential to recognize that women have welcomed the expansion of the welfare state. This may be a result of three interrelated factors: (1) women's powerlessness in both the economy and the family; (2) women's likelihood of requiring state services; and (3) the growing tradition of activism among various types of caseworkers and social work professionals[3] (Piven 1984; Andrew 1984). This does not mean that women have simply taken refuge in the state. Rather, the state may be a "recourse" for women (Piven 1984, 15).

Not only has the existence of the welfare state occasioned challenge to the dominant ideology and structures, but it has provided opportunity for women to gain political resources and influence within legislatures, and has created an infrastructure for potentially facilitating "cross-class alliances" among various groups of women who have different reasons for preserving it (Piven 1984, 18). Indeed, the welfare state may prove to be one of the greatest contradictions of capitalism. Perhaps within women's cultural and historical tradition, the welfare state may be representative of empowerment, struggle, resistance, and change much like the trade union within the working-class male cultural and historical tradition. While it would be inaccurate to over-emphasize the possibility of empowerment and change through welfare state politics, especially in light of the nature and role of the state under capitalism, it is important to highlight women's resistance and participation in the struggle for equity and justice.

WOMEN, FAMILY AND STATE: THE HISTORICAL CONTEXT

The search for a social panacea became increasingly popular around the turn of the century when North Americans[4] faced growing crime rates, massive immigration, unemployment, labour strife, and other problems related to industrialization and urban growth. Between 1880 and 1920, Canada's urban population grew from 25% to 50% of the total population (Kealey 1979, 4). The development of the factory system and the proliferation of technical innovation profoundly affected the cultural and ideological milieux of those who were subjected to important changes in the production process. These changes affected day-to-day reality as more workers were drawn into the factory system's 'innovative' organization of the work process and market system. Not only were people learning to cope with new living arrangements and family forms in the transition from rural to urban living, but they were compelled to work under a new set of codes and practices in the movement from independent farming and skilled craftsmanship to co-operation on the production line. It was during this progressive reform period, 1880–

1920, that the ideological foundations of the family's connections to the welfare state were laid.

By the time of progressive reform, the responsibility for social welfare in Canada had not fully been resolved. The *B.N.A. Act* had not specified federal and provincial obligations. There were almshouses, prisons, and reformatories, but these institutions were scattered and largely unco-ordinated. The provinces relied on church-related institutions, municipal 'goodwill', adapted versions of English poor laws, and the common law to provide various forms of relief. Early programmes of social welfare were largely charitable in nature and mainly were run through or affiliated with churches. They were aimed at preserving the moral order through individual salvation and restitution. Although charity workers pitied those with unfortunate physical or mental afflictions and sought institutional care for them, problems associated with poverty were usually traced to flaws in character and weaknesses in will. This sentiment was reflected in the decision of Upper Canada's legislators to exclude poor laws since, in their view, there were unlimited opportunities in Upper Canada for making a living (Moscovitch and Drover 1987, 15).

Church workers thought that managing poverty was an urgent social concern. The poor were suspect since they characterized the weakness and laziness of sinners. Moreover, a clear connection had been drawn between poverty, crime, and other vices. For those living in poor conditions, the potential for criminal activity, alcoholism, other 'diseases', and behavioural manifestations of personal defects, lingered. It was essential to protect the moral fabric of the community by removing 'degenerates' to institutions where they would be kept on a more or less permanent basis.

By 1850, owing to the increased price of land and massive immigration, there was a growing working class in major Canadian cities dependent on an impersonal and changing labour market. In this situation, families lost many of their functions as producers of food, shelter, and clothing, but nevertheless still represented economic units. While males were the primary wage earners, working-class women and children entered the wage labour market to supplement the male income, to attain an adequate living standard, or simply to manage in the wake of crisis such as illness, injury, or death. Such crises sometimes forced working-class families to give up their children to relatives, orphanages, or other institutions (Bradbury 1982, 110). Coping with the problems of an urbanizing, industrializing society necessitated linkages to a formalized institutional sphere and forced working-class families to recognize and to adjust to their loss of self-sufficiency. The transfer of responsibility for the poor and dependent from families and communities to state institutions was, as Zaretsky (1982, 198) argues, a "direct precursor to the welfare state".

Coincident with these changes in the nature of work and family life was the development of support services designed to quell the fears and concerns of those now living in a world vastly different from the one they had known as children, and to protect new generations from the atrocities of rapid industrialization and social change. Drawing on the notion that poverty and its related problems were cyclical, social reformers demanded social protection, especially for children. For example, some years earlier, Egerton Ryerson agitated for the development of a free, universal, and compulsory common school system in Upper Canada. In his 1846 *Report of a System of Public Elementary Instruction* he reasoned that an educated population would be more manageable and that crime and violence would accordingly be reduced.[5]

The creation of mass compulsory education would serve a variety of functions. The state would play a role in preparing children with the practical skills, habits, and modes of thought to assume future roles within the occupational sphere. At the same time, the practice of schooling itself would serve to place unprecedented importance on children and their pursuits, both within the family unit with the promise of future social and economic success, and within the larger social network with the promise of progress. This, in turn, fostered particular attitudes towards women as natural nurturers and teachers of children, emphasizing the importance of women's role in family life through the home. As a result, a sharp separation was wedged between home and work in the lives of women and children (Wilson 1977). The elevated importance placed on children and the ideology of women's place in the home compelled reformers to seek state protection for women and children as insurance for future social well-being during the last decades of the nineteenth century.

The ideology of social welfare and family protection was promoted during a time when the need for social reform and re-creation of order was apparent. Behind the reformers' search for a panacea was the assumption that under a somewhat confused surface of events lay a harmonious and rational social order. Social problems were thought to persist owing to faulty means of co-ordination among key institutions of society and the dissolution of family and traditional values, rather than because of irreconcilable conflict among parts of society, key actors, and ideological spheres. Curing social ills seemed to be a matter of co-ordinating social institutions, strengthening and protecting traditional family bonds, promoting forums for interaction among various types of social reformers, and establishing support for 'scientific' reform.

In working to establish protective legislation, social reformers adopted the language and method of sociology. Their key concept was that of the "social" (Zaretsky 1982, 207). During the early decades of the twentieth century, social scientists were preoccupied with the nature of society as an entity with a life and purpose of its own.[6] Sociologists sought to establish order and social harmony by analyzing the component parts of modern complex society, isolating particular social problems requiring urgent reform, and organizing a course of action to overcome identified elements of disharmony. The fathers of North American sociology generally agreed on the direction of social change and expressed their fondness for the social, economic, and political patterns of the emerging corporate structures (Smith 1970b; Schwendinger and Schwendinger 1974). Early sociologists sought to preserve what they saw as the 'good society' and provided a rationale for this goal. They argued not only that the 'good society' should be maintained since it benefited all, but that its workings could be perfected through slight alterations based upon further study of human behaviour and methods of social control.

In a society characterized by rapid and profound changes and, consequently, confusion over social values, priorities, and methods for reform, is was the task of the sociologist to sort out the variables that created confusion or limited progress, thereby to provide a path of progressive development and harmony for the community and larger society. Underlying this description of social problems was the assumption that the adoption of normative behaviour was essential to the solution. The prescription for normal behaviour was to be developed by sociologists who would analyze the sources of social problems—difficult economic conditions, the struggle for survival, family breakdowns, and faulty training in morality and social values—and devise solutions. In this scheme, the conception of society was mechanistic, and the solutions offered were no more than simple suggestions aiming at the replacement of dysfunctioning parts. Sociologists justified their strategies as 'scientific'. At a time when science was held to be the perfect panacea, sociology did not merely provide suggestions. Rather its recommendations for change could be tested and evaluated, thus avoiding inappropriately timed or directed changes that would potentially produce social instability (Smith 1970).

Late nineteenth century reform activity drew on sociologists' recommendations. It was essentially protectionist (Zaretsky 1986, 96) and was aimed at maximizing the importance of motherhood. Between 1891 and 1901 there was a 21.4% increase in the female labour force participation rate (Mitchinson 1987, 92). Reformers feared the dissolution of the traditional family structure and agitated for state legislation in aid of families to discourage or prevent women from working and to preserve the bond between mothers and their children. The movement started out as charitable in nature, focusing primarily on disadvantaged families and widows, for example. Gradually it adopted a reformist tone (Mitchinson 1987, 78), especially as it embraced the knowledge and technique of 'scientific philanthropy' and professionalized service.[7]

Middle-class women were key players in this reform movement. Many of these women entered the public arena through extensions of their motherhood role. They never questioned this role, but rather sought to 'feminize' the public arena, clean up social problems, and solve moral dilemmas by charitable acts. Their targets were mainly working-class women and children who were seen as architects of their own misfortune; working-class women were considered uneducated in proper mothering skills. Women did not seek equal status with men, but rather full expression and empowerment in their 'proper' sphere as wives and mothers. Nevertheless, the reformers promoted "gender loyalty" by working to improve women's living conditions (Andrew 1984, 673–74). They raised the notions of voluntarism, social service, reform through legislation and political action, and government responsibility. Within this framework of contradiction, women's associations joined with church and other reform organizations to direct the construction of the welfare state.

The reform movement was heavily influenced by churches, which sought to protect the moral fabric of society by strengthening the family and 'saving' especially the women and children from the 'sins' of a secular, urban life. By the late 1800s, the rhetoric of the religious associations revolved around the preservation of the social good, somewhat a departure from earlier religious interest which was primarily in individual salvation and reform. Specific organizations such as the Women's Christian Temperance Union (WCTU) and the Young Women's Christian Association (YWCA) grew, in fact, under church sponsorship (Mitchinson 1987). Stripped of religious or 'feminist' sentiment and rhetoric glorifying goals of social progress and the preservation of morality, three interrelated themes of the movement emerge.

First, the dominant position of the movement renewed belief in women's primary role in the domestic sphere. The ideology of motherhood and women's place in the home was not challenged. The purpose of the movement was to make the home more comfortable and, therefore, motherhood more attractive. Within this ideological framework, social reformers fought for housing legislation, slum clearance, urban renewal, and the establishment of public health and sanitation departments. Reformers also sought financial protection for the family and often argued in favour of a family wage (an inherently conservative and sexist notion which assumed the dependency of women and children on men), and for family allowances which were treated as tokens of recognition for raising children (Kitchen 1987, 225).

With respect to motherhood issues, there was increased interest in the causes of infant and maternal mortality initiated by the work of prominent reformer Helen MacMurchy (Kealey 1979, 5; Buckley 1979).[8] Recommendations were made with regard to childcare, pregnancy and post-natal care, and education for mothering was popularized (Strong-

Boag 1982).[9] The National Council of Women of Canada (NCWC) essentially addressed these concerns by promoting interest in domestic science education. This education for girls would provide training for future roles as wives and mothers and it would also benefit middle-class reformers by increasing the supply of reliable servants (Mitchinson 1987, 87).

The movement's second theme was the protection of the home as the basis for social stability. The cornerstone of the NCWC's programme was guardianship of the family home from the encroachment of the materialism of the (male-dominated) outside world. Lady Aberdeen and the NCWC "saw women in this critical situation as the divinely appointed guardians of an institution which in its inculcation of the virtues of kindness, love, duty, respect and honour was essential to the best kind of human development" (Strong-Boag 1977, 101). For example, the NCWC sought to protect women and children from "pernicious" literature. Still other groups, such as the WCTU, fought to guard the home against the evils of alcoholism, vices, prostitution, and criminal activity (Mitchinson 1979; Rotenberg 1974).

The third theme was the importance of childhood and the primacy of the mother-child bond. On the one hand, glorifying the child was one way feminists had of highlighting the important roles of women and arguing that these roles should be supported in the public domain. On the other hand, this maternal role was intrinsic to a society characterized by private family units and economic individualism (Zaretsky 1986, 95). The cost of raising children was recognized in Canada's first *Income Tax Act* in 1917 in which taxpayers with children were allowed a $200 deduction for each dependent child under 21 (Kitchen 1987, 223). Along with the intensified interest in child raising and related issues, such as compulsory school attendance, high school education, reformatories, day nurseries for children of working mothers, and kindergartens, child-savers gained legislative ground. Largely through the efforts of J.J. Kelso, in 1888 the *Children's Protection Act* was passed in Ontario, and the Children's Fresh Air Fund and Santa Claus Fund were established (Rutman 1987).

Social reformers insisting on women's rightful place in the home were inadvertently supported by the (male) labour movement's struggle to protect wage levels from the competition of cheaper female and child labour and the state's response to labour's demands. The competition was real. In the late nineteenth century in urban centres like Toronto, together women and children comprised about one-third of the total labour force (Kealey 1979, 4). To the chagrin of employers, the *Factories Act*, passed in 1884 in Ontario, removed the greatest discrepancy between the male and female wage, effectively eliminating some of the competition from the female (and child) labour force for factory jobs. This a and subsequent reform actions by the state, including factory inspection laws, health and safety regulations, hours of work standards, workmen's compensation which extended benefits to the families of injured workers, and Mothers' Allowances, increasingly limited the direct use of female and child labour in the productive sphere. In the case of Mothers' Allowance legislation,[10] the labour movement was joined in its support by social workers, feminists, clerics, doctors, and others who believed that, whether married or not, women's place was in the home with their children. Dependency on the state in this case was an acceptable solution where dependency on a male was not possible (Strong-Boag 1979). Similarly, the 1920 enactment of minimum wage legislation in Ontario was based on women's special needs as future childbearers and mothers rather than on their rights as workers to a fair wage (McCallum 1986). It is clear that changes in both family/welfare legislation and employment/income legislation "were critical in realigning the patriarchal order with the economic system" (Ursel 1986, 159).

The work of the welfare state historically developed as part of its primary function in the enhancement of capital accumulation.[11] Once the state had begun building the technical infrastructure—roadways, railways, bridges, and later hydro generation projects and airports— required by the productive sector, the state undertook a more active role in the regulation of labour. This task was accomplished through education, employment legislation, and family and social welfare programmes.

Until the 1930s, state spending on social expenditures was relatively low. The state resisted many of the reforms sought by labour and women's organizations until circumstances, such as the Depression and the aftermath of war, forced the extension of social expenditures (Moscovitch and Drover 1987, 38). However, prior to this expansion, the state nevertheless intervened in the production process to accommodate certain patriarchal necessities, such as the maintenance of women's subordinate status and the division of labour to restructure and preserve patriarchy's place in the changing socioeconomic conditions (Ursel 1986, 188). In the short run, employers may have continued to benefit from the cheaper female and child labour force. The state intervened to preserve long-run interests of capital by assuring women's subordinate status, thereby marginalizing female labour as a reserve and assuring the primary role of women in reproduction and in the domestic sphere.

The development of the modern state parallelled the shift from "family patriarchalism" or a patriarchal sphere of production to a "private economic unit based in patriarchy" (Zaretsky 1982, 195).[12] Rather than replacing or displacing the family, the modern state and family emerged together as necessary complements of one another (Zaretsky 1986; Barrett and McIntosh 1982; Walton 1986). The state resisted public dependence, but supported the private dependence of men and

children on women's domestic labour, and women's economic dependence on men and the family wage. The state's strategy in facilitating
the shift from large, productive, rural families to "small, single purpose,
self-supporting, private family units" was to create "institutional alternatives"—public schools, social insurance, old age pensions—to some
traditional family functions (Walton 1986, 200–01).

Shifts in state policy, especially over the last 50 years, reflect a social
and institutional adaptation to the needs of the privatized patriarchal
family. These shifts do not simply reflect the work of reformers or
benevolents among state officials, nor do they represent state conspiracy
to produce privatized family units (Walton 1986, 201). The privatized
household, as a consumption unit, enhances capital accumulation. The
state supported this notion by, for example, responding to reformers'
demands for affordable housing by establishing the Canada Mortgage
and Housing Corporation.

Although the welfare state may be regarded in part as the achievement of reformer, feminist, and working-class struggle, when those interests clashed, the state responded in a particular manner to dissipate
tension and to satisfy capital's long-term interests. Moreover, it is important to be aware of the interests of those who argue for decreased
state interference and/or spending in that their activities may work to
renew the family's responsibility for some of the more costly programmes
of the state, such as nursing care for the infirm or elderly (Barrett and
McIntosh 1982). By analyzing the state's response to the sometimes conflicting demands of reformers, feminists, and labour, for equality and
justice, the state's definition of the family and women's place in it becomes
more apparent.

In the next two sections, two key contemporary issues—childcare
and the reform of family law—will be examined in order to demonstrate
how this process functions and to identify the contradictions and constraints within which the state operates.

THE CANADIAN CHILDCARE CRISIS: WOMEN'S CHALLENGE TO THE STATE

Recently a front page story in *The Globe and Mail* (April 30, 1987)
described a lawyer's challenge to the constitutionality of the *Income Tax
Act* in its provisions for childcare deductions. She argues that she would
be unable to practice law without childcare and, therefore, should be
able to deduct its cost (or at least more than the $2,000 allowed) just as
those in business may claim the cost of employing secretarial services.
One of the major focal points in the current Canadian childcare movement is the cost, both direct and indirect, to families, women, employers,
and the state.

The question of childcare 'costs' extends beyond the marketplace and the pocketbook. For the state, there are real financial considerations. Escalating childcare budgets may necessitate the generation or diversion of funds obtained through personal or corporate tax. Through state-sponsored childcare, the state may pursue its legitimation function in the long run, but in the short run it may be criticized by various groups within the dominant class and the (male) labour movement.[13] Employers may be concerned that labour will agitate for workplace arrangements, for subsidization of spaces, or for legislation guaranteeing longer maternity and paternity leaves, or for other such provisions to cover, for example, mothers wishing to continue breast-feeding. For men, whether unionized or not, an adequate childcare system may free women from their marginalized and "reserve" labour force status, thereby increasing competition for jobs. For anti-feminists, publicly supported childcare represents an attack on motherhood, fundamental values, and the tradition of the privatized, nuclear family. For feminists, however, an accessible, flexible, publicly supported childcare system is a necessary first step toward the achievement of equality in the workplace and in the family.

Over the last 30 years, the rate of female labour force participation has more than doubled, from 24% in 1951 to 51.8% in 1981 (Armstrong and Armstrong 1984, 19). Between 1961 and 1981 the prevalence of one-earner couples dramatically decreased from 65% to 16% of all families, while dual income earners increased from 14% to 49% and single-parent families grew from 6% to 11% (Statistics Canada 1986, 7). Data on participation rates for mothers indicate dramatic and continuing increases. In 1984, 52% of women with a child under three, 57% with a child between the ages of three and five, and 64% with school-aged children were in the labour force. This represented increases of 62%, 39% and 29% respectively since 1976 (Statistics Canada 1986, 8). While the participation rates of childless women were substantially higher (in 1984, 73% for those under the age of 55, and 20% for those above the age of 55) nevertheless, the majority of mothers with children of all ages are in the labour force (Statistics Canada 1986, 8).[14] Whatever mothers' job circumstances, "the *majority* of Canadian children will experience some form of shared childcare during substantial portions of their waking time" and in addition, "the *majority* of preschool children experience some form of shared childcare, as do the majority of school-age children, at least during lunch-time" (Eichler 1983, 249).

Women's increased labour force participation is accompanied by only modest gains in overall representation among the higher paying, higher status, professional and managerial occupational categories (Armstrong and Armstrong 1984; Cuneo 1985). The majority of women work out of economic necessity. They work in the clerical, service or retail sectors in jobs that are relatively low paying (as compared to those held by males), with few benefits, few opportunities for advancement, and low rates of unionization. Moreover, approximately 30% of mothers work part-time in jobs in which the pay and benefits are generally poorer (White 1983; Wallace 1983).

Notwithstanding sexual discrimination, sexual harassment, and historical inconsistencies in employment legislation,[15] having children is a major obstacle in achieving workplace equality. Women with children often must accept work on the basis of its flexibility, its proximity to home, childcare, or school; or they must accept part-time work, shift-work, work in the home, non-paid domestic work, or generally less agreeable work to complete their 'double day' of labour. With school-aged children, women must make arrangements with spouses or others for absences from school, emergency situations, dental and medical appointments, teachers' professional development days, school holidays, and for daily care after school, or accept the worries of the 'latch-key kid'. With preschoolers and infants, mothers face high turnover among nannies and babysitters. They must arrange for immunization and other medical care, often with difficulty due to the inflexibility of doctors' schedules, and often must rely on the goodwill of relatives and friends. With two or more children, difficulties are compounded; more than one type of arrangement must sometimes be made, depending on the ages of the children and the restrictions of the services. With all of these childcare concerns, women meet the demand for low-paid, marginal workers, thereby greatly benefiting employers.

Feminists and childcare advocates in organizations such as Canadian Daycare Advocacy Association, have argued that women's equality is dependent upon the establishment of a system of affordable, universally accessible, high quality childcare (Martin 1985). While data clearly support this position, it presents a dilemma for women. One problem is that childcare has been identified as an employment issue rather than a family concern. Clearly families require childcare for reasons other than employment (although employment is the primary reason). Another problem is that childcare has become identified as a 'women's issue', thereby perpetuating the notion that it is women's responsibility to care for children. In reality, in both two-parent and one-parent families, the task of childcare *is* assumed by women, either by remaining outside the paid labour force or by accepting a paid work arrangement that will accommodate the mother role. In addition, the lack of systematic childcare has forced the extension of motherhood for many women who, as grandmothers, are caring for grandchildren.

Currently, the childcare issue crosses class lines. Although the economic and structural circumstances of middle class and career women are substantially different from those of working-class women, there is little difference in their childcare needs (Mann 1986, 242). In struggling for systematic childcare, however, women still face biases stemming from the historical bases of childcare. Historically, daycare was developed by middle-class reformers to care for the children of working and poor women. Implicit in the early movement were anti-feminist and anti-working-class biases. Reformers and professional day-nursery workers believed that these women lacked expertise in child management and care and needed professionalized help. The professionals were seen as more suitable to socialize children than were 'neglectful' mothers who chose to work outside the home. Moreover, the reformers emphasized the importance of motherhood and the normalcy of women's place in the home, thereby pegging the families (and particularly the mothers) of children in nurseries as 'abnormal' (Mann 1986; Strong-Boag 1982; Eichler 1983; Jones 1983).

With increasing emphasis, especially after the Second World War, on the special needs of children and the social and educational benefits of pre-school shared childcare, coupled with the economic necessity of two-family paycheques, organized childcare became more desirable within the middle classes. For working-class and especially middle-class families, this represents a shift in historical relations with the community. Rapp (1982, 179) argues that among poor families there is no radical separation between the privacy of home life and the social world of the community and the workplace. Privatization does not develop among the poor, whose survival depends on sharing limited resources and childcare arrangements within the larger network of family or community members. With the large-scale entry of mothers into the labour force and the need to arrange for childcare, there occurs a shift in the family's degree of privatization (Eichler 1983, 259–60). While this shift is important in affecting community relations—and perhaps for initiating social and political action—at present, the family is a private *economic* unit which must solve its own childcare problem.

The 1986 *Report of the Task Force on Child Care* systematically documents the need for affordable, accessible, quality childcare. It makes 53 recommendations covering parental leaves, training for childcare staff, information and resource banks, taxation issues, subsidization, special needs groups, federal-provincial cost-sharing, licensing, and accessibility. Most of these recommendations, however, are based on the private nuclear model of single or two-parent families. The most critical problem identified by the Task Force is the lack of space in licensed family homes or centres. Currently, the vast majority—more than 80%—of children in childcare are in unlicensed arrangements; therefore, responsibility for monitoring, supervision, and regulation falls upon parents (Statistics Canada 1986, 45). Quality of care varies and is not necessarily related to the possession of a license, but rather may be related to the number of children in the situation, ratio of care givers to children, and the working conditions of the care giver (Statistics Canada 1986; Johnson and Dineen 1981). Options for parents include care in a centre, care in the family home by a relative or sitter, or care in a sitter's or relative's home. Centres may be operated on a profit or non-profit basis and spaces may be publicly subsidized. There are wide provincial variations in the availability of any type of childcare, but four major issues are apparent: quality, affordability, cost, and salaries and working conditions of care givers. These issues underlie lobbyists' programmes.

The state has taken only tentative steps toward developing a childcare policy, based on the recommendations of the 1986 Task Force. Beyond the direct financial costs, the state will resist supporting what may appear to be feminist demands. Inadequate childcare benefits employers, who profit from women's unequal labour force participation. Inadequate childcare limits competition in the labour market. Discouraged due to an inability to make suitable childcare arrangements or because they earn marginally more than childcare costs, many women leave the workforce, and therefore, are not included in official rates of unemployment. Researchers have estimated that women limited from entry into the workforce by the lack of childcare form a significant percentage of the "hidden unemployed" (Social Planning Council 1986).

The current piecemeal system works to maintain class distinctions and promotes divisiveness among women. Childcare has been developed using the welfare principle of selectively subsidized user-fee service. Assessments for eligibility for subsidy are integrated with welfare services. Subsidized spaces are mainly in non-profit centres. In fact, approximately 50% of all childcare spaces in Canada are subsidized, and 95% of all children in non-profit centres are subsidized (Eichler 1983, 154–55). Not only does this segregate children by class, but it divides women. Martin (1984, 11), for example, argues that the selectively subsidized user-fee service "is a form of welfare which rules ineligible many in need of daycare—such as middle-income families and mothers who despite higher 'family' incomes have to pay for their children's care out of their poverty-level take-home pay." Moreover, in the public system, childcare workers, who are mainly women, receive relatively low pay, few benefits, and experience poor working conditions (Statistics Canada 1986; Colley 1983; Johnson and Dineen 1981; Jones 1983). In the private home situation, women desperate for childcare find themselves taking advantage of the low-paid or free labour of sitters, relatives, or friends. Many babysitters simply do not claim their babysitting wages as income, therefore do not issue receipts. In fact, in 1981 only 5.7% of women filing tax claims used the childcare expenses deduction (Martin 1984, 12). Nevertheless, with a $2,000 maximum allowable deduction per child (to a maximum of $8,000 per family or two-thirds of the claimant's income) the government fails to acknowledge the real costs of childcare (Kitchen 1986, 41).

In responding to the childcare issue, the state must satisfy parents (voters), childcare activists, and operators of profit-making centres, while also maintaining capital's long-term interests. The state, therefore, is proceeding cautiously. There is some recognition that childcare may be lucrative for the state. A regulated childcare system may generate revenue through personal income tax. Spouses of babysitters who have to declare babysitting wages as income, for example, may not be able to claim their wives as dependents, and the sitters themselves may face income tax payments. However, since a parent may only claim a fraction of the real cost of childcare (the $2,000 per child deduction), there would be little financial gain for parents.

Promoting childcare may stimulate the small business sector, thereby providing increased job opportunities, albeit in a traditionally low-paid, low-status, marginalized sector. Support for childcare through public or private profit-making institutions essentially removes the responsibility from large employers, and diverts attention away from the possibility of changes in employment legislation, and once again simply privatizes the solution for the individual family. At present the state's objective is to preserve the family as a privatized unit without incurring substantial public costs or obstacles to private profit-making.

The state will take action on the childcare issue by resisting until structural conditions make it necessary to implement change.[16] In the short run, women and families will benefit from the increased number of spaces, larger budgets, and staff training programmes already promised. In the long run, employers will benefit from the state's reluctance to address recommendations calling for an increase in their obligations.

REFORMING FAMILY LAW: THE STRUGGLE AHEAD

Through marriage and family law, the state has persistently maintained the patriarchal family even in the face of seemingly liberal family law reforms in Canada and elsewhere (Gebhardt-Benischke 1986; Ullrich 1986; Kaufmann 1986; Deech 1984; Eekelaar and Maclean 1984; Smart 1984). The problem with family law as it is currently structured relates to the widely accepted liberal democratic or "pluralist" model of law which dominates legal philosophy. In this model, society is viewed as "homogeneous and static" rather than as diverse and dynamic. Law is regarded as neutral and as operating independently for society's good, rather than as "the *result* of the operation of private interest" (Quinney 1978, 41). What therefore developed as a liberalization of family law has been interpreted in ways in which women are consistently disadvantaged.

In 1978, feminists heralded the passage of the *Family Law Reform*

Act in Ontario since this Act formally recognized the injustice of the former law as applied in the notorious *Murdoch v. Murdoch* case (Cohen 1984; Dranoff 1977). In this case, Mrs. Murdoch had worked throughout her marriage on the family farm and had contributed to the original down payment. The court had ruled in 1971 that she only was entitled to $200 a month in alimony as a result of her contribution, but that her years of labour on the farm would not be further compensated since, it was argued, she had done nothing more than the 'usual' work of a farmer's wife.

The principle upheld in *Murdoch* dated back to the *Married Women's Property Acts*, first passed in Canada in 1872. These Acts created the "system of separate property" in which a married man or woman was entitled to acquire assets and register them in his or her own name. To claim a share of the property her husband acquired after marriage, a woman would be compelled to prove that she had directly contributed financially to obtain it. Wives were not entitled by marriage or cohabitation to a share of their husband's property. The Property Acts symbolized wives' financial independence. In reality, most wives were homemakers with no money to buy separate property. With the *Married Women's Property Acts*, what married women had gained was "the 'legal capacity for destitution in their own right' " (Abella 1981, 9). Moreover, since women did not compete for jobs equally with men, had less access to education, and had fewer resources, the "separate-but-equal" property laws were rather ineffectual.

Departing from precedent, in 1978 Mr. Justice Dickson of the Supreme Court of Canada drew upon the argument Chief Justice Bora Laskin developed as dissenting judge in *Murdoch*, "urging the application of a doctrine of constructive trusts in matrimonial property disputes" (Abella 1981, 11) and granted Mrs. Rathwell's appeal in *Rathwell v. Rathwell*. In this case, Mrs. Rathwell left her husband after 23 years of marriage, charging that her husband's alcoholism and abuse were intolerable. Early in their marriage in 1944, the Rathwells purchased a farm with the proceeds of a joint bank account, to which Mrs. Rathwell had contributed $700. The farm was registered in Mr. Rathwell's name; when she questioned this, he argued that it did not matter, since the farm was "ours". In 1974, she applied to the court for one-half the interest in the lands and assets of her husband, because of her $700 contribution, her labour, and her belief that the property, worth between $200,000 and $225,000, was both of theirs. The trial judge ruled against her, arguing that while she was a good mother and housekeeper, she performed the 'usual' services of a farmer's wife. In response to her allegation that her husband referred to the land as "ours", the judge replied:

The fact is now so notorious that I am able to take judicial notice that husbands (other than a foolhardy and valiant few) who desire a life of peaceful co-existence within the matrimonial bailiwick rather than either a hot or cold war, habitually use the diplomatic and ambiguous 'ours' rather than the forthright and challenging 'mine' when referring to anything of monetary value. (*cf.* Abella 1981, 11)

Mrs. Rathwell's appeal both before the Saskatchewan Court of Appeal and the Supreme Court of Canada was successful.

The judgment in the Rathwell case preceded the passage of the 1978 *Family Law Reform Act*. This legislation incorporated Mr. Justice Dickson's sentiments that women's unequal status before the law would not be tolerated, that conditions, values, and attitudes had changed, and that homemaking was a valuable contribution both to the family's economic well-being and to the society as a whole. The *Family Law Reform Act* granted a measure of equality for women in the home, but nevertheless did not alter patriarchal family and power relations.

In 1986, Ontario's *Family Law Act* replaced the *Family Law Reform Act*. This legislation allows judges to limit the duration of settlement awards. Since its inception, husbands are refusing to extend support settlements beyond limited-term agreements. Women should oppose lump-sum or limited-term awards since it is impossible to anticipate future financial needs (Dranoff 1987, H2). The Supreme Court's rulings in three recent cases have shattered notions regarding obligation to marital partner, financial security, and compensation for mothering and non-paid domestic labour.

The cases were Richardson, Pelech, and Caron. In the Richardson case, the wife agreed in 1981 to one year's support of $175 per month, but subsequently could not find work and went on welfare. In Pelech, in 1969 the wife agreed to a final lump-sum payment amounting to about one-fifth of her contractor husband's net worth. He since has become substantially wealthier. Caron's support ended because she lived with another man, but since he did not support her, she ended up on welfare. In these cases, each woman had signed separation agreements that limited their ex-husbands' financial obligations, but later found that their own financial circumstances had changed and that they needed further support since they had become dependent on social assistance. The Court ruled that there was no relationship between their changed economic circumstances and their previous marital relationship, therefore their husbands were not responsible for their current economic well-being.

These recent decisions point to the fact that the law as it currently reads and as it is widely interpreted does not represent women's interests, nor does it address their concrete reality. Like the decision reached in *Murdoch v. Murdoch*, in the current cases there is no recognition of years spent by wives (whether or not they were in the paid labour force) in domestic labour, childbearing, mothering, and managing the family. For many women, these roles have necessitated time away from the paid labour force, participation in the paid labour force in a marginalized position, and the sacrifice of educational or skill-upgrading opportunities. In reality, the interpretation of the current law, which supposedly embodies the principles of fairness and equality, actually divorces individuals from their own biographies, and this is unjust, particularly for women. The current law seems to equate women's increased labour force participation with equality in the family. However, this equality myth is easily shattered by the rate of poverty and financial problems among divorced women. In 1985, female-headed, lone-parent families were reported as having the highest incidence of low income of all family types in Canada. In fact, nearly 48% of lone-parent, female-headed families, as compared to 19.7% of male-headed, one-parent families, had incomes that fell below Statistics Canada's 'low income' designation (Methot 1987, 2–3). As social commentators often note, most women do not realize that they are only 'one man' away from poverty.

In its practical application, "reformed" family law mechanically divides property and assures a fair support settlement. Through liberal ideology, the wife's contribution to the family is acknowledged in terms of division of property. While this does represent some progress in the acknowledgement of the value of the homemaking role, she is not recompensed for her loss of earnings or of career advancements, nor is the settlement necessarily readjusted as property lost or split through settlement increases in value. The 'liberal' treatment of women as equals stands as a mark of injustice (Morton 1987). Reform of family law should begin with the recognition of male-female inequality in society, and the patriarchal structure of marriage and the family, so that property settlements can be awarded on the basis of real circumstances of women's lives rather than on the basis of liberal notions regarding the egalitarian marriage ideal.

The assumption of equality in the federal *Divorce Act* will similarly continue to act as a disadvantage for women. In 1986, Canada's *Divorce Act* was altered to incorporate the "friendly parent" rule. This means that the custodial parent must facilitate the non-custodial parent's access to the children. If the custodial parent (usually the mother) objects or tries to deny access to the non-custodial parent, she may be considered to be 'uncooperative' and therefore may lose custody (Lamb 1987, 22). Sole custody is awarded to the mother in 86% of divorces involving children (Lamb 1987, 21). The new legislation, built on the mediation model, erroneously assumes power equity between the parties in dispute and exacts a high price for unco-operative behaviour or any action that is viewed as obstructing the path of the non-custodial parent. Mothers who choose to protect children from potentially abusive situations may be regarded as conniving. The National Association of Women and the Law (NAWL) suggests that the "friendly parent" rule may disregard the custodial parent's day-to-day roles and preferences in child-rearing, the emotional trauma, and any inequality in the responsibility for childcare during the past marriage. At the same time it implies that the rights and impact of the non-custodial parent override the needs of the custodial parent. Recent cases in the U.S. have demonstrated that this arrangement places women in a situation whereby they may risk their award of custody if they are viewed as vindictive when complaining too loudly, for example, about their former spouse's abusive behaviour. Exposing themselves or their children to further abuse, potential or real, may be their price for the right of continued custody (Lamb 1987, 23).

The reformed *Act* also allows judges more discretion in time-limiting maintenance awards, making it more difficult for women to negotiate changes once the period has lapsed. The ruling is developed on the "clean break" principle, which effectively means smaller payments for shorter periods of time (Dulude 1984, 22). The principle assumes that each spouse will attain self-sufficiency by the time the alimony payment period expires. Divorced women with few marketable skills, with long periods of absence from paid labour force participation, or who are over 50, or living in areas with high rates of unemployment and few job opportunities, will eventually find themselves poverty-stricken under these new arrangements.

While feminists should be credited for their activity in reforming family law and eliminating the separate property principle, the basic issue of definitions—equality, equality of opportunity, spousal contribution—must be clarified (Prager 1982) in light of the state's interest in reproducing patriarchal relations within the family. With the 1978 and 1986 reform in Ontario law and the recent changes in the federal *Divorce Act*, the historical relation of economic dependency on men is maintained, and women, in particular, are penalized for marital breakdown. Concerted action for family law reform—for changes in the legal and economic status of married women—may prove to be a source of women's empowerment. Feminists should take advantage of the contradictions in law to reformulate it from a system of regulation to one of promise and change (Smart 1984). In working to eliminate economic dependency in marriage, women's contributions to males' well-being, as well as to the larger social and economic framework, should be addressed.

CONCLUSION

The welfare state is not just a set of services, it is also a set of ideas about society, about the family, and—not least important—about women, who have a centrally important role within the family, as its linch pin (Wilson 1977, 9).

Through its vast system of laws, regulations, and the institutional structure of the welfare state, the state shapes both personal and social lives. Historically women have both welcomed and resisted the encroachment of the state in the family home. The state at once is regarded as a source of protection and justice and as the basis of inequality. Such contradictions are inherent in a state under capitalism. Although, in the short run, state legislation and policy may appear as liberating and, indeed, may fundamentally alter women's lived experiences, in the long run it reproduces patriarchal relations and thereby sends ambiguous signals regarding the achievement of equality.

Under the rhetoric of progressive liberal reform, the welfare state was developed. The state essentially preserved the family as a privatized, nuclear, economic unit. For some women, the welfare state replaced economic dependency on males with economic dependency on the state. For others, it maintained their inequality in the family by perpetuating the ideology of motherhood and women's place in the home. Despite the state's patriarchal bias, women have drawn upon the ambiguities of the state to struggle for more equitable arrangements. As feminist strategies continue to gain ground, Canadians will witness an increasingly female 'realpolitik'.

NOTES

1. For analysis of the relationship between capitalism, patriarchy and class, see Burstyn and Smith (1985).
2. Welfare workers were expected to note whether (female) clients were sharing their accommodations with males. When it was established that a client was cohabitating, it was assumed that the male was supporting her, and the woman was duly penalized with a reduction in her benefit.
3. Organizations such as Women Against Violence Against Women, local rape crisis centres, women's shelters, and programmes in alcohol and drug treatment, for example, were developed by lay and professional women employing feminist strategies and counselling techniques. Although these concerns often operate on limited budgets, women continue to pressure the state for adequate financing and general recognition of the gravity of such issues. (Levine 1983).
4. The Progressive Reform phase is generally considered to be a North American phenomenon rather than a distinctly Canadian or American developmental period.
5. On this matter, Ryerson (1899, 143) wrote: " . . . a system of general education amongst the people is the most effective preventive of pauperism, and its natural companions, misery and crime. . . . Ignorance is the fruitful source of idleness, intemperance and improvidence, and these the foster-

parents of crime." Ryerson based his argument on statistical evidence from a number of European countries indicating that there was a direct relationship between the availability of education and the absence of crime and pauperism among the labouring classes.

6. This ideology, especially as it was incorporated within practical fields such as industrial sociology, rationalized the purpose of social control, while minimizing the overall significance of the individual worker or work group vis-a-vis the work organization and the production process.

7. For an analysis of the establishment of social service education and its pragmatic focus, see Pupo, 1984.

8. This campaign undertaken by MacMurchy and others had racist overtones in that the reformers urged the government to spend more on infant and material care and less on immigration in the belief that Canada's success rested on the Anglo-Saxon component (Kealey 1979, 5).

9. This was followed by the corporate sector's insistence on the replacement of the 'breast' with the 'bottle' and the psychologists' suggestions for scheduling and training baby.

10. In Ontario, Mothers' Allowance is now referred to as Family Benefits, the long-term provincial replacement for short-term, municipally based general welfare assistance.

11. Struthers (1983) concretely demonstrates this point in his examination of unemployment insurance legislation and the development of the Canadian welfare state.

12. A common theme in some of the recent literature on the family and the state is the argument that the state increasingly encroached upon the family's authority and functions (Lasch, 1977; Donzelot 1979). Zaretsky (1982, 195) however, suggests that the question should not be whether the state eroded the family, but in what form it preserved it.

13. In 1980 the Ontario Federation of Labour adopted a comprehensive day-care policy. With this decision, for the first time in Canadian history, the trade union movement incorporated a key feminist issue and agreed to pursue it (Colley 1983, 308).

14. Besides older women, women who are least likely to be in the labour force are single mothers with children under three; 57% of these mothers are not in the labour force (Statistics Canada 1986, 9).

15. Early unemployment insurance legislation, for example, discriminated against women, whose benefits were based on schedules of contributions that were lower than for men (Cuneo 1980).

16. The state will act in a manner similar to the way in which it responded to demands by labour for unemployment insurance legislation (Cuneo 1979; 1980).

Bibliography

Abella, Judge Rosalie Silberman
1981   "Family Law in Ontario: Changing Assumptions". *Ottawa Law Review* 13: 1–22.

Andrew, Caroline.
1984   "Women and the Welfare State". *Canadian Journal of Political Science* 17 (December): 667–683.

Armstrong, Pat, and Hugh Armstrong.
1984   *The Double Ghetto: Canadian Women and Their Segregated Work.* Revised edition. Toronto: McClelland and Stewart.

Barrett, Michele, and Mary McIntosh.
1982   *The Anti-Social Family.* London: Verso.

Bradbury, Bettina.
1982   "The Fragmented Family: Family Strategies in the Face of Death, Illness, and Poverty, Montreal, 1860–1885". In Joy Parr *Childhood and Family in Canadian History*, edited by Joy Parr, 109–128. Toronto: McClelland and Stewart.

Buckley, Suzann.
1979   Ladies or Midwives? Efforts to Reduce Infant and Maternal Mortality. In *A Not Unreasonable Claim*, edited by Linda Kealey, 131–149. Toronto: The Women's Press.

Burstyn, Varda, and Dorothy Smith.
1985   *Women, Class, Family and the State.* Toronto: Garamond Press.

Cohen, S.
1984   "Family Law in Canada". In *The Family: Changing Trends in Canada*, edited by M. Baker, 162–167. Toronto: McGraw-Hill Ryerson.

Colley, Susan.
1983   "Free Universal Day Care: The OFL Takes A Stand". In *Union Sisters: Women in the Labour Movement*, edited by Linda Briskin and Linda Yanz, 307–321. Toronto: The Women's Press.

Cuneo, Carl J.
1979   "State, Class and Reserve Labour: The Case of the 1941 Canadian Unemployment Insurance Act". *Canadian Review of Sociology and Anthropology* 16 (2): 147–170.
1980   "State Mediation of Class Contradictions in Canadian

Unemployment Insurance, 1930–35". *Studies in Political Economy* (Spring): 37–65.

1985   Have Women Become More Proletarianized Than Men? *Canadian Review of Sociology and Anthropology*, 22:4 (November): 465–495.

Deech, Ruth.

1984   "Matrimonial Property and Divorce: A Century of Progress?" In *The State, The Law and The Family: Critical Perspectives*, edited by Michael D.A. Freeman, 245–261. London: Tavistock Publications.

Dulude, Louise.

1984   "Reforming Divorce Laws". *Status of Women News* 10:2 (December): 20–25.

Dickinson, James, and Bob Russell (Eds.).

1986   *Family, Economy and State: The Social Reproduction Process Under Capitalism.* Toronto: Garamond Press.

Donzelot, Jacques.

1979   *The Policing of Families.* Trans. R. Hurley. New York: Pantheon Books.

Dranoff, Linda Silver.

1977   *Women in Canadian Life: Law.* Toronto: Fitzhenry and Whiteside.

1987   "Women Should Be Wary of Divorce Agreements". *Toronto Star* (July 2): H1–H2.

Eekelaar, John, and Mavis Maclean.

1984   "Financial Provision of Divorce: A Re-Appraisal". In *The State, The Law and The Family: Critical Perspectives*, edited by Michael D.A. Freeman, 208–226. London: Tavistock Publications.

Eichler, Margrit.

1983   *Families in Canada Today.* Toronto: Gage Educational Publishing Co.

Finkel, Alvin.

1977   Origins of the Welfare State. In *The Canadian State*, edited by Leo Panitch, 344–370. Toronto: University of Toronto Press.

Gebhardt-Benischke, Margot.

1986   "Family Law, Family Law Politics and Family Politics". *Women's Studies International Forum* 9(1): 25–33.

The Globe and Mail, Toronto.

1987   (April 30): A1 (July 2): A1–2.

Johnson, Laura C., and Janice Dineen.

1981   *The Kin Trade: The Day Care Crisis in Canada.* Toronto: McGraw-Hill Ryerson.

Jones, Chris.
1983   *State Social Work and The Working Class.* London: The Mac-
            millan Press.
Kaufmann, Claudia.
1986   "Marriage Law Revision—Occasion for Hope?" *Women's
            Studies International Forum* 9(1): 35–40.
Kealey, Linda.
1979   Introduction. In *A Not Unreasonable Claim*, edited by Linda
            Kealey, 1–14. Toronto: The Women's Press.
Kitchen, Brigitte.
1986   "The Patriarchal Bias of the Income Tax in Canada". *Atlantis*
            11:2 (Spring): 35–45.
1987   "The Introduction of Family Allowances in Canada". In *The
            Benevolent State: The Growth of Welfare in Canada*, edited
            by Allan Moscovitch and Jim Albert, 222–241. Toronto:
            Garamond Press.
Lamb, Louise.
1987   "Involuntary Joint Custody: What Mothers Will Lose If
            Fathers' Rights Groups Win". *Herizons* (January–February):
            20–23, 31.
Lasch, Christopher.
1977   *Haven in a Heartless World: The Family Besieged.* New York:
            Basic Books.
Levine, Helen.
1983   "Feminist Counselling: Approach or Technique?" In *Per-
            spectives on Women in the 1980s*, edited by Joan Turner and
            Lois Emery, 74–87. Winnipeg: University of Manitoba Press.
Mann, Susan.
1986   "Family, Class and State in Women's Access to Abortion and
            Day Care: The Case of the United States. In *Family, Economy
            and State: The Social Reproduction Process Under Capitalism*,
            edited by James Dickinson and Bob Russell, 223–253.
            Toronto: Garamond Press.
Martin, Judith.
1984   "Day Care: A National Concern". *Perception* 8: 10–12.
1985   "High-Quality Childcare: A Pre-Condition to Equality of
            Employment". *Canadian Woman Studies* 6(4): 91–93.
McCallum, Margaret E.
1986   "Keeping Women in Their Place: The Minimum Wage in
            Canada". *Labour/Le Travail* 17 (Spring): 29–56.
Methot, Suzanne.
1987   "Low Income in Canada". *Canadian Social Trends* (Spring):
            2–7.

Miliband, Ralph.
1973   *The State in Capitalist Society*. London: Quartet Books.
Mitchinson, Wendy.
1979   "The WCTU: 'For God, Home and Native Land': A Study
              in Nineteenth Century Feminism". In *A Not Unreasonable
              Claim*, edited by Linda Kealey, 151–167. Toronto: The
              Women's Press.
1987   "Early Women's Organizations and Social Reform: Prelude
              to the Welfare State". In *The Benevolent State: The Growth of
              Welfare in Canada*, edited by Allan Moscovitch and Jim Albert,
              77–92. Toronto: Garamond Press.
Morton, Mary.
1987   Dividing the Wealth, Sharing the Poverty: A Feminist Anal-
              ysis of the Role of Law in the (Re)formation of 'the Family'.
              Paper presented at the Canadian Sociology and Anthro-
              pology Meetings, June.
Moscovitch, Allan, and Jim Albert (Eds.).
1987   *The Benevolent State: The Growth of Welfare in Canada*. Toronto:
              Garamond Press.
Moscovitch, Allan, and Glenn Drover.
1987   "Social Expenditures and The Welfare State: The Canadian
              Experience in Historical Perspective". In *The Benevolent State:
              The Growth of Welfare in Canada*, edited by Allan Moscovitch
              and Jim Albert, 13–43. Toronto: Garamond Press.
O'Connor, James.
1973   *The Fiscal Crisis of the State*. New York: St. Martin's Press.
Panitch, Leo.
1977   The Role and Nature of the Canadian State. In *The Canadian
              State*, edited by Leo Panitch, 3–27. Toronto: University of
              Toronto Press.
Piven, Frances Fox.
1984   "Women and The State: Ideology, Power, and the Welfare
              State". *Socialist Review* 74 14:2 (March–April): 11–19.
Piven, Frances Fox, and Richard A. Cloward.
1971   *Regulating the Poor*. New York: Random House.
Poulantzas, Nicos.
1973   *Political Power and Social Classes*. London: New Left Books.
Prager, Susan Westerberg.
1982   Shifting Perspectives on Marital Property Law. In *Rethinking
              the Family: Some Feminist Questions*, edited by Barrie Thorne
              and Marilyn Yalom, 111–130. New York: Longman.
Pupo, Norene J.
1984   Educational Promises and Efficiency Ideals: The Develop-

ment of Management Education in Ontario, 1900–1960. Ph.D. Dissertation. Unpublished. McMaster University.

Quinney, Richard.
1978   "The Ideology of Law: Notes for a Radical Alternative to Legal Oppression". In *The Sociology of Law: A Conflict Perspective*, edited by Charles Reasons and Robert M. Rich, 39–71. Toronto: Butterworths.

Rapp, Rayna.
1982   "Family and Class in Contemporary America: Notes Toward an Understanding of Ideology". In *Rethinking The Family: Some Feminist Questions*, edited by Barrie Thorne and Marilyn Yalom, 168–187. New York: Longman.

Rotenberg, Lori.
1974   "The Wayward Worker: Toronto's Prostitute at the Turn of the Century". In *Women at Work: Ontario, 1850–1930*, edited by J. Acton, P. Goldsmith, and B. Sheppard, 33–69. Toronto: The Canadian Women's Educational Press.

Rutman, Leonard.
1987   J.J. Kelso and The Development of Child Welfare. In *The Benevolent State: The Growth of Welfare in Canada*, edited by Allan Moscovitch and Jim Albert, 68–76. Toronto: Garamond Press.

Ryerson, Egerton.
1899   Report on a System of Public Elementary Instruction for Upper Canada, 1986. In *Documentary History of Education in Upper Canada, 1791–1876*, edited by J.G. Hodgins. Toronto: Warwick Bros. and Rutter Printers.

Schwendinger H., and J.R. Schwendinger.
1974   *The Sociologists of the Chair: An Analysis of the Formative Years of North American Sociology, 1883–1922*. New York: Basic Books.

Smart, Carol.
1984   *The Ties That Bind: Law, Marriage and The Reproduction of Patriarchal Relations*. London: Routledge and Kegan Paul.

Smith, D.L.
1970a   "Some Socio-Economic Influences on the Founding Fathers of Sociology, 1865–1917". Ph.D. Dissertation. Unpublished. State University of New York at Buffalo.
1970b   "Sociology and The Rise of Corporate Capitalism". In *The Sociology of Sociology: Analysis and Criticism of the Thought, Research, and Ethical Folkways of Sociology and Its Practitioners*, edited by L.T. Reynolds and J.M. Reynolds, 68–84. New York: David McKay.

Social Planning Council of Metropolitan Toronto.
1986   "Hidden Unemployment Updated". *Social Infopac* 5:5
            (December): 1–10.
Statistics Canada
1986   *Report of the Task Force on Childcare*. Ottawa: Minister of
            Supply and Services.
Strong-Boag, Veronica.
1977   'Setting the Stage': National Organization and the Women's
            Movement in the Late Nineteenth Century. Pp. 87–103 in
            S.M. Trofimenkoff and A. Prentice (eds.) *The Neglected
            Majority: Essays in Canadian Women's History*. Toronto:
            McClelland and Stewart.
1979   "Canada's Early Experience with Income Supplements: The
            Introduction of Mothers' Allowance". *Atlantis* 4(2): 35–43.
1982   "Intruders in the Nursery: Childcare Professionals Re-Shape
            the Years One to Five, 1920–1940". In *Childhood and Family
            in Canadian History*, edited by Joy Parr, 160–178. Toronto:
            McClelland and Stewart.
Struthers, James.
1983   *No Fault of Their Own: Unemployment and The Canadian Welfare
            State, 1914–1941*. Toronto: University of Toronto Press.
Swartz, Donald.
1977   The Politics of Reform: Conflict and Accommodation in
            Canadian Health Policy. In *The Canadian State*, edited by
            Leo Panitch, 311–343. Toronto: University of Toronto Press.
Ullrich, Vivienne H.
1986   "Equal But Not Equal—A Feminist Perspective on Family
            Law". *Women's Studies International Forum* 9(1): 41–48.
Ursel, Jane.
1986   "The State and The Maintenance of Patriarchy: A Case
            Study of Family, Labour and Welfare Legislation in Can-
            ada". In *Family, Economy and State: The Social Reproduction
            Process Under Capitalism*, edited by James Dickinson and Bob
            Russell, 150–191. Toronto: Garamond Press.
Wallace, Joan.
1983   *Part-Time Work in Canada. Report of the Commission of Inquiry
            into Part-Time Work*. Ottawa: Ministry of Supply and Services.
Walters, Vivienne.
1982   "State, Capital and Labour: The Introduction of Federal-
            Provincial Insurance for Physician Care in Canada". *Ca-
            nadian Review of Sociology and Anthropology* 19: 2 (May): 157–
            172.
Walton, John.
1986   *Sociology and Critical Inquiry*. Chicago: The Dorsey Press.

White, Julie.
1983   *Women and Part-Time Work.* Ottawa: Canadian Advisory Council on the Status of Women.
Wilson, Elizabeth.
1977   *Women and the Welfare State.* London: Tavistock Publications.
Zaretsky, Eli.
1982   "The Place of the Family in the Origins of the Welfare State". In *Rethinking the Family: Some Feminist Questions,* edited by Barrie Thorne and Marilyn Yalom, 188–224. New York: Longman.
1986   "Rethinking the Welfare State: Dependence, Economic Individualism and The Family". In *Family, Economy and State: The Social Reproduction Process Under Capitalism,* edited by James Dickinson and Bob Russell, 85–109. Toronto: Garamond Press.

Index